LETTING GO

A 12-Week Personal Action Program to Overcome a Broken Heart

LETTING GO

A 12-Week Personal Action Program to Overcome a Broken Heart

Dr. Zev Wanderer
and Tracy Cabot

G. P. Putnam's Sons • New York

Second Impression

 Published simultaneously in Canada by Longman Canada Limited, Toronto.

SBN: 399-12136-6

Library of Congress Cataloging in Publication Data

Wanderer, Zev.
Letting go

1. Bereavement—Psychological aspects. 2. Separation (Psychology) I. Cabot, Tracy, joint author.
II. Title.
BF575.G7W35 1978 158′.2 77-26616

Printed in the United States of America.

The Authors wish to express appreciation for permission to quote from the following songs:

Acknowledgments

The authors want to thank the following special people whose valuable experience, advice, research, encouragement and support have meant so much to us:

DR. GEORGE BACH
MELVIN BELLI
DR. ALEX COMFORT
DR. DONALD F. COWAN
DR. ERICH FROMM
ROBERT LEIGHTON
NANCY SHIFFRIN
PROF. B. F. SKINNER
DR. MANUEL "PETE" SMITH
HEDY AND LIONEL WHITE
DR. JOSEPH WOLPE

Dedication

To the memory of my three earliest teachers,
My father Jacob,
My mother Annie, and
My brother Bernie.
To my teachers and colleagues,
And to my students and patients, from whom I have learned most of all.

–Z.W.

Dedication

To my first teachers in the art of loving,
My father, Ben Blank, who showed me how to
recognize the truth and
My mother, Ruth Blank, who taught me to
smell life's flowers.

—T.C.

Preface

A Personal Note from the Authors

Each time we became victims of a change of heart on the part of our lovers, we realized the incredible, unrelenting pain involved. And until each particular relationship fell apart, we suffered from "neurotic security," thinking each love was the one that would last forever.

At the Center For Behavior Therapy in Beverly Hills, hundreds of patients had been treated for depression caused by the disintegration of their love lives, unrequited love, or even the death of a loved one. Always it seemed as though, in spite of the best efforts, time was "the best medicine" when it came to treating a separation trauma.

Finally, after suffering just one heartbreak too many, we decided that it must be possible to bypass the usual time-and-sympathy-will-cure-approach. Using ourselves as guinea pigs, we began experiments. The same behavioral treatments that had been so successful with phobias, addictions and obsessions at the

Center as well as at university clinics around the world were applied to our own loss-of-love symptoms. Since behavior therapy had cut the usual treatment time from years to months in the former cases, we saw no reason why a love cure should take longer.

By using the staff's various innovative behavioral treatments for loss of love on our own symptoms, a "Letting Go" program was designed that erased all the painful memories of a lost relationship within a three-month period. Interviews with patients and friends who had also suffered from depression, feelings of inadequacy and loss of self-esteem after a divorce or breakup revealed that the average time it took a person to get on with the business of living and not be haunted by memories of their lost love was usually half the time the relationship had existed. In other words, a ten-year marriage or commitment would typically take five years to get over.

Grieving lovers who have completed the "Letting Go" program report that almost all their symptoms disappear within the three-month period, no matter how long they have been carrying their pain around, or how long their relationship lasted. We have every reason to predict your successful recovery and a happier future for you as well.

—Zev Wanderer and Tracy Cabot

A NOTE ABOUT STYLE: Until there are more appropriate nonsexist pronouns in the English language, the authors have opted to use the words "them" and "their" in place of specific gender identification throughout the text.

Contents

Introduction

by George R. Bach, PhD., author of
CREATIVE AGGRESSION, THE INTIMATE ENEMY and PAIRING

In my own books I have developed and fully explained the pairing system, which is an effective self-help program for intelligent and sensitive men and women to improve their coupling skills and joys. In over thirty years of clinical experience, I have applied my system in counseling hundreds of couples in how to live and play and stay together. But when what the pairing therapy program tried to keep together and alive tears apart, dies in spite of my best professional counseling efforts to preserve that love bond—then I have to shift my therapeutic strategies from holding on to letting go procedures.

At this often tragic turning point in the quality of a pairing relationship, I have turned to Dr. Zev Wanderer's lost-love therapy program and applied it myself to the mending of broken hearts with much success. The rejected, grieving, shocked lover seeks practical ways to better survive one of the most psychologically traumatic crises of intimate living. He/she desperately needs a reassuring self-help program to lighten the acute stress, to lower the pain, to heal the psychic wound and to prevent an acute disappointment from lingering into a chronic depression and withdrawal!

Through this book, based on solid scientific principles matured by Dr. Wanderer's many years of clinical experience as a psychotherapist, the authors have now made available a survival guide for constructively managing the agonizing side of the vicissitudes of human romance. For as all lovers know only too well, at any moment the passion, the joys, the excitement mutually felt by the intimate pairers can turn into a battle. And in these battles of the sexes, one or both combatants may get seriously hurt, unless they learn not only how to fight *for* genuine love, but also how to fight their way out of self-destructive, pathogenic relationships.

It is unhealthy to hang on to a destructive attachment based originally on the many collusions, like unrealistic expectations, that "nice" lovers tend to practice. To bemoan too deeply and for too long its toxicity, its unworkability, to dwell on the pain of disappointed expectations, invites the growth of a crippling neurosis.

Do not become a love cripple! Read this book and learn how to use healthy aggression to overcome the pain, the anger, the self-doubt, the guilt, the acute loneliness and sense of loss that are the symptoms of a broken heart. This book shows how you yourself can not only just survive a broken heart, but also learn from the experience how to prevent traumas in your future.

And should the reader find difficulties in applying the Letting Go program alone, the authors have provided specific criteria for when and how to seek professional consultations. This ethical perspective distinguishes this book from most simplistic, psychological, do-it-yourself popular books that irresponsibly minimize the human need for professional counsel in crisis situations.

Prologue

For as strong as death is love
Violent like the nether world is jealousy
Its heat is the heat of fire
A flame of God.
Many waters are not able to quench love
Nor can the rivers flood it away.
—Song of Songs
The Old Testament

1
THE PAIN

What have I got to do to make you love me
What have I got to do to make you care
What do I do when lightning strikes me
And I wake to find that you're not there?

—ELTON JOHN
"Sorry Seems To Be the Hardest Word"

When you feel helpless, unable to function, overcome by pain, like you just can't get yourself together because your loved one is gone, you've got "it." Love sickness!

All your life, people have been telling you love is the answer. Love will bring you security, happiness, joy, ecstasy.

But you're in love, and you're miserable. That's because the love pushers never mention what happens when the person you love goes away.

A huge proportion of the happiness that comes from being in love is in being loved back. You love your parents, and they love you back. You love your dog, and it loves you back, but loving another person doesn't guarantee you'll be loved back.

If your parents die, you're unhappy. You grieve. You go to the funeral and you maintain your loving feelings for them, but you know there is no possibility of getting them back. You accept the loss. You know they didn't go away because they stopped loving you.

If your dog is missing, you don't feel a personal rejection; you know it's not because he doesn't love you anymore. You can advertise or check the pound or offer rewards for his return. There are things you *can* do. But what can you do when a person you love simply doesn't love you anymore?

The problem is, you still long for the love you had, know where the person is and that they're available—but not to you. It's frustrating, degrading, causes anxiety and leaves you in a state of limbo.

Suddenly you find yourself obsessed with being in love. Nothing else matters. You discover that the love you lost is the only thing in life that can give you satisfaction, that adds real meaning to your existence. Your job, your friends, your family—nothing they can give you will make up for your loss.

You can't advertise to get your lover's love back. You can't offer a reward for it, although stories of bribes to get a passion started again aren't unusual. You may feel as if you would give anything to make things go back to the way they were, but nobody's taking. You feel forsaken, deserted and alone.

Unrequited love is a real Catch-22. Keep it and you're miserable, but nobody knows how to get rid of it. The library is full of books on how to remake yourself, become lovable, make new liaisons, live fully and fall in love. You've done all that. Now the question is, "How do I fall out of love?"

The Letting Go program is the answer. By following the

twenty-four-session, twelve-week course, you will be able to relieve all of your acute symptoms and anxieties in three short months. You will no longer feel as if you are "falling apart," and you will be free to love again.

THE FIRST WEEK

Session One: Self-Diagnosis

Loving is a good thing, but being "in love" with someone who doesn't love you back isn't.

Being in love, even when you are loved back, is often accompanied by an altered state of consciousness and an altered state of perception. People in love report an extended high feeling, like a drug experience. They sometimes get out of touch with reality, seeing both the world and their lover through a rosy kaleidoscope. It's the fairy-tale aspect of the love experience, not the reality, that the abandoned lover misses.

Frequently, the being-in-love feeling is accompanied by paranoia ("People are always trying to take my lover away"), self-aggrandizement (as if being in love makes you and your loved one better than others), jealousy and suspicion.

The person who is in love is deluded, thinking their love one more attractive, more intelligent, and even more loving than he or she really is. Part of the post-affair depression is the unrealistic feeling that nobody else in the world is as wonderful as the ex.

Okay, you agree, maybe you've got "it," the sick part of being in love. How do you get rid of it? If only someone could simply wave a magic wand and make you fall out of love. If only you could take a pill and get rid of the driving need for "that" person.

Then you could get on with the business of living—*if* you weren't so irretrievably "hooked," so blindly, so incurably in love. If you just didn't have that irresistible urge to be near your former mate, to hear their voice, to see them.

Or, even better, if you could only have them back.

Friends tell you to bury yourself in work or recommend an immediate replacement. But the obsessive vision of your lost love is too blinding, your self-esteem is too low and you're often too busy being hysterical. That's why neither of the usually recommended "cures" works well.

Friends will assure you that "time" will help. It will, but philosophically, time exists only as a series of events, as motion in space. By identifying the events that take place when someone is "getting over" a relationship successfully, and then by causing these events to happen on a programmed schedule, you can abbreviate the time and accelerate your recovery.

You could wait for "time" to help, but case studies have shown that recovery usually takes about half the time the relationship existed. Even then, many people still carry around about ten percent of the painful memories caused by their lost love.

You could opt for years of conventional psychotherapy to change your whole view of the world, to transcend your ego or become more mature through intensive analysis. You could relive your life to find out what's wrong with you, why you can't have a successful relationship, why "it" failed, and why you need "that" particular person in your life.

Or you could accomplish for yourself what others have taken years of suffering to do. You can get unhooked. You can let go of the impossible situation that's keeping you from enjoying life.

It's easy to get friends to take you out, to console you and even to "fix you up." But assuming you can get yourself together enough to go out, you know you'll probably wind up alone in bed anyway, unable to sleep and obsessed with thoughts of your ex. Even while your friends are busily arranging to take your mind off your troubles, while everyone's having fun, you find yourself wondering where your ex is, rerunning both your good and bad times together like an endless matinee, wondering what he or she is doing and wishing they were doing it with you.

Getting lots of sympathy isn't an answer either. While everyone's assuring you you're a real human being for feeling your pain so deeply, you still hurt.

For most people, the first week alone is a hazy blur of tears and disbelief. That's when the most acute symptoms of love sickness occur. You feel the most helpless, the most hurt and the most desperate.

It's important to realize that the emotional upset caused by loss of love is not an unusual or rare occurrence. The following symptomatology was compiled based on reports from hundreds of people suffering because a loved one had deserted them. The complaints are universal.

To find out just how serious your attack of love sickness is, rate yourself on a scale of one to ten for the following indications. Ten means the symptom occurs more than once a day. One means you experience it once a week or less.

When you recognize some of your own symptoms on the list, don't panic. You're not the only person to ever feel that way. If there are a lot of symptoms you don't have, you're better off than you thought you were.

The Checklist

Obsessive Symptoms

- I can't concentrate.
- I watch the telephone and jump expectantly when it rings.
- I listen to sad songs and think they're about me and my ex.

- I imagine I see my ex everywhere. His/her car is all over.
- I spend long hours devising schemes, making scripts of imaginary conversations.
- I can't think about anything but my loss and how to recoup.
- I remember the loving things my ex said and wonder if they were all lies.
- My whole concern is centered on him/her.
- I think I may get fired.
- I wonder if there's another man/woman. I can't stop thinking of them together.
- I feel guilty over all the things I did wrong.
- I wonder if we could start over.
- I think about killing myself to end my pain and wonder how sorry my ex would be.
- I know the love I lost was the most perfect one for me, my destined true love, and I blew it.
- I want desperately to contact him/her, but am afraid of more rejection.
- I think about ways to get even, of making my ex suffer.
- I dream about my missing lover coming back.
- I imagine if I looked different, I'd win my mate back.
- I remember our loving times together and overlook the bad ones.
- I'm giving up responsibility for my life. Whatever happens, happens.
- I can't make decisions. I doubt almost every move.
- I can't relieve the constant pain.
- I think about going crazy, being committed and taken care of.
- I can't stop thinking about "the one" and how my ex was it.

Compulsive Symptoms

- I actually pursue strange cars or people in the hope it's my ex.

- I question and probe mutual friends for information.
- I mainly talk about my lost love and seek consolation, support and/or advice.
- I've suddenly turned spiritual, to God, Jesus, a church or cult or the religion of my childhood.
- I pray to get my lover back.
- I constantly seek advice on how to get my lover back.
- I keep eating junk food and sweets.
- I'm drinking too much or taking too many drugs.
- My only goal in life is retrieving my lost love.
- I keep buying things that don't make me happy.
- I've started smoking or increased my smoking.
- I can't help listening to the words of love songs.
- I'm always checking for phone messages.
- I drive by my ex's house, school, place of business.
- I buy "friendship cards" to convey my message.
- Whenever I pass a store, I look for something to buy as a "make up" gift.
- I buy clothes that I imagine will entice my mate into coming back.
- I call my lover on the phone over and over again.
- I keep all my former mate's favorite foods ready in case he/she shows up.
- I make preparations for the time my mate and I will get back together.

Depressive Symptoms

- I can't stay awake.
- I doze at my desk when I'm supposed to be working.
- I want to spend all my spare time sleeping or in bed.
- I don't want to go anywhere or do anything.
- I'm not interested or excited about anything or anyone.
- I'm not taking care of my body or my house.
- I neglect my pets, children, work or plants.

- I get tickets and don't pay them.
- I've been letting my bills pile up.
- I cry a lot.
- I feel as if nothing's any use.
- I think I've failed in life.
- My finances are going downhill. My credit rating has probably dropped.
- I can't cope with simple problems like flat tires or traffic jams.
- I feel helpless.
- I cry over leftover memorabilia, pictures of us together, gifts he/she gave me.
- I reject other offers of love.
- My life has become like a nightmare.
- I feel fat, skinny, unattractive, even ugly.
- None of my clothes are right, my house is loused up, I never look right.
- I've thought about killing myself.
- I've planned how to kill myself.
- I've attempted to kill myself.
- I feel disconnected, like I don't belong anywhere.
- I want to give things away because they have lost their meaning and value to me.
- I feel like a fool.
- Nothing could be worse than what's already happened, so I take foolhardy chances.
- I've lost interest in sports, dancing or exercise.

Phobic Symptoms

- I feel like everything is closing in on me and I can't stand to be in close quarters.
- I panic at the thought of meeting new people.
- I have to be with someone all the time.
- I want to leave all the lights on and all the doors open.

- I'm afraid I may be losing my mind.
- I'm afraid that now I'll be alone forever.
- I'm losing my looks.
- I'm afraid I won't be able to support myself.
- I'm afraid I'll get sick and there won't be anyone to take care of me.
- I'm afraid of getting old alone.
- I avoid places I went to with my lover when we were happy together.
- I want to run away.
- I want to sell everything and move to another city.
- I'm afraid that I've ruined my life.
- I'm afraid that I don't have enough to offer someone for a long-lasting relationship.
- I'm afraid no one will ever love me again that special way.
- I'm afraid I might kill myself.
- I'm afraid I can't attract anyone as good-looking, smart or loving again.
- I'm afraid of my friends and relatives and what they'll think and say.
- I'm afraid I won't be able to afford the life-style we had together.

Psychosomatic Symptoms

- I have attacks of heartburn or diarrhea.
- I feel nauseous at the sight of food.
- I feel like everything gives me physical ailments.
- My sexual appetite is gone.
- I'm impotent or "frigid."
- I get chest pains.
- I have rapid heartbeat.
- My blood pressure is up.
- My ulcers are acting up, or I feel like I'm getting ulcers.
- I have dandruff.

- I have pimples, psoriasis or unexplained rashes.
- I'm having "female" problems or "male" problems.
- My hair is falling out.
- I get cold sores, hives or acne.
- I have an onslaught of physical illnesses like flu and colds.
- I have headaches.
- My back hurts, my neck has a kink or it hurts when I walk.
- I have on occasion lost control of my body functions.
- I've begun biting my nails. My hands and cuticles are dry and ragged.
- My allergies are acting up.
- I have bronchial attacks.
- I wake up in the middle of the night.
- I get indigestion whenever I eat.

Hysterical Symptoms

- I get irritable at the slightest provocation.
- Little things that go wrong throw me into a panic.
- I forget important things I'm supposed to do.
- I lose things, my keys, wallet, driver's license.
- I run around all the time accomplishing nothing, just trying to keep from having to be alone.
- I lose my temper regularly.
- I'd give money, gifts, reformed behavior, anything, just to get my lover back.
- Noises drive me crazy; loud music, construction, even freeway traffic and airplanes get on my nerves.
- I can't stand to have the television off or the stereo silent. I must have noise.
- I can't get warm.
- I want to scream out.
- I feel like smashing and breaking things.
- My emotions flare uncontrollably.
- I drive aimlessly, miss turnoffs and sometimes get lost.

- I miss and cancel appointments.
- I imagine killing my former lover.
- I am careless and have accidents.
- I hurt myself physically all the time, cooking, working around the house or just walking into things.
- I go into giggles or uncontrollable laughter.

Anxiety Symptoms
- I'm finding it increasingly harder to fall asleep.
- I can't eat.
- I have accidents, dent my car, drop and break things, spot and tear my clothes.
- I've been getting traffic tickets.
- I can't breathe deeply enough.
- I have tension headaches.
- I grit my teeth.
- I grind my jaw.
- I feel "butterflies" in the pit of my stomach.
- I perspire excessively.
- My hands and feet are always cold and clammy.
- My face is tense.
- My brow is getting deep wrinkles.
- I am nervous and touchy.
- I worry all the time about everything.
- I blow things out of proportion.
- I think I've lost important things and panic.

Scoring

If you rate yourself a five or higher (out of ten possible) on *most* of the above listed symptoms, you are suffering in the acute stages of love sickness. You will notice, as you progress on the program, that more and more of your symptoms disappear or become less severe.

If you score seven or higher on *most* of the above listed

symptoms, you may need a licensed health professional like a psychologist, a behaviorally oriented psychiatrist, or a clinical social worker to monitor your progress on the program.

The Addiction

In order to overcome your symptoms, you have to admit that you are no longer involved in a Romeo and Juliet tragic love story, but are now suffering the withdrawal pain of an addict.

The first week of separation is the hardest. Suddenly you find yourself without the gratifying supply of love. You've been cut off "cold turkey."

Being "in love" is being addicted to the loved one. You get used to having that particular other person around all the time, to thinking of living your life as a unit with them. You've done things together so much that it's hard for you to think about doing things alone or with someone else.

In the past, when you've taken pride in your appearance, it was to make yourself more attractive, more lovable in your beloved's eyes. Doing it for yourself just isn't the same. Who will enjoy your clean house? Who will laugh with you at the movies? Who will share your triumphs and disasters? You are suffering from withdrawal pain—the withdrawal of love by the one person who got you hooked.

It's easy to say you'll find another person who will love you as much, but imagine telling an alcoholic that the world would look better sober than it does when he's drunk, or even a drug addict that being high on nature is as good as being high on drugs?

That's what making it alone sounds like to you.

The same principles of behavior therapy used successfully to treat people who are addicted to foods, drugs, alcohol and even sexual compulsions can be applied to your addiction to your former lover.

Behaviorists believe in stopping the pain, not wasting years delving into the subconscious to find out what *could* have caused it. Behaviorists work to change behavior by replacing old habits with new, more gratifying ones.

Your immediate problem is how to stop the withdrawal pain. The immediate symptoms (the insomnia, the obsessions, the paranoia and mostly the feeling of being totally helpless) are keeping you from living a normal life.

You can't go to the grocery store without remembering when you went there together, so you don't go. You imagine that nobody has ever felt as badly as you do about being left, so you're embarrassed and try to hide your pain. If you were to ask your friends, you'd probably find that one out of three has actually thought about killing themselves over a lover. The feelings you have aren't unique, except to you.

In order to think straight about your problem, you have to break the thought-addiction to your former lover. The obsessions, the things that go through your mind all the time about the person who has left you, things you would say to make them come back, explanations you would give for the supposed wrongs you did, apologies you want to make, fantasies of all-is-forgiven, loving conversations, even the constant image of "the" missing face—you can conquer them all.

Soon you will stop crying over sad songs on the radio, eat something besides junk food, get yourself together and your life in order. Now that you have diagnosed your symptomatology and understand its basis, you are ready to begin to take positive steps toward your recovery.

Session Two: Conquering the Need to Communicate

Sure you want to talk, to know why you were left. Was there someone else? When did it happen? What did you do wrong?

Knowing the answers may not make you feel better, but could you really feel worse?

Advice and Information

Getting information from the wrong places would make you feel worse. People love to give advice. It makes them feel essential, needed. And the person who is love-addicted is compulsively driven to seek advice and information from everyone.

Most people won't give you good advice because they don't know the answers, but they'll try. Some people will even like you better when you're suffering. They love to nurture, to sympathize.

The truth is that the more you talk about your ex, the more you will reinforce your thought-addiction. If you can, don't get advice. Don't indulge in long, commiserating conversations with well-wishers. Don't ask them why they think it happened, what you should do or how to win your lover back.

Even unsolicited information, the casual "By the way, I saw your ex last night," can trigger a depression. The rest of the story might be even worse. Don't leave yourself open to it. A simple "I prefer not to discuss it" will close the subject with most people. Constantly talking about your addiction is just as addicting as the addiction itself. You become addicted to talking about your loss. You renew your hope and wind up in a more perplexing, push-me-pull-you, it's-on-it's-off kind of situation.

The Telephone

It's driving you crazy. Every time it rings, you're sure it's "the one." You feel the adrenaline rush.

Classic advice to the lovelorn is, no matter how badly you want to, no matter how good the reason, no matter what, don't contact the person you're yearning for. "Don't give him/her the satisfaction," friends counsel. But what about your satisfaction?

If you could never call your ex or think about them again, it would be great for you and you wouldn't be so smitten, but chances are you can't do that right now. There's probably a telephone number playing over in your head at this moment. Your fingers seem drawn to the dial.

Go ahead, make the call, and don't put yourself down for being "weak," either. It may make you feel better just to hear your old lover's voice, even if you know your reception will be cool. Don't expect anything great. Be satisfied if you get the momentary satisfaction of knowing where your ex is without humiliating yourself by driving "accidentally" past their house.

Two months after Robert left her, Janet found herself in the unflattering role of spy. She would park near the place he worked hoping to see him come in or out and even drive by his house to see whose car was there.

"I couldn't help it," she explained to her therapist. "It was as if I just had to know." Twice a day she telephoned Robert's home or office. As soon as he said hello, she'd hang up without identifying herself.

"I hate myself for doing it," Janet berated herself. "I feel humiliated and I'm terrified he'll catch me, and yet I can't stop. I have to hear his voice, but I'm afraid to talk to him." Feeling weak and helpless in the face of her compulsion to talk to Robert only reinforced Janet's bad feelings about herself. Don't let that happen to you.

It's okay if you call your ex during the first week. *You* are the one in pain, and you are the one that has to be considered. If calling your ex on the phone six times a day and hanging up will make you have less pain, do it.

The worst has already happened. The love is gone, so there's no threat of loss. If calling makes you feel better, call—but don't expect sympathy or support.

You don't have to hang up either. You could actually talk. Maybe your former mate will say something really rotten and help you get disillusioned with them. Part of the problem is that your lover has become disillusioned with you, and you haven't had an opportunity to do the same. *You* still imagine you have lost the most wonderful person in the world.

There's even a chance that you're being missed and the relationship can be rekindled. Certainly you have nothing to lose and everything to gain.

Janet was able to call Robert after her therapist desensitized her to her secret fears—either that a woman would answer Robert's phone or that he would hang up on her in disgust. By repeatedly imagining both these situations while relaxed (See Stress Inoculation, Chapter Eleven), Janet developed an immunity to her fears.

When she did talk to Robert, she felt better. Giving up her tacky spy role helped her regain her self-respect.

"Sure," you say, "but if I called every time I felt like it, I'd be on the telephone twenty-four hours a day. Even when we do talk, I think of another thing I should have said almost as soon as I hang up, and I want to call back again."

Certainly your ex isn't going to spend every hour of every day talking to you, and it wouldn't be good for you either, but there is an alternative to adding an outrageous phone bill to your problems—an emotional bankbook to store them in.

The Bankbook

This is a special notebook and a special pen used exclusively for writing those things you want to say to your ex. Questions you want to ask, solutions, promises, apologies, even name-calling invectives belong here.

The next time you talk to your former lover on the phone, you can pull out the notebook and go down the list. You may find that you don't really want to communicate everything you've written, and eventually the entire Bankbook will begin to sound repetitive, embarrassing and boring, but that comes later.

There are five important reasons for the Bankbook.

1. It will save you the humiliation of calling your ex each time you have a thought you *must* share.

2. By writing things down, you get them out of your head. You don't have to walk around all day saying to yourself, "The next time we talk, I have to remember to point out such and such."

Using the Bankbook technique will free your mind of some of the obsessive thoughts. You won't be repeating them to yourself to remember, and by the simple act of repeating them, learning a new habit. The Bankbook will relieve you of the burden of carrying these messages around in your mind.

3. By limiting your thoughts to the Bankbook, you will automatically cut down the time you spend on them. All the nostalgic and even bitter thoughts about your lover will be confined to one place. This helps keep you from "flashing" uncontrollably all day long. Very soon, you will learn how to confine your nostalgic thoughts and communications with your ex to just a short period of time each day and finally to no time at all.

4. Your Bankbook will act as a cooling-off period for anything you *think* you want to say to your ex. It will keep you from grabbing the telephone and saying rash things that might be embarrassing later.

5. You'll begin to self-limit your thoughts—if having to write them down is the price for having them. It gets to be a lot of trouble after a while, especially when you discover that you're writing the same things over and over again. This is called *response cost* in behavior therapy. Writing is the cost for your

having nostalgic thoughts about your loss, for dwelling on them. The higher the cost to you (i.e., the more you have to write), the quicker you will self-modify the costly behavior.

Thinking about your old lover and your ruined love affair tends to aggrandize them both. That's why it's important to have an "in person" meeting.

The Meeting

It's essential that you have a meeting as soon as possible. A meeting with the ex is much better than a phone call because it gives you a better chance to become disillusioned. Sporadic telephoning after the first week can result in an *intermittent reinforcement* situation. The phone call only builds your hope and reinforces the fantasy that your gratification has to come from "that" person.

In laboratory experiments, it's been proven that mice work harder to get food from a machine if they only get it intermittently—not consistently or constantly. By getting intermittent attention or love from your former mate, you react like a lab mouse and work harder for the intermittent reward.

If it's at all possible, insist on a confrontation. The meeting could be a comfort to you and prove he/she really does care. Or it could show you that your ex isn't so great after all.

Announcements

It's not a good idea to make announcements to all your friends (either mutual or otherwise) and family that your relationship is over—at least not until you have one meeting. Sometimes, a few days' "cooling off" period is all a couple needs. You're going to feel silly if you've made statements that you and your ex are finished and you get back together again—particularly if you've been broadcasting all the awful things that happened.

If all you really needed was a "cooling off" period, work out a reconciliation agreement so you can learn how to stay together in the future. Most couples do try at least one reconciliation, and some succeed.

If you do, you're one of the lucky ones, but remember, as Swami Satchidananda told his disciples, "When you win a war with your power . . . you have won the war but not the heart. Real victory is to win the heart."

2
RECONCILIATION

Think of what you're saying. You can get it wrong
and still you think that it's all right.
Think of what I'm saying. We can work it out and get
it straight, or say good-night.

—JOHN LENNON AND PAUL MCCARTNEY
"We Can Work It Out"

You really wonder if it's worth a try and most of your friends say no, it won't happen, or it still wouldn't be any good. But deep down inside, your secret dream is getting back together and working things out, restoring your relationship or even making it better.

Don't count on a reconciliation working. Most don't. Things can never be the same as they were before. You have both said and done things that hurt. Those things will definitely make you change in your actions and thoughts toward each other. The relationship has to change if you want it to work.

Reconciliation attempts are advantageous even when they don't work. There are two reasons why you should make an effort to get back together. The first is that you will get a chance to see the reality of your lost love and your former relationship.

Part of missing your habitual addiction to "that other person" in your life is the aggrandizing of their qualities. If love is blind, lost love is deaf and dumb, too.

In your imagination, you have probably given your ex physical, emotional and intellectual qualities that don't really exist except in your imagination. You have emphasized the loving qualities of your former lover to the exclusion of their not-so-perfect and endearing character traits. A reconciliation attempt gives you a chance to see the truth.

The second reason for a reconciliation attempt is that it probably won't work. Even though you're sure you could seduce your ex into loving you again if you only got the opportunity, it's highly unlikely.

In most cases, no matter how much you've changed, no matter how loving or perfect (to your ex's specs, of course) you've become, you can't *make* another person love you. Nor will you be able to keep up a charade by attempting a monumental surface change in your own behavior.

Yes, you say, but what if the miracle occurs? What if you meet, fall into each other's arms sobbing forgiveness and swearing you both want to make it work?

It's not totally impossible. If it does happen, negotiating a behavioral contract, perhaps with the help of a professional counselor, is the best success possibility. But try it by yourselves first.

THE SECOND WEEK

Session Three: The Behavioral Contract

The behavioral contract, developed by Dr. Richard Stuart of the University of Utah, is one of the newest and most successful tools used by psychologists and marriage and family counselors to help couples reconcile what seem to be irreconcilable differences. In order to have a working contract, you must have two people who are both willing to work at changing admittedly undesirable traits in themselves for the good of the relationship.

If you and your partner can agree on enough points that you each feel you need to change and that you want to change, you can make your own behavioral contract.

The first step is to make a list of things you want corrected by your partner. Your mate must also make a separate list of things he or she wants you to change. The list should be made up of the most important things that bother you about your mate—not red-herring issues like putting down the toilet seat, taking hairs out of the shower drain or putting tops on the toothpaste tubes. Your lists must be positive, not negative.

Each item on your list that reflects a negative quality in your partner must be converted to a positive request.

For example, instead of, "I want him to stop yelling about things," you might have a positive request of, "When I irritate him, I want him to sit down and discuss things with me calmly and quietly."

Or instead of, "I don't want her to nag me with problems about what went wrong at home the minute I come in from work," you might request, "I want her to wait until after dinner to discuss household problems with me."

The important thing is that each person must agree that they will be correcting something that is undesirable in themselves. In the above example, the man must agree that yelling at his partner is not a good quality, and the woman must agree that bombarding her mate with problems the minute he comes in the door isn't a good idea. These agreements are basic to a good behavioral contract.

Time limits are important. You might specify that your partner save problem discussions until two hours after you come in. The net outcome is that you put each other on a mutual positive reinforcement program.

The behavioral contract is a quid pro quo contract, an even exchange of value for value. Everybody gets something they want. Your partner's reward for changing undesirable behavior is your own agreement to change or modify your behavior in some productive way. Your reward is what they agree to do in exchange.

Julia and Rick are a good-looking couple, both in their early thirties. Rick is a salesman who's on the road a lot. Julia stays home with her five-year-old daughter from a previous marriage. When they came for counseling, they had been living together three years.

Their relationship had deteriorated over the last six months. Julia was bored and felt neglected. Rick, on the other hand, felt great, flush with success over a newly acquired higher income bracket and disappointed that Julia didn't share his elation. They fought all the time, but wanted to stay together.

One of Julia's biggest complaints was that Rick excluded her from too many parts of his life. "He works all the time, then wants to take off and go fishing with the guys on his vacations. He wants to play golf with his buddies on Sunday and basketball on Saturdays. He bowls during the week and goes on business trips alone all the time," were her negative complaints. With a counselor's help, she changed them to the positive request, "I want Rick to spend more time with me."

Rick complained bitterly about Julia's extravagances. "All she does is spend money. She has more clothes than any woman I know, and she's still buying stuff all the time. Our bills are outrageous, especially the telephone bills. She spends hours talking with her girlfriends on the phone, long distance."

Their therapist explained to Rick and Julia that Rick is indeed a sovereign being with no one to account to for his time. However, as a mature person, Rick needs to be sensitive to Julia's feelings when he's not with her and to take them into account when he plans trips.

"If only he'd spend more time with me," Julia sighed again. "I wouldn't have to go shopping all the time or spend so much time on the phone because I wouldn't be so lonely or bored."

Rick and Julia's therapist pointed out that as soon as Julia said the word "if," there existed what behavior therapists call a *contingency contract*—a contract where one thing is dependent or contingent on something the other person will do.

Rick offered to be home more and to take Julia on more trips with him. In exchange, Julia offered to spend more time with him as a substitute for shopping and talking on the telephone.

Within a very few weeks, the telephone bill and the credit card slips decreased measurably, and Julia and Rick took their first vacation together in over two years. They had also learned a method for staying together.

Not all couples have reconcilable differences. In these cases one or both partners categorically refuse to change those undesirable behaviors their mate finds unbearable.

What happens if you find too many unbargainable points? Your partner may not agree that the things you want changed are really unlovable and disagreeable, or they just may want to stay the way they are.

Session Four: Working Out Details

Arnold and Marie had been married ten years when they came for counseling. Marie is thirty-five, vivacious and attractive. Arnold is forty-two, balding and slightly overweight, yet attractive, too.

Marie loves her job as a receptionist in a large manufacturing plant. She enjoys the attention from all the salesmen that come in and out all day. It was obvious from the way she dressed and acted during her therapy that she fosters a sexual and flirtatious image of herself. Marie was unwilling to give up her job to be home cooking three meals a day for Arnold during his "slow" periods.

Arnold is an actor, a bit player who does a nightclub act during slow periods. He might make $2,000 in two weeks on a movie and then not work again for months during the day. Sometimes he goes out on cruise ships as an entertainer for weeks at a time. Usually he is home all day with nothing to do.

Marie wanted Arnold, a certified accountant by schooling, to take a regular job with regular work hours and to bring in a regular paycheck. She really was saying it was either acting or her.

Arnold wanted Marie to stay home. He had the urge to start a family, but she felt it was too late for her to have children and that his career wasn't secure enough to raise a family.

Neither partner was willing to see their jobs as undesirable qualities and neither was willing to make their work a negotiable point in their behavioral contract. Eventually they separated.

If you find that you are trying to build a behavioral contract with an uncooperative partner and can't reach an agreement on contractible points, you may have to face the simple fact that you and your mate are truly incompatible. That you have different values and different needs. That you can't supply each other with the thing the other person needs most.

If that does happen, it's not so terrible. If you come to the realization that you can't live with the other person's necessary actions, the things they feel they must do, then your loss isn't as great as you thought it was.

Gilbert and Elaine had been going together for two years. Elaine was twenty-eight and had never been married. She was an elementary school teacher who spent every day in the school yard, yearning for children of her own. With tears in her eyes, she confessed to her therapist that she wouldn't feel complete as a woman unless she could have a child.

Gilbert, dashing and suave, in contrast to Elaine's rather pretty but plain looks, said he wasn't going to give up his bachelor life and his freedom to be *trapped* into marriage, as he put it. Kids, he said, made him nervous; he wanted to travel and have no obligations to take care of anyone but himself.

Since Gilbert refused to marry her and give her children, Elaine broke up with him. Gilbert was heartbroken until he realized, while trying to negotiate a behavioral contract with Elaine, that she wasn't really the woman he wanted. They had different life goals.

Elaine realized that she would either have to give up her dreams of having a home, a husband and children, or give up Gilbert. Although they both felt that they cared for one another, they were able to separate on more friendly terms because they each realized they couldn't live with the other's terms. They were truly incompatible.

If you find that you and your partner wind up with too many important unnegotiable points on your positive request list, or if you find you can't live up to the things you've agreed to change, you might want to get in touch with a professional behavior therapist.

Almost every city has a society of licensed psychologists,

psychiatrists or clinical social workers. Call them and tell them you want to see a behavior therapist, and they will refer you to someone. You can also contact your local university or college for the name of an appropriate professional in your area, or you may want to write the authors for a referral.

Your reconciliation may or may not be successful. Odds are it won't. If it is, there will be a lot of hard work and a lot of leftover pain to deal with. Even if your behavioral reconciliation does work, it may take many months before your relationship is on an even keel.

Suppose your partner categorically refuses to attempt a reconciliation in any way? What do you do then?

Perhaps they've found someone else to love, or maybe you've lost your love by death, divorce or desertion. Does that mean your life has to end? Of course not.

3
WHEN THERE'S NO HOPE

There are no tomorrows for this heart of mine,
Surely time will lose these bitter mem'ries
and I'll find that there is someone to believe in
and to live for, Something I could live for.

—KAREN AND RICHARD CARPENTER
"Goodbye to Love"

You know you'll never get your loved one back, and suddenly your life seems worthless. The battle for emotional stability isn't one you're ready to deal with. You begin to think about painless methods of ending it all.

It's not as silly as it seems. Suicidologists report that lost love ranks with heart disease and cancer as a cause of death. Suicide prevention centers across the United States report that almost 80 percent of the cases they come in contact with involve loss of love. The incredibly high teenage suicide rate can be almost exclusively attributed to terminated relationships.

Even if you don't feel suicidal, you are in danger. When you're suffering in the acute stages of "broken heart," you are risking your health and your life. Not only are you in danger of killing yourself by committing suicide, but statistics show that many people going through the changes caused by a loss of love (even by death) develop life-threatening diseases like cancer or risk their lives in a flurry of "accidents." Naturally, there is no way to prove that a newly divorced woman develops breast or cervical cancer solely because she feels unloved, or because her life-style has changed significantly, or because she is depressed, but she is in a higher risk category statistically.

Depression of any kind is often accompanied by illnesses, and a post-affair depression is no different. When you break off a love relationship, you are likely to fall prey to a surfeit of psychosomatic ailments.

Ulcers are caused when your aroused body secretes too much digestive juice and your irritated stomach and intestines lose their resistance. You begin to burn a hole in your own gastrointestinal tract. Muscle tension is the psychosomatic cause of backaches. Tension headaches can be caused by chronic contraction of the scalp and neck muscles due to emotional tension. Hypertension (high blood pressure) and even heart disease could all result from your anxiety over your lost love.

Nobody feels good when they're sick. A few days of flu, a backache or an upset stomach could make you even more depressed than you are. At the first sign of illness, you have fantasies of yourself much sicker, in the hospital, and alone.

It's not just the physical upsets that make people feel like killing themselves when they lose their love, it's the seeming relentlessness of everything going wrong combined with the helplessness in the face of the obsessive thoughts about the ex.

It seems as if your entire life is centered around that one thing—your lover who's no longer available.

It's relentless. Every morning and every night you are haunted with thoughts and visions of your former mate. It doesn't seem to be going away; it only gets worse. You feel as if there's no way out. You've done everything you can think of to appeal to your former lover and now you figure, "I'll do anything to show how much I care, how deeply I love. Even kill myself." You feel that's the only thing left that would have any impact.

Suicide prevention centers report that twice as many men kill themselves over broken hearts as do women. There are three theories as to why fewer women actually succeed in killing themselves than men.

One reason for the lower female suicide rate is that women are more in touch with their emotions and are more sensitive to the subtle signs that a relationship is over, while men are more often unprepared and shocked by the apparent suddenness of the ending.

A second theory for female survival is that women are more capable of handling separation trauma because they are dumped more often than men. Each experience has desensitized, prepared and strengthened them for the next. Men are still the leaders in dumping partners and when they're dumped they just don't know how to handle it.

But the most likely reason women don't succeed as often in suicide attempts is because they usually get custody of the children and feel more responsibility to life. Who will feed the kids tomorrow? The thought of their children, alone and abandoned, is a strong deterrent to female suicides.

THE THIRD WEEK

Session Five: Suicide Prevention

Tom Sawyer Fantasies

The Tom Sawyer suicide funeral fantasy is the most popular when loss of a lover is involved. The abandoned lover imagines their own funeral, who will come and who will send flowers, and most of all who will cry.

"If I kill myself," thinks the suicidal lover, "then they'll be sorry for the way they treated me. Then they'll feel as awful as I do. Then they'll suffer, too." It's a way to punish the one who drove them to suicide—by using "I killed myself for you" guilt induction.

"He/she will be haunted forever. They'll never forget me if I kill myself over them," is a common presuicidal fantasy. Or, "He/she didn't realize how serious it was, how much I really loved him/her, or they wouldn't have left me. Will he/she be sorry when they find out."

Homicidal Suicides

Anger is a major cause of suicide, but not necessarily anger at oneself. Suicidologists point out that suicide is 50 percent homicide and 50 percent suicide.

If you've thought about killing yourself, you probably have a lot of suppressed anger—not, as you would suspect, with yourself, whom you want to kill, but rather toward that other person. Perhaps you'd like to kill the one who left you, but you're not really a murderer, so you pick on the easiest and most convenient substitute—yourself.

You imagine your lover will pay for your death by emotional suffering and guilt, that you'll have your revenge from the grave. Actually your suicide will only make your former lover feel important and by taking your own life, you will prove how impossible a relationship with you would be. You will justify their leaving you.

The harsh truth is that if you kill yourself over your separation, your mate might even be angrier with you for causing them pain and problems. Besides, imagine your ex at a cocktail party one day saying, "Someone died for love of me." Or seducing a new lover with the sad tale of you, the tragic love. Naturally their version of the story will have a different slant, probably how they lost their own true love in a Romeo and Juliet tragedy.

Do you want to immortalize that other person by sacrificing your life for them? Is he/she really worth it?

Suicide-Safe Support System

Although this book is set up in a carefully laid out three-month treatment plan for completely overcoming love sickness, your current emergency situation requires immediate first aid. Many recommendations for your third week of separation are simply stopgap measures to keep you from doing irreparable harm, and first aid to lift you from your current despair. The detailed treatment that will cure your pain and restore you to the complete, functioning and loving human being you were before this tragedy will take place over the next nine weeks.

Even if it's just for a brief moment, everyone suffering from abruptly terminated, postrelationship blues thinks that life is just not worth living anymore. If you're in that spot there are a few suicide prevention techniques to be aware of and take immediately.

1. Give your guns to a trusted friend.
2. Flush your sleeping pills down a toilet or give them to someone to keep for you and dole out as needed.
3. Keep emergency phone numbers by your bed—your

mother, your psychological counselor or local suicide prevention center.

4. Have handy the phone numbers of three friends you can call in the middle of the night. Confide your suicidal inclinations to them and resolve that you will call if you find yourself having serious self-destructive thoughts. The reason you need three is in case somebody's not home.
5. If you get in trouble, call the suicide prevention center, local help line or university counseling center. They'll help or refer you to help. In life-threatening emergencies, call your local police department or fire department.

If you need help, suicide prevention centers do a good job, although they're not as good as your therapist or a close friend. You don't have to worry if you call them. They *don't* send police, or ambulances filled with men in white coats, nor do they come banging on your door themselves. They *will* talk to you. If you've already done something harmful, they are trained to get you help.

People at suicide prevention centers across the United States are in contact with free and pay-what-you-can clinics in their cities. They'll aim you toward regular and reasonable help when your crisis is past. Some cities have twenty-four-hour psychological help lines.

Often, just letting the other person know that you are thinking about killing yourself takes some of the drama out of the situation. Many suicide attempts are simply gestures to let the other person know how much they really mean, how serious things are.

You don't have to kill yourself to let your lover know you care. You don't even have to make a dramatic gesture. You can do it with a telephone call.

Instead of planning a suicide attempt, call your lover and tell them you feel like killing yourself. Probably, you'll make the disconcerting discovery that the other person doesn't really care if you do. They may even tell you to go ahead and kill yourself. If your ex is unsympathetic, immediately call and tell a close friend your problem, someone who will assure you they *do* care.

On the other hand, if your ex cares enough, they may come running to your rescue. Or, if they care, but don't want to change their mind or encourage you about the relationship, they might send a friend.

If you've made even vague suicidal plans, set up immediate obstacles to their fulfillment. If you're obsessed by driving your car off a certain cliff, don't go near that cliff until the obsession passes. If you want to jump off the Golden Gate Bridge, find a way to make it hard to do.

Set up a pattern of "must make" phone calls that you agree to make before taking any steps. You must talk to two important friends and one therapist. When you call people, don't be afraid to tell them what you intend to do and to *ask them to help you not to do it.* If you are afraid to call your lover and say you feel like killing yourself, in case he or she doesn't care, make your close friends or therapist a substitute for the lover call. You know they care.

Learned Helplessness

The main cause of suicidal depression is the discovery that you are helpless. No matter what you do there is no way to make the other person love you.

The tragedy of a lost love is the helplessness of not being able to do anything to change the other person's mind. In the past you were able to influence that person in every way.

Now you've broken up. Nothing will change your ex's mind. Not gifts, playing hard-to-get, withholding love, honesty, silence, flowers, temper tantrums, bullying tactics, even courting.

Manipulations don't work either. Nor does jealousy, seduction, rage, threats, tears, cajoling or even sex.

It's a shock to find out that all the things you've done in the past to maintain the relationship no longer work. Messages through loved ones, children, pastors, friends. It's all for naught. You're doing the things that always worked before, and nothing's happening. You're depressed because you feel there is nothing to do. You feel helpless.

You may or may not get your old lover back, but even if you don't, you'll be okay. If you are thinking of killing yourself, or even if you have thought about it in the past, hold off. This book can save your life.

Don't even try a dramatic, attention-getting suicide gesture. Many deaths are accidental successes, and you're really not helpless. It's not true that there is nothing to do. There is plenty to do to help yourself. This book is full of tasks, assignments and projects that when done as prescribed will shut off your pain, save your life and prevent the destructive illnesses that are likely to follow your breakup. You have learned to be helpless. You can unlearn it.

Dr. Martin Seligman's experiments with rats proved the startling effect of learned helplessness. A light in a box where the rats were kept went on a few seconds before the rodents were given a mild shock. There was a lever that turned off the shock. It wasn't long before the rats learned that if they pressed the lever as soon as the light went on, the shock wouldn't happen.

After they learned to stop the shock by pressing the lever after the light went on, the lever was disconnected. The rats pressed the bar and got shocked anyway. Soon, the depressed rodents curled up in the corner of the box, not bothering to press the lever when the light went on. They accepted the shock and acted like depressed patients who don't want to do anything except sit and whimper. The rats' depression was caused by learned helplessness.

Just as you have learned you can't do anything to get your

mate back, the rats learned that they were helpless to change their predicament in any way to stop their pain.

To counter your depression, attack the learned helplessness. One way is to consider: what are the things your ex did for you? How can you do them for yourself or get someone else to do them for you? You can only continue to feel helpless when you continue to be dependent on the person you've lost. By proving you can provide things you thought only that other person could give you, you start dismissing your learned helplessness and also a lot of your depression.

Thin Schedule of Reinforcement

Another cause of suicidal depression is being put on a thin schedule of gratification. It was easy to feel appreciated and gratified when you were loved and someone was always there to tell you, at least by their presence, how wonderful you were. If your ex gave you a lot of strokes for every third good thing you did, your normal gratification schedule is one in three. Now you're alone and there's no one to give you those strokes. You may have to do ten or twenty good things before someone comes along to appreciate them. Instead of waiting and suffering from a thin schedule of reinforcement, give *yourself* strokes for closing a deal. Invite a friend over to see your new lamp. Find an occasion to show off your new hairstyle. It's not easy to get used to a thin schedule of gratification. You'll react like the lab mouse who always got a food pellet when he pressed the bar and suddenly finds the pellets come only once in twenty-six presses. It's depressing. Like the dollar devaluation.

Don't brave it out alone. Invite overnight guests and visit friends where you can stay with them. Don't miss out on couples and families. They have each other all the time and are glad to help, if only for the diversion of a new person and something new to talk about. Remember, everybody has lost a lover at least once, and so they will be very understanding. You don't even have to spend all your visits telling your troubles to your friends and relatives. You could just swim in their pool, read on their sundeck, play cards or just gossip.

If you break up over the holidays, and it's amazing how many people do, things will seem even bleaker. Being alone during Christmas and New Year's is about the worst thing that can happen, even to a well-adjusted, normal person whose lover hasn't just left them.

No matter what holiday is coming up, throw a party. Be sure to have a co-host or hostess and tell them to invite their friends. To avoid the depression of missing your ex's help, plan clean-up help afterwards.

The party is to take care of you, so set it up that way. If you can, arrange for your co-host to stay over. The house seems terribly empty after a party.

By throwing a party, you accomplish two things. You keep your mind off your troubles while you're making party preparations, and you have an excuse to call all the people you haven't talked to for a long time, to make those important reconnections with the world. Even if it's right before Christmas, you'll be amazed to discover how many of your friends have nowhere to go on Christmas day. You'll also drum up a reciprocal invitation for New Year's or whatever the next holiday is.

Regaining Control

A third cause of suicidal depression is the feeling that your life is totally out of control. When you lose your love, it feels like everything is going wrong. Your bank statements read overdrawn. The IRS wants to audit you. The kids are failing and causing problems at school. The roof leaks, and even the weeds in the backyard seem to be attacking you. You're bombarded by everything. Traffic tickets, five-day phone cutoff notices, utility rate increases, gas leaks, invasions of green bottle flies, a sick dog and a spot on your new suit. You wonder why everything goes wrong now.

Everything is going wrong because you've been neglecting so many of your obligations and responsibilities while trying to save your waning relationship. Since it broke up, you've been on even more of a downer and neglected things even worse than before. That solves the mystery of why the plants picked now to die.

One at a time you have to gain control over your backed-up problems. Pile up your bills and sort them into the most pressing—lights, gas and water. It's even okay to tell some creditors you can't pay right now, but that you will. Pay off the smallest bills and pay little amounts, just tokens, on your large ones. Never miss a month paying *something.* Your credit will miraculously get good. If necessary, get a job, anything, even temporary work, to see you through.

It may feel like the whole world is out of control and you have to fight everything at once. You think things have gone haywire because you lost your love and that's why you're overwhelmed. But the truth is that everybody feels bad when they can't pay their bills.

Don't try to boldly assault all your problems at once. Instead, do one thing at a time. One reason people consider suicide is because when "everything" is wrong, death seems an easy way out. By attacking things one at a time, you'll find that you can cope and regain control of your life. Soon "everything" won't be out of control. Do maintenance tasks first (water dying plants, balance overdrawn checkbooks, pay something on the bills), then take the rest in order of priority and easiness to complete.

Lack of Nurturance

The need for love isn't something you made up. It's real! In a classic English study, war orphans died without human love and warmth. A kitten's spine will actually shrivel if it's not licked by its mother cat or touched and fondled and stroked.

Stroking is important. Even mice react to handling. An "experimental group" mouse that is handled learns better and faster than a "control group" mouse that is left alone. Neurologically, all creatures need stimulation, especially humans.

Physical stimulation is essential to your survival. That's because the nerve tissue along the spine can actually die if it receives no stimulation. Even the nerve tissue that makes up your brain will die if it's not stimulated regularly. That's why solitary confinement is the most feared punishment in prisons.

To counteract your lack of nurturance, seek out physical affection. Try increasing the amount of physical affection you give and receive each day. Getting affection will be easier for you than sex right now and will be comforting as well.

Make your first goal to get at least one hug this week. Each week increase by one hug, until you are getting at least four warm cuddly bearlike squeezes weekly. It's not as hard as it sounds. Ask a friend if they've had their four hugs for the week. Chances are ten to one that they haven't. You supply it. It's a sly way to get one back. Or you could tell them you haven't had *your* four-hug quota for the week. "I need a hug" is irresistible.

Substitute a kiss on the cheek, a warm arm on the shoulder or a brief embrace for your usual handshake. Become more physical with both sexes. Kiss your same sex friends. Hug them, too. Touch people when you talk to them, and they'll automatically feel warmer toward you. After all, you're stimulating their nerve tissues and giving them those life-prolonging strokes.

• • •

Sensual Deprivation

When a relationship falls apart, people tend to let themselves go, to pretend their physical being just doesn't exist. Often, they feel that the body that couldn't keep a lover, husband or wife doesn't deserve to be well treated, so they punish it with neglect.

The cure is simple. Take a bubble bath. Spread suntan lotion all over and go to the beach. Go to a matinee of a movie you've been dying to see. Eat buttered popcorn, drink Cokes and wallow in junk food. Give yourself a facial. Get a manicure. Go to a health club. Spend an entire day on your own body. Have a pedicure. Get a massage.

Remember, you don't have to have sex to cure a case of sensual deprivation. Do at least one sensuous thing for yourself each day this week.

Dependency Needs

Dependency comes from delegating your responsibility to get things for yourself. When you rely on *one* person to do things you really can do for yourself or with the help of community resources, you make yourself dependent.

If there are "special things" your ex did for you, list them from smallest to most important. Then beginning with the easiest, think of some way to get what you need by yourself. If it's love, get a puppy or a plant. If it's sex, buy a vibrator. If it's money, earn or borrow some. If it's repair work, hire someone.

Because you haven't been getting all those things—whatever they were—from your ex, you've been feeling deprived. Feeling deprived of anything that you're used to having makes you depressed. If you don't want to feel depressed, don't allow yourself to be deprived.

One of the things that made your ex important to you is that you became dependent on him or her for so many things. Men tend to become dependent for more (believe it or not) material things—like taking care of their house, cooking, taking clothes to the cleaners or simply running the daily trivia of living so they are free to go out to work and earn a living.

Women usually depend on men for things like the illusion of emotional security, financial support, social respectability, general rescuing and the opportunity to play the highly touted family game.

A man gets a lot of gratification from his work, but unfortunately the average woman's only source of emotional and intellectual stimulation is often the man in her life. On the average, her dependency needs are stronger than her mate's.

A woman is often more socially dependent because in our culture, most women aren't wealthy enough or confident enough to go out alone.

Fortunately, financial dependence on men is becoming less necessary as more women find they *can* make enough money to support themselves.

Sexual Dependency

The other important thing women depend on men for is sex. When an affair breaks up, a woman is likely to withdraw from sexual activity, feeling that no man will ever be able to satisfy her as much as the one she lost. Even if she has an orgasm, it's just not as good. Part of the thrill is missing. It's just a warm body in her bed, but not a "special" one. Culturally, women have been taught to get pleasure from only one man (monogamy) while men are often admired for multiple sex contacts.

You will learn how to break the sex hook to your ex-lover in chapter five, but for now simply accept that there's a difference between sexual relief and making love in a meaningful way to an important person in your life, with whom your body has been "in tune." You can't expect it to feel the same.

People of both sexes report that when their lover leaves

them, they're just not "turned on." Right now, nobody is going to live up to the inflated ideas you have about your ex. Well-tuned interaction takes time.

It's okay to have *just* physical relief with sex right now. And it's also okay if you're not interested in making sexual contact now. But that doesn't mean you have to sit home and feel sorry for yourself either. Take yourself someplace you've always wanted to go. See if you can find a friend to go along. Treat your single self just as well as you did when you were part of a couple. Spend money on yourself. Go somewhere fancy or expensive. Coffee at the Hilton is always more fun than a whole dinner at Howard Johnson's.

Getting Off

You get your emotional nourishment and strokes from your close family, your new pet and your good friends, but what if you're still concerned about your sexual needs? Masturbation isn't making it for you. You don't feel loved unless you have intercourse.

Remember, hamburgers are still better than hunger. If you notice that your sex activity has been decreasing, don't panic. It's just that your supply has been cut off and you have to find a new source. Every sensual experience doesn't have to be a peak experience—like the ones you had with your ex. Some people never have that kind of thrilling sex, and yet they survive on the old everyday fare. Surely you didn't expect a gourmet meal every night, even when you were in love. Now you're not in love, bells may not go off when you have sex, but it's better than nothing.

Lovemaking can give you lots of physical stroking right now, and that's important for your welfare. Built-up sexual tensions can feel like increased anxiety, so don't worry if you're not in love. It's okay to have sex with somebody just because they're there and they're nice.

Sex Sabbatical

After a breakup, sex may not be as much fun, and there are real reasons why. The first shot with someone new is rarely good. It probably *was* better with your old lover. Your bodies had time to get in tune.

Good sex takes practice. If you find that you don't get any satisfaction from making love with someone else now, you may feel that it will go on forever and that you will never be as sexually satisfied again. You will, but not right now. You may not want to have sex at all right now, and that's okay, too. Take a brief sex sabbatical. You can be sure that eventually you will desire sex and it will be good again, too.

Even under the best of circumstances, even with your ex-lover, there were times when you had an empty feeling after sex or it just wasn't up to par. No wonder it's worse now.

You may find fault with a new person's aroma or with their hair or their coloring. Probably the person isn't as bad as you think, and sometimes it's possible to just feel and not look, so if you need to make love, do it, but don't be disappointed if it's not up to your expectations. Snuggling could be even better for you now than actually getting laid.

Make friends with your own body. Buy a vibrator and learn how to use it. If you find yourself fantasizing and thinking of making love to your ex, buy sexy magazines and books and look at them while masturbating. Develop new fantasies.

Treat your body sensuously. Rub it with oils. Burn incense in the bathroom while you admire your naked self. Turn on to your own body if you can't find another one to make you happy. A glass of wine or even recreational drugs like marijuana can help you relax. Don't use drugs or booze if you feel depressed, only if you're horny.

If it seems as if every time you have a dream, it's about your ex, don't worry too much. Everyone who ever gives up an addiction has dreams about it. The alcoholic dreams of booze, the drug addict of heroin, fatties of hot fudge sundaes. Your dream is a combination of wish fulfillment and gratification. Dreamland is one place where you get what you want the way you want it. There's also the fear that is caused by the dreams that you'll never have it again—that you've lost the thing you dream about.

Insomnia

If you wake in the middle of the night, suffering from a nightmare about your former lover and depressed because you're alone and it was just a dream, don't panic. And don't lie there trying to go back to sleep either. That causes more obsessions and eventually insomnia. Insomniacs fear not being able to sleep and so they can't sleep. So instead of lying around building resistance to sleeping and fantasizing about your ex, get up and do something good to yourself or for your self-esteem. There's no law that your eight hours has to be in a row.

It makes no difference that it's two in the morning. Get up, mow the lawn if you want. Call a friend. This is the time for unusual activity. Read about how to play backgammon, or improve your card game. Go out and get something to eat. Don't worry if your time patterns seem a little out of sync right now—this isn't the time to worry about a regular schedule.

You'll probably lose a little sleep, but it's statistically normal right now. Just don't lie there in bed in the dark. Do crossword puzzles, watch television. Do anything that will make you sleepy, but don't stay in bed. Be sure that by the time you do go back to bed, you're so tired you won't be able to stay awake.

Triggers

Your obsessive thoughts about your ex are due to the withdrawal symptoms of having your love connection taken away. Addicts are always thinking about scoring, getting a fix. Why should you be any different? The addict, like the abandoned lover, can't stop thinking about his fix. As Professor Irwin Lublin observed in his research at California State University, people who stop smoking dream about cigarettes.

You dream about your loved one, imagining them returning to you. You think about it all the time. Next week, through "thought stopping" and "aversion," you'll learn to control and actually stop the urge to think about your lost love.

You have become addicted to your loved one, and certain things trigger your urge for the addictive substance (contact with the ex). In treating any addict, the first thing is to remove the triggers.

If someone overeats and is a food addict, you take the sweets away. You don't fill the refrigerator with cream pie and ice cream. In the same way, you don't want to keep your lover's picture on the piano, because each time you see it, you'll want him or her. In a Pavlovian way you will have trained yourself to "salivate," or, in this case, to yearn at the sight of the photo, increasing the difficulty of your battle against your own addiction.

The love songs you hear are calculated to make you cry. Song writers sit around cynically thinking of words to jerk your tears. Don't listen.

You feel sad when you take off a wedding ring you've worn for many years or put away a favorite photo, but are they really worth having if they cause you pain? You can have all your trinkets back later when you'll be able to enjoy them without feeling badly.

Memorabilia

Among the things that will trigger your sadness to the point of feeling like killing yourself, that keep you awake at night or tossing with dreams of your ex, are the memorabilia of your times together. Even if yours wasn't a "live-in" arrangement, you'll find that there are little momentos and reminders of your relationship all around your house. Gather them all up immediately and put them away in a special box or place.

Wagnerian Toothache

If you don't hide the triggers that cause you to feel sad, and leave them there until your "Implosion Day" (chapter eight), you'll probably fall victim to the Wagnerian Toothache. That's when you put away the ring your lover gave you and then make the mistake of taking it out a week later and putting it on—just to see.

Putting that ring on and checking it all the time to see if it still hurts you to look at it, if it still brings back those painful, tear-jerking memories, is like poking your tongue into a cavity or sucking cold air onto it or biting down on a new filling to see if it's still tender. That favorite photograph of the two of you together or the one where she looks oh so cute or he has that special love sparkle in his eye is an even more tempting toothache test.

Don't indulge a masochistic urge to look at an object connected to the old relationship, just to see if it still has the power to make you feel sad.

It probably does. One patient left his former girlfriend's picture on the wall of his apartment and every time he went by it he fell to the floor sobbing.

A lot of your friends will tell you to leave the memorabilia in sight. "Grieve," they'll say. "Feel the pain . . ." Others will tell you to call the Salvation Army and get a tax deduction on it all. Some will advise dumping it on your lover's front porch with a note.

But don't do that. Those things can be useful to your cure.

Save them, but out of sight, for now. You don't have to throw out your senior prom picture, or the chair "he" always sat in, or the Boston fern "she" hung in the john, or the picture of herself she painted and gave to you, or the table he made. But you could put them away in your "griefcase," a box, drawer, storage locker, bin or any out of sight room or closet until they are diffused by "Implosion" (chapter eight) and can no longer trigger your longings.

Don't be tempted to try the Wagnerian Toothache routine by taking something out before it's time. That's like picking your scab and just makes the healing process take longer.

The Implosion Box

Gather up everything that reminds you of your ex–gifts, favorite clothing, souvenirs from trips, photo album, favorite pictures, records–all the sad "broken dream" objects–and put them away.

Save everything, especially photos. Don't look at them now, because they'll just hurt you. Simply sort them out and throw them in a box.

When you go anywhere to buy a greeting card, you'll notice many that express the exact thought you want to communicate to your former mate.

How do you resist buying them? Don't try! You'll be tempted by "friendship" cards because what you've got is an epidemic. Millions of others are suffering the exact same pain you have, and the card companies know it. If you want to, buy the sentimental message, but don't send it. Put it away in your Implosion Box.

Every new popular song you hear seems to express your longing. Buy the records and put them in the box, too. Don't send them as "messages." Your ex will just feel that you are annoyingly hooked.

Your Implosion Box can be anything from a carton to a corner of the garage. It doesn't really matter, but it must be someplace where you won't run into it as you move through the daily tasks of living.

Use your Implosion Box to overcome the reminders that maintain the obsessions, to stop yourself from thinking about your lover and from crying over your loss. Put away as many things as you can that remind you of your lover.

If there's a favorite chair "he" or "she" always sat in and that you can't afford to throw away or replace, cover it with a furniture throw of a wildly different color.

All the little gifts, the presents, the books, even the wedding ring must be put away as soon as possible. Stop torturing yourself. Take down and put away all the photos of you and your ex together, even the ones of you that your ex took. Put them in your Implosion Box.

Naturally, it's hard to give up all the things that remind you of the happiness you once had, but now they can only cause you pain. You walk into a room and there's a picture of the two of you together, smiling happily and obviously in love. Of course, that sets off your yearning for the good old days.

The simple act of putting these things away will help you discover that you're not helpless. Maybe your lover refuses to talk to you on the phone, or go to a marriage counselor or a shrink, or try to work things out with you, but putting all the memorabilia away is something you can do for yourself and by yourself. Try putting away a couple of obviously upsetting things. See how it feels. Then hide everything possible.

After your Implosion Day, a month from now, you will be able to bring all those things back into your life, and they will simply be fond (not painful) memories.

If you listen to the words on the radio (especially the soft rock stations) you'll find that almost 90 percent of all the records played are about broken hearts and deserted lovers. For now, turn the dial to another station.

Tune your car radio to either all news or classical music, jazz or sports. Not the things you listened to with your lover. For instance, if your ex was hot for chamber music, avoid it. Right now, avoidance will help you to become depression-free.

Clear out the medicine cabinet. Put away your lover's pills. Sweaters, socks, even underwear. If you're a woman, make your place feminine again. If you're a male, get rid of the feminine frills.

Rearrange your bedroom. Change your environment as much as possible. If your ex was allergic to flowers, fill the place with them. If your ex didn't like you to wear see-through shirts or double knits, wear them now. Anything you can do to change the stimulus cues that set off your depression will make you feel better.

You have become conditioned to thinking of your former lover whenever you hear certain music or whenever you see certain things. If you fed your dog out of the same dish all the time, it would begin to salivate at the sight of the dish whether there was food in it or not. Your cat will drool over the sound of the can opener whether you are feeding him or not.

That's called a conditioned reflex, discovered in Pavlov's famous experiments. A conditioned reflex is an emotion triggered automatically by a button that gets pushed in you by something in the environment.

In his studies on digestion, Pavlov measured the amount of saliva secreted by a dog at the sight of food. He soon discovered that not only would the dog salivate at the sight of the food, but he would also salivate at the sight of the research assistant—the one who brought the food.

The lab assistant was a signal to the dog that the food was coming, in the same way that your lover's special brand of coffee brewing could signal their presence.

By ringing a bell just as the food was given to the dog, Pavlov tested his theory. Eventually the dog salivated to the sound of the bell, without there being any food at all. The dog was reacting as if the bell were food.

In the same way, when your lover leaves stuff around and

you have learned to yearn for that lover, that "stuff," the clothing, the razor, the toothbrush, will actually trigger the same emotion and longing you would feel if the person were there. By removing your bells, by changing your environment, you will remove your longing.

When Pavlov changed the ringing bell to a flashing light, the dog didn't salivate. So if you can change your environment somewhat, your yearning for your absentee lover will also be reduced.

You will also stop the nostalgic sad thoughts from interfering with your everyday activities. The trouble now is that you can't confine your sad thoughts. There's no way to stop the painful memories if you allow yourself to be bombarded with triggers all day long. If you maintain too many triggers in your environment, you will be more obsessed and yearn even more for your former mate.

It even helps to have the phone company change the bell on your telephone to a chime if you find that you miss the calls you used to get from your ex and jump in expectation every time it rings.

Places That Make You Sad

You'll suddenly find that certain places, maybe an entire area of the city, make you feel awful. When you go there, your heart sinks and the lump rises in your throat. Even if you've only been there together once or twice, it doesn't make any difference. If you didn't go there with other people and spend significant time there with others, if the place hasn't been diluted in your memory by other competing memories, you'll notice that those places act as emotional triggers, just like the memorabilia.

If you go to the sad places now, you will get resensitized, feel your fear and sorrow again, and become habitually sad at just the thought of that place. It can become your trigger and you'll act toward it the way the dog responded to the bell. So, temporarily, don't go to sad places, especially alone. You will leave feeling worse. The next time it will be even harder to go back because you will have found out that that place does indeed hurt.

The phobic Catch-22 about places that remind you of your ex is that if you avoid all the places you ever went to with your ex, you may become agoraphobic—afraid to go anywhere. Or you may feel so good about getting away with not going there that you will want to reinforce that good feeling by never again going to the "bad" place. You may become afraid to leave what you consider safe plaes—places where your ex doesn't live, eat, work, drive, or visit. Your geographical limits may be become smaller and smaller.

Although it is advisable to avoid the places that make you sad right now, don't count on avoiding them forever. Avoiding them now is like putting the memorabilia in an Implosion Box—first aid. In chapter eight (competing response and systematic desecration), the eighth week, you will learn through specific Letting Go treatment techniques, to face the nostalgic places and make them yours again.

Running Away

Just as Pavlov's dogs salivated to the sound of the bell rather than the smell or sight of actual food, you will "salivate" for your loved one simply because of the constancy of the old cues in your environment. Looking at his or her empty side of the bed or the empty seat at the breakfast table can make you yearn for your ex. Also, you have become used to having all the loss of love symptoms in that particular environment, which means that just staying in your house can trigger your unhappiness. Your current environment triggers the memories and the urge to be with the missing lover.

The best way to change your environment, if you can afford

it right now, is to move. It may be to your advantage to move now to a less expensive place if you were financially dependent on the support of your ex. The physical activity of moving will act as an energy outlet that may otherwise be spent in hysterical outbursts. Moving will give you impetus to clean up your house and get rid of a lot of old things that bring back unhappy memories. That will give you a sense of accomplishment. You might be able to sell your house and even make a killing in the real estate market. Surely you'll feel good about that.

The least you should do is rearrange your furniture, redecorate, trade or repaint your car, and plan a trip, now. Start planning right away because you should find someone to go with and a successful trip takes forethought. Even if you don't feel like going right now, make tentative plans in case you get the travel bug when you are over your lovesickness—in just a couple of months. Take out inexpensive cancellation insurance. That way you can always cancel out; but chances are you won't.

There are two kinds of trips. One is where you loll on the beach in beautiful romantic Hawaii or Tahiti. These are places which you should avoid until you have a new lover to go with you, someone who's at least as lovable as the one you lost. Otherwise, you may find yourself disappointed halfway through your trip and missing your ex even more as you watch the loving couples all around you.

The second kind of trip is very involved and keeps you busy every minute seeing and doing new and exciting things. Well-organized, mostly singles places like Club Med can be good, especially if you're not used to travelling. That way *nothing* can go wrong. You won't find yourself wishing you had someone to talk to or that your ex were there. An archaeological dig, a safari or a skin-diving expedition are fine choices.

Even if you're lucky enough to have found someone to go

with you, you should recognize that it's not going to be the same as it would be with your old lover. But if you go to a busy place with a lot to do, it won't matter. Pick a travelling companion who is up, happy and exciting, not a sad-sack type or even someone who is going to allow you to wallow in unhappiness missing your ex. An old lover or even a close friend of the same sex might be fun. You can level with them when you feel sad, and they can help you by pulling you out of it. And don't go where you went with the ex! Not just yet. Details on how to visit *those* places will be explained in chapter eight—just a few weeks from now. Romantic, calm places where life is still and there are beautiful sunsets and places you wish you could be sharing with your former mate are the ones to avoid right now. This is the time for the excitement of Paris or Rome, not a romantic sail up the Nile or a trip to the place where you spent your honeymoon.

It's better to go on a wilderness survival trip in the mountains than a quiet still place where romantic temples stand out against the sky and the air is filled with mimosa and the sights are so incredibly beautiful that you regret not sharing them with the one you love. It's hard to think about your ex when you're climbing a mountain with a pack on your back or your life is in danger hang-gliding.

Thrilling things like skydiving, hunting, parasailing, anything with physical danger will quickly take your mind off your sadness.

Research done by the authors including interviews with travellers in Mexico, Hawaii, Canada, Egypt, Tunisia and Europe showed a full 80 percent of travellers were running away "from a terminated relationship." And four out of five of those were miserable if they were in passive vacation spots.

A girl who went to Europe sightseeing reported that everything was so unusual that she wanted her former boyfriend to see it, so she spent every day storing things in her mind to tell him. At the end of each day she spent hours recalling the sights she'd seen in long letters to him. She should have written one post card as soon as she left home, mailed it from the airport and forgotten him for the rest of her trip.

A man who went to Egypt "to forget" didn't. He spent his entire vacation trying to find a suitable gift for his ex, one that would show her how much she was loved, how special she was to him. Even in Egypt he was haunted by his addiction.

Sure you'll want to buy a gift. Do it as soon as you get to where you're going. Make sure it's small enough to stick in the bottom of your luggage and forget about. You don't want to spend the entire trip lugging around a huge statue for your ex that must be carried separately for fear it will break. If you can, mail the gift. Get it over with quickly.

Don't write long letters, just a nice card, the kind you would send to your high school teacher. Don't sign "Love." "Cheers," "Salud," "Salaam," or "Au Revoir" are far more appropriate.

Relocating

Now is the time to apply for a job across the country. If you live in California, go to New York. There are no ties now that will keep you in the place you're living in. You can start over without that other person influencing the decision you make. It's all up to you now. Maybe you could get a job in Paris or Rome—or study at Oxford.

Moving offers the advantage of once and for all getting all the triggers out of your life. It's a way to "strike the set" of your life. You can have a garage sale and get rid of everything that doesn't apply to your new life. It's like starting fresh.

Start planning now, but don't go until you finish this book, or you'll find that you only have to take some of that same old yearning with you. Most people who move as a "running away" gesture or a maneuver to get their ex back quickly return, because they find that the one thing they couldn't leave was themselves. Until you're together where you are, you won't be together somewhere else.

Hysteria

Hysteria is the number one symptom most women and some men report for their being unable to function and to do things which will rebuild their self-esteem after a relationship falls apart.

Hysteria may be scientifically seen as the "respondent for being put on extinction." If laboratory mice get fed every time they press a bar, and suddenly the food stops coming no matter what they do, they go into a burst of bar pressing, run around frenetically, jump, bite the bars of the cage and defecate, before they finally get fatigued and quiet down—all of which looks very much like the emotional outbursts of hysterical humans.

That's similar to your tendency to be "extra good" to the lover who has just cut off your supply of love, sending a lot of flowers and love letters and gifts to the lover who left you. You're pressing the bar, frantically looking for the love pellets you always got before.

Lovesick hysteria takes many forms. Agonizing nights spent over what you or they should have done or said. Prayers. Those terrible tearful midnight phone calls. Frantic flights. Desperation offers and impossible deals. Schemes and charades and lies. Running around, yet unable to concentrate sufficiently to actually get anything done. Getting irritable and "biting" toward everyone. And the worst, self-abuse and neglect.

Hysteria may be seen as the body's hyperactive reaction to the nervous energy generated by emotional tension. One remedy for hysteria is physical activity. Running around the block, hitting golf balls, riding a bike or even cleaning house will tire you out, allow your body to blow off excess carbon dioxide and take in fresh, relaxing oxygen.

A person who is having a hysterical reaction will feel wired.

Often they will find themselves caught up in meaningless running around—as if they had a big shot of adrenaline.

Swimming or a cold shower can also help if you feel hysterical, because of the distracting feelings against your body. Whatever you do, you must do until you hyperventilate or pant.

In the laboratory experiments, research students are told not to feed their experimental mouse, even when it does become hysterical after the feed pellets are cut down. The reason the students are told to ignore the hysteria is because if they were to feed the animal at that point, it would quickly learn to become hysterical in order to get food. That would only reinforce the hysteria. In the same way, if you are able to make a renewed contact with your lover because of your hysteria, you will also reinforce your hysteria.

The hysteria in the lab animal always passes, and so will yours, especially if you find alternative ways of giving your body the activity it needs to get rid of the upsetting tension energy.

Patients who experience hysteria for the first time because of the loss of a lover will often assume they've gone crazy and even ask their therapist to have them committed. It's important to realize that you're not crazy if you suffer from hysteria, but are merely reacting to being put on extinction; that is, you are having a natural reaction to being suddenly deprived.

Depressive Delusions

When you are suddenly shocked out of the love delusions that you had, it's important to realize that you're like someone who took LSD all the time and imagines and believes that the grass in the front yard is moving. When the acid trip finally ends, it's a shock to find out that the grass isn't really moving. And the same thing is true of love—the grass doesn't move unless you're "in love."

That there is one great love for everyone, a Mr. Right, a Ms.

Perfection, is a culturally induced delusion. The illusion that you *were meant* for each other is just that, an illusion!

Romance, like the LSD-induced moving grass, is real when you're in the throes of an affair and not real when it's over.

The Colorado Indians experienced a similar culturally induced delusion when they climbed to a mountaintop to fast until the Great Spirit came to them. Every Indian boy who had to pass through this rite of puberty wasn't allowed to eat anything until he reported that the Great Spirit spoke to him. Every young man in the tribe actually hallucinated hearing and seeing the Great Spirit. But his hallucinations were not psychotic; it was simply something that the whole culture believed in to the point of mass delusion.

By setting up models like Romeo and Juliet and Tristan and Isolde, even the Doris Day–Rock Hudson movies, our culture reinforces false beliefs inherent in romantic love delusions. Even Cinderella gets her prince—we learn it from earliest childhood. Romantic love is part of being "in love," not necessarily reality. Now that you can't get your love fix, you shouldn't expect to maintain the same delusions. Like the Indian on the mountain who sees and talks to the Great Spirit, you don't feel the same hallucinatory high that you did until you are "in love" again.

One cultural delusion is that "marriages are made in heaven." Another involves the promise of "forever" whispered between lovers.

Reality is that all relationships end, but everyone thinks that theirs won't. Everybody who gets married thinks they'll be together for a lifetime. Realistically, they have about a sixty-forty chance nationwide, and a fifty-fifty chance in California.

If a younger couple wants to get married and the man is under twenty-five, the couple has an 85 percent chance of divorce. It's like jumping out a window and believing you'll fly. The odds just aren't in your favor.

Be grateful you flew as long as you did. Predestined one and only soulmates only exist in mythology.

My Soulmate

The feeling that your lost love was your soulmate and that you will never find another because there is no other "perfect" person for you is a culturally induced delusion, too. If that were true, then what would happen if the person died? In the old days women killed themselves with their husbands, but since we no longer throw wives into graves with husbands, the conclusion is inevitable that there's not just one man for every woman, that it's definitely a false belief.

In order to defeat a false belief, you need Cognitive Restructuring. Even if you're a birdwatcher, a nonconformist or kinky, and so was your ex—don't worry. There are more deviants out there waiting to meet you.

The Melted Snowman

The "forever" and the "one and only" myths combine in our culture to create "The Myth of the Melted Snowman."

It's upsetting to feel like you've been had.

Your cherished belief in your investment in this "Pygmalion," whom you've lifted from her salesgirl job to the respectability of career or the fulfillment of motherhood, has been crushed. How could she sell out to shack up like some hippie or run off with a tennis coach? How could she just give up what's best for her? You torture yourself trying to figure it out.

And how could that man you've supported and encouraged through graduate school just drop out? How could he desert the wonderful future you planned? You feel like someone stepped on the model airplane which you so patiently and lovingly built. You believed this was "the one," and that the snowman never melts.

When romance is blooming, these culturally induced false

beliefs enhance, excite and endear. But when the love-drug is unavailable, it's a restorative tonic to realize that although the myths are very powerful, they don't reflect reality. "The one" doesn't exist. *Nothing* is "forever." When the seasons change, the snowman melts.

Transferring Sad Feelings To Angry Ones

In order to stop feeling sad, the best thing to do is to start feeling something else.

In the brain, there are two different brain centers for anger and sadness, but both brain centers share the same common nerve pathway. When one center is using the pathway, the other can't.

To stop your sad feelings, all you have to do to block the sadness is use the mutual sadness-madness brain pathway by filling it with anger. The trick is to dwell on all the bad, thoughtless things that other person did to you, not the good, loving ones. Instead of feeling nostalgia for the time your lover took you to a special place, try to feel angry with them because they aren't taking you there now, or because they're taking someone else, or because when they used to take you there, they promised it would be "our place."

Every time you have a romantic thought about your ex, push it off your brain pathway with an angry thought. Your friends can help. Tell them everything your lover did to you—the things that were so terrible you were ashamed to tell anybody. The time he hit you. The time he showed up with another girl to hurt you. The time you caught her in bed with another man. The time she charged a gift for another man on your account. The time he was late for your birthday. You'll be surprised how many of your buddies secretly agree that you had a bad deal. Or that the person you thought was so loving and faithful had begun to use you, dangle you on a string, take you for granted. You may even hear some new terrible things about your ex, but if you can feel anger instead of hurt, you won't be depressed.

Ask everyone, "What did you really think of him?" The answers may surprise you. Nobody's ex is as wonderful as they remember them. Being in love makes everyone look better.

Session Six: Loneliness

Sundown Syndrome—Handling the Fear of Being Alone

Most rejected lovers can handle the daylight hours. They go to work, keep busy most of the day, do errands, shop, or even visit with friends. It's toward evening that the trouble starts.

Suddenly, you're afraid of the dark. You hate coming home knowing nobody's there.

As the sun goes down, bereft lovers are overcome with feelings of depression and loneliness. Plan to be with someone at sundown. A walk in the sunset, a glass of wine or a cocktail. Or have evening plans that make it necessary for you to spend the sundown time getting ready.

Remember when you were little and afraid to be alone in the dark? How much better it was if you could just be near someone?

When the sun goes down, you automatically think of warm family gatherings. Of sleeping with someone, of dinner together, of just communicating the thoughts and happenings of your day. That's why you've *got* to be with someone or, even better, have someone over.

If someone does call and invite you to go somewhere, don't turn them down even if you're too tired, or too messy, or just want to go to bed. Why not take time to get fixed up instead? A quick shower and some primping can be an upper. It might be fun, and it's surely going to be better than sitting at home and suffering from sundown syndrome.

Plan ahead for sundowns. Calling someone at six o'clock because you just had an attack is a bad way to get a date for seven. It's easier to keep a commitment when someone's on their way over. You know you have to get your shit together. But it's harder if you're the own who's going somewhere. The temptation is just to curl up and forget about it.

People Who Need People

Being alone a lot all at once isn't the way to overcome fear of loneliness. In the beginning fill your time with people.

If you find yourself panicking one night, don't be afraid to call someone and ask if you can sleep over. It's amazing how much better everything seems once you're out of the environment that frightens you.

Have long conversations on the phone. Believe it or not, there are probably lots of other people sitting home on Saturday night, and they might welcome a long chat with you.

If you don't know anybody to be with, sign up for discussion groups or group therapy, where there are always lots of lonely people, where part of the cure is to talk and help each other. Put yourself out to go places where you will be made into a better person and where you will also meet people who are in the same boat you are. Nobody feels as bad when he finds there are lots of people out there who feel the same as he does. It's just feeling that you're the only one in the world who's lonely that's torture.

Local high schools have adult education, the community college has night classes, the university has extension courses, there are sure to be photography courses and even classes like skin-diving that mean you have to take a trip somewhere to do it. The YMCA has classes, the airport gives flying lessons. Even just sending for the brochures for the different things will open up new ideas to you. You'll find that there are indeed ways not to be alone.

At first, and as a stopgap measure, schedule so much that you have very little time to yourself. The times you're at home at night, invite someone over. Be alone gradually, first in the daytime and then at night.

Weekends are the roughest. Schedule them really full, especially in the beginning. Next to Saturday night, Sunday mornings are the worst. Make plans for your "lonely" times. Subscribe to the daily paper so that you will have something to do every morning when you wake up.

Keep charts of your activity. Use an appointment book and fill it with lists of things you have to do. It's important for you to have real physical evidence that you are making progress in controlling the fear of being alone. Just looking at your book filled with dates and appointments, shopping lists, notes of special places you want to check out can make you feel more confident.

You may quickly find that you've made so many plans to be with so many people to do so many things that every minute alone becomes precious, a time to pay your bills or read the paper. You'll thank God for a cancellation.

Put a dimmer switch on your bedroom light if you can't sleep in the dark, and mark how low you dim the light each night. You will see progress. As you become more in control of your life and environment, you will have actual evidence by the marks on your dimmer switch.

Going Out by Yourself

If you run into a night when there's just nothing to do, take yourself to a first-run movie or even a play. One ticket is almost always available, even for a first-run, sold-out performance.

Concentrate on doing something you like, so it won't matter whether you meet someone or not. Don't spend your evenings at singles bars or singles dances. The trouble with those things is that you go there expecting to meet someone. If you don't, you feel like you've failed. The good thing about doing things you'll really enjoy is that even if you don't meet someone there, you won't be disappointed because that's not the reason you went.

Stay out late. Shop until you're really tired. Come home exhausted. You won't be so likely to feel bad; you'll just want to fall into bed and go to sleep. Try to schedule all your fun activities in the evening, because that's the time that always hurts the most.

Nights Are Forever

Those lonely nights can make you feel crazy. Some patients report classic claustrophobic reactions the first few nights they spend alone. "It seemed as if the entire house was closing in on me," a thirty-year-old artist reported. "I couldn't paint, I couldn't breathe. There I was in the middle of winter with all the doors and windows wide open and every light in the house on. It was two A.M. and I was panicked."

If you experience a claustrophobic feeling, open everything up. Then close doors and windows one at a time as you feel safe and in control.

The way to overcome a fear is gradually. If you find that you have obsessions when the lights are out or feel as if you're going crazy, don't sit in the dark and suffer. Sleep with all the lights on one night, and turn one off each night until you are down to a tiny night-light. You may want to keep that one going forever. So what! You're in control, and that's the important thing.

Learning to Like Being Alone

There are basically two ways to overcome the fear of being alone. One is to not be alone. One patient was so afraid she would be alone when her boyfriend left her that she immediately went to the community college and signed up for courses almost every night. When she didn't go to class, she made plans to do things with friends. Unfortunately, she never took the next step and learned to like to be alone.

Many people never do. They have such a deep-rooted fear of being by themselves that they never pass the stopgap measure of filling all their time. For them, the next step is always a new romantic interest that often ends up exactly like the last one—a time-consuming, all-encompassing romance that fills all the empty hours.

The patient who signed up for night classes every night met a new boyfriend within two months of classes. She immediately gave up all the classes so that she could spend every night with her new friend. When he eventually left her, she was right back in the same place again, only worse. She still hadn't learned to enjoy her own company.

How many times have you heard a broken-hearted man say, "What I need is to fall in love. Another girlfriend, someone I can get close to—that's the cure for me." And how many men have done just that, jumping from one relationship to another, falling in love fast and furiously simply to avoid being alone.

Of course, eventually they'll be alone again, and because they haven't learned to like their own company, they will once again suffer. The only true danger with rebound affairs is when you're still totally dependent on someone else for your happiness, still afraid to be alone.

The advanced way to deal with the fear of loneliness is to *not* run out and fall in love again, no matter how many people advise it. Instead, learn to make being alone very gratifying.

When people are dating or married, they typically put off things they would like to do. It could be sorting and filing your old papers, organizing your clothes, sewing, getting involved with lessons, gardening. Things you can do by yourself. Even making Christmas gifts way in advance. Try a craft. Make a needlepoint that you just can't put down, or build a harpsichord from a kit—anything that you feel driven to finish, either because you can't wait to see it work or because you've invested so much money in it that you don't want to just throw it out.

Take lessons that will tap your talents—playing an instrument, painting. Anything you can do alone and that you have put off doing because you were involved.

You can offer to make dinner for people, and they will reciprocate. It's a good stopgap measure, but the truth is that you can't keep doing it forever. Eventually you're going to get tired of running around, and you're going to have to face the sundown syndrome and live through it. Once you find that you really won't die if you spend an evening alone, or sleep alone, or even spend several evenings alone, you'll be okay. A lot of the fear will be over.

Believe it or not, you could learn to enjoy being alone. Even for a whole day. Wake up on a Sunday morning and go back to sleep for as long as you want. Don't clean the house until you feel like it. Sit around reading a junk novel or the Sunday papers without having someone ask, "Where's my socks?" or "What's for dinner?" or "When will you fix the garage door?" or "Why are you always late?" You haven't been by yourself for a long time. This is the time to get to know yourself. Be selfish.

You can be good company for yourself. See how much pleasure you can get. Buy the latest best-seller and spend the weekend soaking in a hot tub, reading the newest book, gossiping with old friends on the phone—ones you haven't seen or talked to in a long time.

Watch all the new television shows that you've missed and make yourself a huge bowl of popcorn. Indulge yourself, and you'll begin to like your own company.

The Soap Opera

Decide now which friends you want to keep, the ones you

think will be loyal to you and not your ex. People are going to be nosy and curious. They'll want to know what happened, and some may even be so bold as to call and ask you. One way to keep yourself busy and to remind yourself how badly you were treated, how you were used and abused, is to tell everybody about it.

People love to hear gossip, and you've got some of the best. Use it and gets lots of attention now. Eventually even you'll get bored by your sad tale. In the meantime, you'll be nurtured by others' sympathy.

When your more honest friends get tired of hearing about it, they'll tell you. You are suffering from the repetition compulsion, the urge to repeat something frightening to overcome it. Too much sympathy will reinforce your illness, though, so if you find yourself feeling worse after getting tons of commiseration and strokes from friends who admire your capacity to feel deeply, try to cut it off. Or spend time with someone who has a touch of cynicism. Many of your friends will suddenly admit they never liked your ex, that you were too good for him/her and that your ex had no class, no savoir faire, no warmth, was self-centered, etc. It's good for you to hear those things right now because you still have an exaggerated perception of how wonderful your former mate was.

Let people's sympathy work for you by saying, "Yes, I do feel awful. I would feel better if you would go to the movies with me." Suggest something fun. You can even tell sympathetic friends you're lonely and ask them to fix you up.

It's best to contact people who didn't know your ex at all. Of course, they'll ask what you've been up to and you'll have to tell them you were going with someone for "x" amount of time and got dumped. Picking friends who don't know your ex will insure that they will be on your side.

Soon you will realize how much of a soap opera your story is. There's often another lover in the picture when a mate leaves.

There's disillusionment, disappointment, hurt and hate. Your story isn't original. Your friends have heard and experienced it many times before.

Sympathetic Sad Sacks

Mutual friends and relatives—in-laws, etc.—will all want to meet with you and discuss the breakup. Stay away from inquisitors. You'll be talking your heart out trying to explain what happened and only hearing hurtful news about your ex.

For the time being, go back to the friends you knew before you met your old lover, not your mutual friends. If that's not possible, really put yourself out to find new friends, ones who don't know your ex.

Get a loose-leaf telephone book and change your regular listings from alphabetical to rank order—starting with the person you'd most like to see.

Call old lovers. Some will sympathize and some may even feel hurt that you spent all that time with your ex while they were waiting around for you. Call some person you know will be lonely and anxious to see you.

To a certain extent you can avoid all the people who make you feel badly, but there are always going to be some. What do you say to the neighbor who asks how come she doesn't see your boyfriend's little red car at your house these days. Did he get a new one? And well-meaning friends will delight in bringing you news of the ex.

The Press Release

Some people will advise you to cover up your shame, to lie, to tell people that the relationship just wasn't working out or wasn't making progress and so *you* called it off. That way you never have to admit you got shafted. Men are more likely to advise buddies to do this than are women, but it's a bad idea in any case.

For a man who is willing to admit that he lost his love, there is lots of sympathy. Women will know that you're a real human being and will share your tears and sadness. They'll compliment you because you are big enough to say you were rejected.

For a woman who admits she's been left, there are always friends who'll say the guy wasn't good enough or he should have been grateful to have such a wonderful mate and what a jerk he was.

You have to realize that a lot of the people you know are going to be either *your* friends or your ex's friends after the breakup. Try to make as many of them yours as possible. The best way to do that is to say that you're really the hurt one. Everybody sympathizes with the one who was hurt. It's okay, too, to say that talking about it makes you too sad.

Don't worry about people thinking you are a loser, that you were victimized. It's okay; it's happened to everybody at least once, whether they admit it or not.

Building Self-Esteem

A person who wants to self-destruct obviously doesn't put too much value on him or herself. Suicide signals an abysmally low self-esteem.

Reverse your low self-esteem by thinking of the things that would make you feel good if you did them. They could range from cleaning a closet to having a poem published somewhere. Or even simply writing a short story.

Don't panic at the thought of your list. You don't have to do any of those things if you don't want to. Just making the list will show you there are possibilities.

Pick the one thing on your list that is most important to you. Not necessarily the thing that will impress someone else, but the accomplishment that will make you feel best about yourself. If you are overweight and being thinner would make you feel terrific, make your first goal to lose only one-third the amount you need to take off. Or drop one size. Or fit into a pair of too-tight pants. If you want to firm up, don't try going to the gym five days a week. Start with one day. Don't set unmanageable tasks for yourself, only those you know you can succeed at.

It really doesn't matter what your goal is. It might be something spiritual like going to church, or social, like learning disco dancing. Or artistic, like painting or learning to play an instrument.

If you've always wanted to play the guitar or piano, the first step would be to find a teacher or a class. Check the classified ads in your local paper for a few days. Look in the yellow pages next. Then call one or two of the different teachers. Find out how much it will cost, what you will learn and how long it will take to play your favorite song. Then visit a class. If you don't love it, find another one.

Pick the teacher or group *you* like best. Arrange to go as often as you want. If you find, after trying something, that it's not for you, quit without guilt. Go on to the next thing on your list. Your enjoyment and pleasure is the key.

Winning

Make a written "Winner's Plan." Divide up your goal into very small tasks you can accomplish each day that will lead to your target. Don't get discouraged if you don't do a certain thing on the appointed day. For example, if you violated your diet, simply start again the next day.

One of your tasks might be to fill out an old insurance claim. Day One could be calling the insurance company and asking them to send you the necessary forms. Day Two could be getting all your receipts together. Day Three, making a list of everything you want to claim. Day Four, filling out the forms. Day Five, running around for signatures, notaries, etc., and finally, Day Six, mailing your claim.

Each small accomplishment proves you *can* do something. Combating learned helplessness is a certain ego builder. Everything you do for yourself increases your self-esteem.

The important thing about self-esteem is what you believe about yourself. For instance, if you know you're highly intelligent, it wouldn't bother you if someone told you you were stupid. Real self-esteem comes from knowing what other people say doesn't matter because you know you're bright, or attractive, or competent.

It seems impossible for people to break up any kind of relationship, either business or personal, without each half of the partnership hurling insults and accusations. Who did what to whom and why often seems more important than salvaging either person's self-esteem or whatever remains of the relationship.

When you're the one who's breaking the thing up, you have an urge to justify yourself, to give reasons, to say you're leaving because you just can't endure that terrible person anymore. If you're the one who's being left, you might be tempted to believe that you really were awful. The truth is that the one who is doing the name-calling wouldn't have been with you or gotten involved with you in the first place if you didn't have some very unique and valuable qualities. But it's hard not to feel like a shit when the person you loved insists that you are.

Friends may tell you that's ridiculous, that you're a fine person—but that's not enough. You need to over-correct to change your sad feelings and negative self-image. You need lots of people to tell you that you have specific value. It's not enough to get vague compliments right now.

You need immediate specific evidence of your value, and the best way to get it is to do something you do well and get positive feedback about it.

To find someone who will think you're wonderful for doing a

specific thing, you'll have to do something wonderful first. Just walking around telling yourself you're not really that bad doesn't make it.

If you can, start a sexual relationship. It's okay, too, if it's someone you just like; you don't have to love them.

If that seems too hard right now, it's not necessary that it be a sexual relationship, just a good friend who cares about you and will give you positive evidence that you're not a louse by taking you out or spending time with you.

Missionary Work

It'll make you feel better if you help someone who is in a worse love situation than you are. You won't be jealously yearning for a nonexistent perfect relationship like you thought your friend had, and you can be a valuable help to anyone suffering from the loss of a love.

You can share the techniques you've learned in this book. Even if they haven't recently broken up, there are a lot of people who are still carrying around 10 percent of their pain. Maybe they have one favorite photo that always makes them feel sad, and you could advise them to put it away for a while.

If you have an urge to offer help to your ex, don't. Don't clean his or her house. Clean yours instead. Don't balance his or her checkbook, take care of your own.

If you are inexplicably driven to buy things and do things for your ex, buy them for someone else. Do a favor for someone else, as a loving thing, just to prove to yourself that you don't have to stop all loving gestures toward others. Give a small gift to someone who has been nice to you. That way you'll get the appreciation you miss now. You will feel good about having given. Your ability to be loving hasn't been cut off, and it's important that you discover that making loving gestures to another person can be even better than making them toward your ex, who would only reject you in some new way.

Roots

Another way to increase your self-esteem, especially now, is to visit a family member. It's as reassuring as crawling into mother's bed at night when you were scared as a kid. It could be a brother, a mother or grandmother. Now is the time to discover your roots and to spend time with the member of your family that you enjoy the most. They'd probably enjoy a visit from you, and you'd be doing a good thing for yourself.

Most suicidal people are alienated from their families. The reason they find it easier to kill themselves is because they're not thinking about whom they will really hurt. A visit home can show you whom you are really responsible to and who would really cry at your funeral. Since feeling unconnected and irresponsible is a reason people kill themselves, it's important to find out that people will care and miss you, that you belong.

You may find yourself unable to go home simply because it's too far away. Use the telephone; call. Contact anyone else who would think a visit from you would be really marvelous and a great event. Knowing how much they think of you will act as a suicide deterrent. Even an ex-boyfriend, ex-wife or ex-husband is a good person to contact now. Reestablish connections with people you've cut off.

Don't worry about being a burden. Everybody likes to help, and helping you is insurance in case they ever need help themselves. Besides, some of them might already owe you favors. If your nuclear family is out of the question, form an intentional family from those you know the longest—even old loves.

Instant Gratification Hotline

This is a list of friends or even a therapist whom you can call for good positive feedback. People who will lift you up and give you encouragement. Only those who think you're great belong here. People who will be willing to hear you in the middle of the night. Keep your IGH with you and near your bed.

4
THE WAILING WALL

I've done everything I know to try and change your mind, And I think I'm gonna love you for a long, long time. 'Cause I've done everything I can to try and make you mine, And I think I'm gonna love you for a long, long time.

—LINDA RONSTADT
"Long Long Time"

You want to cry all the time. A sadness pervades everything you do. You wake up crying, you go to sleep crying. At work, the choking feeling is in your throat and you find yourself blinking back tears. Driving on the freeway, a sad song on the car radio starts an uncontrollable waterfall.

Even at parties, movies, plays, the circus, tears come welling out. Nothing keeps you happy for very long, even a phone call from the ex—after that, it's even worse. You don't feel safe, you never know when the sad feelings will take over.

It's embarrassing, humiliating, and your ex probably isn't suffering at all. Knowing that makes you cry even more.

Your crying is usually triggered by a thought that you have, like "How could she do this to me?" or "How could he give up all we had together?"

THE FOURTH WEEK

Session Seven: Anti-Depressive Techniques

Thought Stopping

The first thing you have to do is find the sentence that most frequently pops into your head and makes you cry. Once you find your "cry" sentence, you can erase it from your consciousness by making it unappetizing.

Pick a time when you're not upset. Relax quietly, then begin to say the trigger sentence that makes you cry. There may be two or three. Try to say them out loud without crying. Don't worry if you can't, you soon will be able to.

Begin with just one sentence, like "How could he leave me for her?" Say it out loud. As you speak the last word of your sentence, "her," interrupt the thought by either shooting off a cap pistol, slamming a ruler on a desk or simply clapping your hands. Repeat the sentence, moving the thought stopping interruption back one word at a time.

It will go, "How could he leave me for her?" Bang! The second time: "How could he leave me for" Bang! The third time: "How could he leave" Bang! The fifth time: "How could he" Bang!

And eventually the noise will precede the thought, interrupting it before you even get to think the word "How." Just keep cutting off the last word of the sentence each time, until your sentence is gone. Sometimes it helps to have a friend do the banging during the thought stopping training.

The noise or other interruption of your sad thought trains you to stop the thought before it is completed. By interrupting a particular sentence often enough, you will find that you have gained control over that sentence. Then the next time something in the environment triggers your emotional attachment to your ex, and his or her face pops into your mind, and the sad thought starts to happen, you may say, "How," but before you get to the word "could," you'll automatically interrupt the thought yourself.

The noise or bang will occur in your mind. If it doesn't happen the first time, start the training all over again. By faithfully isolating and erasing each sentence that makes you feel sad, you will be training yourself to stop the sad thoughts. Stopping the sad thoughts will stop a lot of the tears. Your expectation of hearing a frightening loud noise at the sad thought will become stronger than your urge to cry.

Aversion

Aversion is another form of thought stopping that you can use to train yourself not to have sad nostalgic thoughts about your ex. Aversion treatment is good when unexpected sad thoughts occur.

You might be out driving when an ad for a resort you and your ex-mate had visited suddenly blasts from the car radio. You remember how happy you were there and wish it could be that way again, and you begin to cry for your lost happiness. That's the time to use aversion. Inconspicuously and even in front of people if you need to, you can stop your tears.

Actually put a raw egg out in the sun for a day. It'll rot and stink, and the odor will be nauseating. Take out the contents of either a Benzedrine inhaler or a Zippo lighter and refill either one with cotton that's been soaked in the juice of the rotten egg.

Take the lighter or inhaler with you wherever you go. When you have the sad thought or nostalgic wish, "Oh, I want whatsisname back again," pull out your inhaler and take a sniff, or open the lid of the lighter and breathe deeply. The rotten-egg smell is an aversive way of interrupting unexpected sad thoughts that haunt you at inappropriate times. Imagine! You'll get nauseous at the thought of your missing lover.

If you can't handle the rotten egg juice, get a little bottle of smelling salts (spirits of ammonia). Keep it handy in your purse or pocket, and whenever you have a sad thought, open the bottle and take a deep whiff. It's a painful but actually harmless aversive technique. Keep it near your bed if you cry a lot there! The painful smell will interrupt your sad thoughts and inhibit your crying.

The rotten eggs and smelling salts are emergency aversive conditioning measures to get you through the day.

The Crime Sheet

If you can think clearly now for a little while, you'll realize it's about time you admitted your ex wasn't all you've built them up to be. That there were always things you didn't like about him. He was too short, cheap, fat, bossy, thin, grouchy, hairy. Or about her. She was too fat, thin, extravagant, messy, argumentative, tall.

No relationship is ever smooth sailing all the way, and everybody overlooks a certain amount of irritation from time to time. Certainly you did. Remember the lies you caught, but decided to overlook. The times you felt mistreated, talked down to, ignored or simply taken for granted. The ruined evenings, the missed lovemakings.

The Crime Sheet is a detailed listing of specific things that your ex did wrong, not necessarily limited to things having to do with your breakup. As a matter of fact, it's better if the "crimes" were committed before your breakup. Remember how he/she embarrassed you in front of people? Was rude to your mother? Made passes at your friends? Those things.

The way he/she pushed you around, the way they made you feel bad. The time you were sick and he/she didn't come. The time he/she passed a phone number in front of you. The broken promises, the disappointments, the angry scenes. Re-create each instance in your imagination. List each one separately on its own three-by-five card.

The Crime Sheet does more than just remind you of all the lousy things your ex did. Psychoanalysts interpret depression as internalized anger. Assuming that is correct and your depression is really misplaced anger—against yourself instead of against your ex—you must redirect your anger where it belongs to lift your depression.

A deserted lover's anger is often internalized. The awful things their ex did are too easily forgotten. The need to have the old mate back, the yearning and nostalgic *weltschmerz* make all the bad times fade into the background. How can you be upset over the times he screamed at you for losing the keys when that seems like such a little thing compared to the fact that he's gone? Or the times she was late, now that she doesn't come at all? Somehow, you've decided your ex was perfect and only left because you did something awful, or didn't do something you should have. It's all your fault, you feel. Your ex was really the greatest person in the world.

At first it'll be hard for you to make up your Crime Sheet. You may still be having your delusions. But surely if you try, you can think of *one* thing they did wrong.

Start with the most awful. The worst lie, the time you were the most humiliated, the coldest thing you ever saw them do. What was the worst thing he/she ever did? To you? To someone else? Making a Crime Sheet will help you convert your tears to anger. It will also do away with the delusion that your ex was perfect and you did everything wrong.

As you note each incident on a separate piece of paper (three-by-five card), picture the details vividly and jot them down, too. One girl's boyfriend ran over her puppy on his way to see another woman. Her card simply had a photo of him holding the puppy. Certainly when she looked at the picture she felt angry. Yours may not be so vivid. Maybe he hit you. Maybe she broke a date with you to go out with someone else.

What you're looking for on your Crime Sheet are incidents that will indicate to you that your former lover had character traits that are inconsistent with your romantic illusions of them. Write down all the things that happened. All the bad feelings that you had. The deceits, lies and half-truths you discovered.

The card shouldn't read, "I caught her in bed with another guy." It should also say, "And I felt really stupid. There I was at the door with flowers in my hand, just an hour early. And I really loved her that day. I can see her coming down the stairs all flustered with a towel wrapped around her and nothing else on. And I even remember how I volunteered to come back later."

Physiologically, being angry will block the pathways to the "sadness" brain center. Emotionally, all you have to do is pull out your stack of cards and start going through them when you feel like crying. The anger will stop your tears. Certainly you'll feel better.

Grieving

All your friends will tell you that it's best to grieve and cry whenever you want, that if you hide your sadness, you'll get ulcers from keeping your emotions in too much. There's no scientific evidence for that rumor. You're more likely to get ulcers if you continue to suffer. Also, no one grieves as completely as they should. Even when a loved one dies, we no longer have the many days of circumscribed ritualized grieving our ancestors had.

Mourners once tore their clothing and grieved for many days. Elaborate burial services and religious rites and even prayers for the dead are a comfort to the bereaved.

Anthropologically, we can also speculate that depression is indeed anger turned in, by pointing to the rites of many people whose grieving is accompanied by slashing their own bodies, pulling their hair out or scratching their faces in grief, as Shakespeare's heroines did. Punishing themselves, they could actually feel the anger turned inward.

But suppose you don't lose your love by death? Of course people would think it was silly for an abandoned lover to set aside a week to sit home and grieve over all the memorabilia, to have friends in, to weep until it was over. You're expected to carry on your life as if nothing happened. You don't get to exorcise your sadness with socially acceptable grieving or mourning.

By not setting aside a specific mourning period to wear black and grieve for your lost lover (and our society would definitely frown on something so uncool), you don't really get the deep sadness out of your soul. You could spend years, even the rest of your life, carrying around 10 or even 20 percent of your sadness over an old lover. The idea of grieving is not only to do it, but to also get *through* it and *past* it. And it can't be done right unless you do it as a full-time job for a prearranged period of time.

You may be having a sad nostalgic memory of your ex, maybe even be just about to burst into tears when the telephone rings. It would be embarrassing to answer the phone with tears in your voice, especially if it were a prospective new lover instead of your best friend, so you hide your tears, you squelch them, and they are still there. Because grieving for a lost lover is never completed, it recurs at most inopportune times.

You will need a period of time when you can get through your grief and past it, and we will structure that for you in chapter eight. But for now, as a stopgap measure, put aside as many of your sad feelings as you can, using thought stopping, aversion, the Crime Sheet and the Implosion Box.

The Hope Trap

It seems impossible for anyone who is left to give up the fantasy that their lover will come back. Hoping is also a denial of the reality of the situation, and having hope acts as an intermittent reinforcement.

If you allow your hope to be fulfilled by seeing your ex-lover just once in a while, you are going to feel worse. If you get a cool reception, you'll be disappointed. If your ex is nice, you'll be encouraged to hope things could go back to the way they were.

To hope and get nothing is better for you than to hope and get little doses of love. Then you'll try even harder to get your love back, hoping through every disappointment that the next meeting will be the one.

Each disappointment maintains your crying and sadness, but you can't get disappointed if you don't have hope.

Once you realize the situation is hopeless, you let go. It's important to give up hope of getting your relationship back, but it seems that people have the hardest time of all deciding that a love relationship is hopeless.

The odds are that your relationship can't be restored to the way it was, so if you hope for that, you're going to become even sadder and more disappointed. Hoping to get your lover back also makes the thoughts you're trying to stop occur more often. If you don't think you'll ever see the jerk again, you're not likely to be haunted by thoughts like "When so-and-so realizes what they've lost, they will beg me to come back."

Having hope that you'll get your lover back, or even

fantasizing about happy reunion scenes and thinking of ways to make them happen, can set you back. It's as if your mate were actually coming back and making you believe everything was fine and then leaving you—over and over again. It reinforces your belief that you will be a pair again.

In experiments with lab animals it was shown that "intermittent reinforcement" causes serious emotional upset and loss of control, with longer-term efforts to please the researcher. The animals were fed a food pellet every time they pushed a bar. Then they were only given the pellet once in a while. That seemed to make the animals work for the food pellet even harder and longer. The animals began madly hitting the bar, seemingly desperate for the food pellets, although hunger was not at issue. They had become slaves to their newly learned "hope."

In the same way, hoping that your lover will come back reinforces the fantasy that you will indeed be together again and keeps you hooked instead of getting on with your own life. You will remain tied securely to your ex and your fantasies of getting them back, while they are off enjoying themselves with someone else. That's why you have to "let go" of the hope.

You may be uselessly racking your brain, torturing yourself over why you were left, what you did wrong, when the truth is he wanted a blond with blue eyes, and you're a brunette. Or she wanted a tall, good-looking athlete, and you're a short, fat intellectual.

Don't let yourself get tricked into thinking the problem between you two is something you can correct in yourself. Instead, get out of the hope trap. Then you can find someone who likes you the way you are.

The best thing to do is avoid any contact at all with your ex. Seeing them or talking to them will only make you yearn to have them all the time as you once did. They weren't willing to reconcile with you, and now getting a little love from your ex once in a while only makes your hope stronger that you will get them back—for keeps.

You're like a gambler in Las Vegas who keeps playing a slot machine and losing, but stays because once in a while a few coins dribble out.

The little victories keep the suckers coming back and putting their nickels in the slots, hoping to hit the jackpot. You must realize that if you thought about your ex-lover as married and moved to another state, far away or even dead, then you would approach your situation differently. You would still be sad, but not hooked. You wouldn't expect a reconciliation. The unhappiness you feel now is the gap between your expectations and reality.

It's important to your happiness that you realize you can never have your ex back, at least not in the kind of relationship you really want. But there is the possibility of having that relationship with someone else . . . as soon as you give up the old hopes. It's not the expected relationship you aren't going to get, it's just that you won't get it with that particular person.

Making phone calls to make things better, dressing up so that your ex will see you and want you back and showing up where you will "accidentally" meet all make things worse. Simply planning an encounter or thinking about one will activate your own hope that you really can change things. Once again, the hope will be unfilled and you will be disappointed and unhappy.

Everyone who's been left seems driven to change their ex's mind, to scheme and plan and spend hours devising ways or methods to make them sorry. Game-playing runs rampant. Maybe if only your ex thought you were dying of cancer, they'd come back, if only they saw you wasting away, if only they thought you were going to marry someone else, "if only." Use thought stopping to control your urge to think "if only."

By trying to get your ex back, you can become even more of

a victim. While you're planning how to make them love you again, they may be simply taking advantage of the time to keep you on the string, "in case." Your cooking a special dinner for him or taking her to the ballet won't help. Sure, they'll come for a special dinner or a show, but when they go away afterward, you'll only feel worse.

Your ex may even be encouraging you to stick around. Why not? Why should they say to you, "it's over," when you're so willing to hang around and take leftovers.

Giving up hope will eventually make you feel better, and it is a necessary step to your cure. Maintaining a fantasy that your husband doesn't really like his secretary—even though he's living with her now—is destructive. Maintaining a fantasy that your ex will come back as soon as he/she gets over some temporary infatuation makes no sense. Your ex will either stay away or come back on their own and it won't have anything to do with what you do. Schemes and plots to get a lover back are embarrassingly obvious to everyone but the person who runs them.

You'll find yourself doing all sorts of embarrassing things if you maintain your hope, and you'll be driving yourself deeper into depression with each disappointment.

Your ex is probably feeling sorry for you or maybe even guilty, but certainly annoyed at your humiliating phone calls.

Losing weight or dressing up and doing a remake on yourself is good so that you'll feel good about yourself, but don't do it to impress your ex. It'll only be demeaning when you discover that in spite of how good you look, or how good you act, they may not even notice, and they still don't want you.

Even if your ex responds favorably to you, it may not mean that he loves you, only that he just closed a big deal and feels generous, warm and loving toward the whole world. Or if she is sweet and passive, it could be because she just finished making love with someone else. The most dangerous time for you is when he is having a breakup with the new girl. Remember, it is just a temporary fight, and you will be left looking silly with your tongue hanging out.

Your yearning to get even intermittent reinforcement from your ex is a simple animal response. Like people who play the slot machines until all their money is gone, you could continue to plan your life and hopes around your ex until all your self-respect and energy are gone.

A hope situation is terribly destructive. The truth is that if you hammer away long enough and hard enough, you will get some feeble response. And that will keep you hooked and in pain longer.

Trading Old Hopes for New Ones

Your new hope is that the next relationship will be better, and of course it will. If you look back, you will see that the next important relationship is always better because you have learned new interpersonal skills from your old relationship.

The loving will be better, and so will the sex. That's not a fantasy at all, because the fact is that both loving and sex are skills that are improved with practice. The practice you got in your old relationship will work to your advantage in the new one. The odds are that you will be more mature and sensitive in your next big love affair.

By following the Letting Go program, you will also find that in your next relationship you will be a winner instead of a victim. You will develop new independence and new interests of your own that will make more interesting people want to seek you out instead of your chasing them.

The new hope is based on experience. The very next lover you try may not be "it," but the next big love experience will definitely be better, especially in terms of sex. Bereft lovers who thought only *that* man or woman could give them a satisfactory orgasm report that they have discovered it's not true. And you will, too, even though right now you may be still sexually hooked to your ex. In the next chapter we will show you how to break the sex hook and get on with your personal sensuality.

This is the time for you to trade the hope of getting your old lover back for a new hope—that you will feel fine without them. Getting over your depression makes you a more desirable person to everyone. Nobody wants to be with someone who is on a constant downer. Once you are over your depression, people will be attracted to you. The very act of doing something constructive for yourself about your own depression will make you feel powerful and a winner.

Pretend you made an investment—say in the stock market. If you bought at a high price, say a hundred dollars a share, how long would you wait before you sold as you saw the stock was going down? When it got to fifty, twenty—or would you wait until it was down to zero? Of course not.

Imagine your lost love affair in the same way. Your love was at a high. Now, how much has it lost? Isn't it time for you to cut your losses there, too? Don't throw good energy after bad.

Salvaging What's Left

Of course you want to dispose of your old lover's stock before it's totally valueless. But what about the things that are left? Can you totally ignore the friendship that developed over your ten-year marriage? The time spent learning about another person and having another person know about you? Of course not. We don't say that you will never see your ex or never be friends with them. But not now. In chapter twelve, we will set up specific circumstances for you to reconnect with your ex in a constructive way so that you will still exchange some friendship dividends without reinvesting your entire heart.

Right now, you are in a position of wanting to get close enough to your ex to get the goodies you used to get, but the relationship has deteriorated so badly that if you get that close you are likely to get some of the flack, too. Stick around and chances are you'll get dumped on. Don't worry, though, you haven't lost him/her forever. Just for a couple of months. You can then choose to get close enough to get what you want and keep your self-esteem while doing it.

Unless your ex has died or moved into voluntary oblivion, you will be able to see them again if you want to. There is a future relationship for you, but not now. Meanwhile, everyone you talk to tries to give you news.

Your Friendly Neighborhood CIA

All those people who were once friends of you both and who now supply you with information about your ex—that they're happy, doing well, doing badly, etc.—are your CIA. You seem driven to talk to these people, to exchange thoughts on why your ex left, to send messages or even to make them jealous.

Unfortunately, getting information from the CIA costs. Talking to them, no matter what they tell you about your ex, will only set you back. The truth is, hearing news and transmitting messages through the neighborhood spy systems is simply another way to keep your old lover in your life. Avoid the gossips. Tell them you're not quite ready to meet. Even if you have been part of a couple so long that all your friends are friends of you and your ex, you can find someone who won't stoke your fires.

Even chance meetings with the CIA are dangerous. They'll be tempted to give you news, for which you know you're hungry, and you'll be tempted to plant news. Some people even send picture postcards to mutual friends, hoping that news of them will get back to their ex's. Don't use anyone as a telegraph service to make your ex feel bad or to show them that you're all better and that they should see you now.

CIA communication with your ex through mutual friends is the worst kind, because it's indirect. It's impossible to transmit real feelings through friends, no matter how honest you try to be. You'll find yourself sending messages that you think will get your ex back. And in turn, your ex will send things that he/she thinks will make you go away, feel bad, or even worse, keep you hooked.

It's hard enough to communicate with someone after you have broken up, even when you do talk directly. It's impossible if you do it through friends.

Don't try to reconcile through friends, either. It never works, and you may wind up losing the friends, too. Right now, you must cut off communication (even indirect communication) with your ex. When you're tempted to call the CIA, use the Instant Gratification Hotline you set up in chapter three.

No matter what you hear from the CIA, you won't feel better. Suppose you discover that your ex has fallen in love and is just as happy as you are miserable. Your self-esteem drops when you realize that that other person can indeed be happy without you, but you aren't happy without them.

Or you may find out that your ex is miserable, but still doesn't want you back, an even greater insult to your self-esteem.

Or you may fan the flames by saying to yourself, "Of course, he/she can't be happy without me and will soon want me back." You lose either way because you're staying hooked.

You may be in the unfortunate circumstance of working with friends of you both, or going to school with them or simply having *all* mutual friends. What do you tell these people? How do you stop the intelligence reports?

It's not easy. First of all, you'll have to control your own natural urge to seek information and to hear the intelligence reports. The best thing to do is to make it clear on your first contact that you don't want to hear anything, before they start to tell you things about your ex "for your own good."

"I like you, and I want us to remain friends," you should say, "but I don't want to hear any news about John." Or, "I just want to make sure that we can be friends now that I am no longer part of a couple. Right now it's not good for me to hear news about Judy. Before we meet, I want to make sure that we can just exchange news about you, me or anything but my ex." Or, "Let's have lunch, but my analyst says not to talk about Mary right now."

You'll find that some of the people you knew will prefer remaining friends with your ex, either because they always were closer, or because they're geographically more convenient, or because they never really liked you that much anyway. Eventually, everyone you both knew will have to make a choice. You don't want to be invited to parties where your ex will show up cuddling with the new person in their life. So you, too, will have to make choices.

If you think a friend may be inviting you to a party your ex will attend, the best thing to do is to be magnanimous. Say that the friend should invite your ex, and you'll see your friend another time.

In most cases, if you ask whether your ex is invited, the answer will be something like, "Gee, I don't know . . ." If you're generous about it ("I think I'll come to the next party") you can usually wind up going to that party and being protected from your ex's presence. The friend will like you because you didn't create a problem, and you will be reaffirming the breakup.

It's okay, too, to ask people to stop talking to you about the breakup, if they are. Simply tell them it's not good for you and makes you unhappy. Nobody wants to be around an unhappy person, and they're sure to shut up if you say that.

If you are compulsively seeking information, you might even ask friends to help you, a la Alcoholics Anonymous. Tell them to remind you that you are reinforcing a bad habit by even asking about your former mate when you start saying, "Have you seen . . ." Tell them you'll only feel bad no matter what the news is. Again, nobody wants to make someone feel bad.

The Communications Blackout

If you can run away, it is the best cure for the communications blackout frustration. Even though you are taking your old sad self along on the trip, you will at least cut off the temptation to call your ex all the time and to seek news about him/her. Involving yourself with something new keeps your mind busy.

Many people report that they just can't stand "not knowing." Where is he/she? With whom? Doing what?

If you don't know where your ex is or how to reach them, you're lucky. Your ex cut off communications, and if they did a good enough job, your Letting Go therapy will progress faster.

If your ex is still close, you will have to cut off the communications yourself. The best way is to move if you can, or change your phone number. Make it difficult for your ex to reach you. Get an answering service, and tell them not to tell you about calls from your ex, or even buy an answering machine. Don't return calls if you get them.

You may say, yes, but what if they want to make up and come back? The answer is if they really want you, they can find you. And it won't matter how hard it is.

It's natural to have thoughts you feel you *must* communicate or that you can't keep to yourself.

The Last Love Letter

This is where you put all the thoughts you have that you are obsessed by, like brilliant ideas to make your relationship work again, or yearnings you want them to know about, or apologies for whatever you imagine you did wrong, or telling them off for whatever they did wrong.

Your Last Love Letter should be kept in a special journal. Or if you type, you might even want to type it each day and file the pages away. You think now that someday you'll present it to your ex, but chances are you won't. Believe it or not, all those incredibly obsessive thoughts you must communicate to your ex will disappear from your mind.

By writing the Last Love Letter you will purge the obsessive thoughts that inhibit your everyday activities, the thoughts that you think you must remember to tell your ex—if you ever get a chance. Now you won't be responsible for remembering them—you will have them all written down.

The Last Love Letter is a continuous thought journal, and the things you say in it are up to you. Your letter could be shockingly ugly, full of threats and hateful thoughts. You may have a vision of your ex lying dead, or you may feel like killing them. You may want to grab them and make them listen to you. You may hate them. Or you may have yearning, loving thoughts, things you want to say. Happy times when you were together that you wanted to remind them of. Things they said to you or things you said to them. What about those old Valentine cards that said "forever"?

Whatever it is, you can write it in your Last Love Letter without there being any permanent damage. You won't communicate thoughts that will make you look silly or lose respect or dignity, but they will be there. You won't be carrying them around in your head, either.

Don't even wait until you get home if you don't want to. You can carry your Last Love Letter around with you to jot down things during the day. If that's inconvenient (yours is very large), or you're afraid someone might see it, carry a small notebook so you can make notes to transfer into your Last Love Letter during the Sob Hour.

In the next session you will learn specific ways to use your Last Love Letter as a therapeutic device.

Session Eight: Confining the Hurt

The Sob Hour

When do you get to cry? You can't cry during the day, you have been using thought stopping and aversive therapy to stop that; you can't cry over sad songs on the radio, because you have learned not to listen to music stations.

The Sob Hour is the time for all your crying. This will be a time, perhaps an hour a day, that you will set aside to spend crying over your ex. It's a perfect time to write your Last Love Letter.

Sad thoughts like "If only I could see you tonight . . ." and "Why don't you want me, I could make you so happy." You can think them all you want and write them in your Last Love Letter. Eventually you'll find that you're writing the same things over and over again.

The Sob Hour has to be scheduled at an inconvenient time, a time when you would rather be doing something else. That's so that you won't get to like it.

The Isolation Booth

Set up an inconvenient or uncomfortable circumstance (like with your feet in a cold tub of water, or locked in the bathroom, or sitting in a corner with your face toward the wall) for your Sob Hour.

Suppose you indulge each thought as it occurs to you during the day, say in the morning, or just before you go to sleep at night, or as soon as you come home from work, then those places and times of day become associated with thinking about your ex. Let's say you always do your crying over breakfast, or while shopping in the same store you always shopped in, or walking on the same walkway you always walked on. If you indulge the emotional outburst right there and then, whenever it happens, then that place and time of the day become even more associated with the emotional link to your ex.

Eventually, just as your cat learned to salivate at the sound of the can opener signalling dinner, you'll learn to feel sad for your ex-love at "your" supermarket or on "your" beach. To sever the triggering connection with your ex, jot down the thought in your emotional Bankbook, save it for the Sob Hour and continue shopping, sleeping or eating.

Your cure is already taking place simply by doing this faithfully each day. You are regaining emotional control by self-limiting the time you think about your ex. You aren't spending all day long feeling sad, but only one hour of each day. Eventually you can limit it to a briefer time allotment. It's very frustrating to think that you're devoting your entire day thinking about someone who doesn't care about you. How much time a day will you devote to your ex? It's up to you, but for now, you must start with a maximum of one set hour a day.

Soon it will become a drag to do an hour stint locked in the bathroom writing Last Love Letters and thinking sad thoughts. Right now, it may sound like just the thing you want to do, but it does wear off.

Instead of thinking about your ex everywhere you go, there will only be one special place for doing it. That's why you should do it in an uncomfortable place, one you're not likely to spend a lot of time in—like the garage or the cellar. The more uncomfortable the situation is, the more you will be able to cut the crying time. You won't want to spend a lot of time crying if it's cold or hot or damp.

If you have trouble getting started, write at the top of the first page of a special notebook these words: "Dear [ex's name], I don't know if you will ever read this but . . ." Go on from there. Or, "Dear [ex's name], Everything is fine but . . ."

During the Sob Hour, you may choose to be standing, not sitting. Make it uncomfortable—maybe in the sun if you don't like the heat, or indoors if you'd rather be out in the sun. Take out your emotional Bankbook. Read over what you've written. Have imaginary conversations with your ex. If you feel angry, beat on a pillow with your fist. Cry or scream, but only for one hour a day.

"Yes," you say, "but I could do it all day long. How can I limit it to one hour?" Try. Set a timer. Tomorrow's another day and there will be another Sob Hour for you to fill. For this week, you should maintain the same amount of time you started with. Soon, you will get bored and will automatically cut down your crying time.

5
THE LOVE FIX

Love has no pride
When I call out your name,
There is no one but myself to blame.
I'd give anything to see you again.

—Bonnie Rait
"Love Has No Pride"

You should be over most of the severe depressive symptoms by now, but you may still yearn for the love your ex once gave you.

There's nothing wrong with being addicted to love, as long as you're loved back and you are functioning well in the world. But if being love-addicted has become a problem for you, it's time to kick the habit. That doesn't mean that you should give up being in love forever—just for now and just with that one particular person.

If you suddenly discovered that you were drinking too much or smoking too much or had gained a lot of weight from overeating, you might want to stop drinking or smoking for a while or go on a diet (consult your doctor). That doesn't mean that you'll never eat, drink or smoke again—but it'll be your choice.

The love high is great while you're on it, but sometimes there's a hangover when you come down. You're not high anymore, and the world looks pretty bleak. You've been unexpectedly (no one every really thinks their relationship will break up), and probably without too much ceremony, tossed back into reality.

The altered state of consciousness, the delusions, what Freud called the temporary psychosis, the enhanced perceptions and the general good feeling of being in love are wonderful. But since you've lost your connection temporarily, you'll have to live in reality until you score again.

Even though you may face the reality that you can't have the fix from your ex-lover, and that even if you did, it would be bad for you, you may still be yearning for love. There isn't a chemical that you can take to do away with the yearning, but there is "psychological methadone" in certain behavior techniques.

There will be things that make you yearn for the love you used to get. It could be a simple thing like Saturday night, or a party coming up and you don't have a date, or waking in a lonely bed on Sunday morning, or when it gets dark, or when you come home to an empty house.

It could be more specific like when you need help, or when you wish you had someone to eat out with, or when you ride your bike alone, or on your anniversary or birthday. And, of course, you might be missing sex.

You might be triggered by seeing another person who has a particular quality you always admired in your ex, or by meeting a new person who is conspicuously lacking in that quality. Going to a wedding or a party. Seeing a happy couple. It sometimes seems as if you had just quit smoking and everyone is lighting up after dinner.

A woman might start to get dressed for an evening out and automatically stand in front of her closet imagining what her ex would like to see her look like. It's what she's always thought about when she's dressed, or even put on makeup.

A man comes home from work and the house is empty. He makes his own instant coffee in the morning instead of brewing for two. Any normal event can be the trigger, the thing that makes you feel nostalgic longings for your ex's loving. It's often an event rather than a thing that causes your trigger to activate.

There are even ways for you to control the sad triggers that crop up unexpectedly, the things you can't hide in your Implosion Box, like the freeway sign that points in the direction of your ex's house.

THE FIFTH WEEK

Session Nine: Kicking the Love Addiction

Ratcheting

Delaying the urge for immediate gratification for just a little while, or ratcheting, makes the urge go away temporarily. If you're on a diet and have an urge for a hot fudge sundae, you can delay it for at least a little while and may forget about it. If you immediately indulged every urge for everything fattening, you'd never lose weight. An urge to see, contact or even telephone your ex for a love fix will seem less pressing if you can delay for just an hour. You could find that you won't need the fix so badly then. You don't have to depend on will power alone. Do something to take your mind off your urge. You wouldn't go to a candy store if you were trying to diet. So if you have the urge to telephone your ex for a love fix, don't sit with your hand on the dial. Go somewhere. Buy yourself a present. Do something that will make you feel good or useful, or go somewhere where there are no phones.

Everyone has had the experience of having to urinate at an inappropriate time or inconvenient place, and everyone knows they can postpone it. That's the "ratchet effect." When you discover that the department store bathroom is four floors up, and you pass a sale on the way, you probably will forget about the bathroom.

If you will try to postpone driving by your ex's house by substituting another activity, especially something interesting, the urge will disappear—at least for the time being. Since the urge to see your ex isn't a physiological urge, like urinating, it won't come back even stronger. Since you don't really "have to" see the other person, and since you have been able to postpone it once, you will gain a sense of mastery over your addiction by using the simple ratcheting technique.

Learning that you can control your urge is reinforcing your faith in your own powers.

Simply wanting to control your urge is not enough. As Dr. Nathan Azrin's research on enuresis (bed-wetting) concludes, you must also reward yourself by substituting something you would like. If there is something special you want, like a trip, a massage, a dress or even a ticket to a special event, you might award yourself one dollar toward it each time you control your urge through ratcheting. Make your goal a luxury that will involve you in a bigger reward than the probable put-down you'd get from a contact with your ex.

Indulgence of the Urge

Indulgence is the urge to get the fix, acted out. Driving by an ex-lover's house for a fix just reinforces the addiction and creates a new bad habit—driving by your ex's house more often. As every addict knows, every time you get a fix, it strengthens the likelihood that you'll need the fix again and again.

Indulgence of that kind of urge won't do you any good at all. You might run into your ex and be embarrassed. You might see them with another lover, or you might discover another car parked in their garage. Probably nothing will happen, but you could be hurt and will certainly feel empty afterwards.

How silly you'll appear calling your ex to find out whether your lost perfume bottle or razor is there. He'll know it's not for the perfume. She'll know it's not the razor you want.

And if you don't get caught driving by their house, or if you're lucky and you call and they're not there, what then? You become like a petty thief who didn't get caught. You got away with it that time, and there's a certain exhilaration in getting away with something. You feel relieved and excited. The second time is even more dangerous. The more you get away with it and the more exciting the risk becomes, the more you will try. Eventually you will get caught, but in the meantime you are becoming addicted to getting away with something, like a teenager who shoplifts for the excitement.

A man who knew when his girlfriend would get out of nursing school each day stationed himself near the school and watched for her. Then he followed her home. Every eighth or ninth time he did it, she would see him. Sometimes she'd shout at him to go away; other times she'd point him out to friends with a shrug or a giggle.

He would be embarrassed, but he kept doing it. Getting punished once in a while isn't a deterrent. Instead, the times he didn't get caught became reinforcements that he would get away with it again. That in itself was his reward—plus the attention he got one way or another.

Session Ten: Love Casualties

Sex was a big part of your old relationship. Probably it was very good with your former partner, or you wouldn't have been with him or her so long and you wouldn't still be yearning for them. Everyone needs physical love and warmth to survive.

Both men and women suffer missing their former lovers in bed because that's where they spent so much of their time together. Many men judge how worthwhile they are by their sexual capabilities and by how much they can turn on a woman.

When a woman says goodbye to a man who has been trying to satisfy her sexually and give her what he imagines she wants, he feels a sexual slur—as if his sexual prowess hadn't been good enough. His masculinity is in doubt in his mind, and because of our macho-influenced culture, so is his personal value as a human being. He may even become sexually dysfunctional, suffering premature ejaculation or impotence. He feels he isn't a man because he couldn't keep his woman. His fantasy is that she stayed around because he satisfied her sexually, because she was in love with his penis and his prowess as well as himself.

For a woman, a similar fantasy exists. She may become asexual because she feels that a man would have stayed around if she were really satisfying him with her body. Her fantasy is that he can't live without her loving breasts, open legs or welcoming vagina. She feels that she has been unsatisfactory as a woman, that she gave him everything and he didn't want it. She feels as if her entire being has been rejected.

You may notice that you have lost your sexual appetite. Just as certain people, especially adolescent girls, develop a distaste for food to the point that they can't eat and aren't hungry, you may develop a distaste for sex. You just aren't turned on.

Impotence and Inabilities

Not getting an erection and coming too soon or way too late are upsetting problems, but for a man who is suffering an emotional loss as well, they soon become only secondary problems.

His sexual dysfunction is almost automatically tacked onto his list of problems. He fears that it will happen again and again, and that he'll never be sexually adequate unless he can have his old girlfriend back. The fear-caused impotence is the very thing that makes his impotence happen over and over. Added to his feelings of being rejected and of being not worthwhile because he couldn't keep the woman he loved with his sex is the fear that he cannot have an erection with anyone. He retreats from sexual and even social encounters. Just one occasion of impotence convinces a man that his problem is that he is "impotent." He may have had his erection while kissing and lost it when they got undressed, or just as he was about to make love, or even after he had started, or just at the moment of penetration. Something the new girl did or said that was different, or even the same as the old one, could have triggered his impotence. Or it simply didn't feel as good.

If a man has one instance of premature ejaculation, while kissing or rubbing against a woman, or at the entrance to the vagina, or after one or two strokes, he may think he was too excited, which is rarely the case. Or he may immediately assume he has become a premature ejaculator forever, as may the retarded ejaculator. If he can't come just one time, he assumes he will only be able to come with his ex, or that he never will be able to come with a woman again.

All of the major male sexual dysfunctions that appear after the breakup of a relationship are maintained by the fear that they will occur again—regardless of how they started. Like a stutterer who stutters because he is afraid he will stutter, a man can develop secondary impotence, or premature or retarded ejaculation out of fear.

By the time a man with a sexual dysfunction gets to a psychologist's office after his affair breaks up, he is already suffering from secondary sexual dysfunction symptoms, so much so that his problem even occurs if he goes back to his first lover. At this point his fear of sexual performance failure is as much to blame for his problem as the initial rejection by his ex.

One reason for the fear and anxiety that causes sexual dysfunction in both men and women is that the body's defensive reflex system takes over and makes sex physically impossible. The defensive reflex nervous reaction is the one that prepares your body to either fight or run away in time of danger. It also keeps you from being hungry or sleeping or having sex or thinking clearly by taking over from the orienting reflex, the one that usually is operating and that allows you to eat, think, sleep and be physically and emotionally comfortable.

If you were in the middle of making love, and an earthquake started, you might lose your erection if you are a man or find yourself no longer lubricated if you're a woman. That's because your defensive reflex takes over in emergencies, pumping the blood away from the genital regions and into the large muscles of the legs and body in preparation for flight. It's nature's way of preserving the species.

As man progressed from caves to civilization, those with the best defensive reflex responses survived. If a cave-style bacchanal were going on, and suddenly a saber-toothed tiger appeared, only those whose defensive reflexes took over survived. The others would continue eating and drinking and making love because their "fight or flight" nervous systems failed to react. Only the ones who got turned off sexually and ran away lived to have sex again, to have children and to become our ancestors.

Any normal physical urges to urinate, to eat, to make love

are instantly inhibited when your defensive reflex takes over. If you're picnicking and it starts to rain, you'll probably lose your appetite in your rush to get out of the rain.

Once you develop a fear of any kind, your body can't tell the difference between *real* danger and *imagined* danger. All it knows is that fear equals turnoff. You may be afraid you'll be impotent and get turned off. Or you may be afraid of a new relationship and you'll feel sexually indifferent. Your body is only acting as if your social fear were an actual physical danger. Your defensive reflex is taking over and cancelling your desire.

A woman may fail to lubricate or a man may not get an erection, if true fear takes over. Men may suffer premature ejaculation because that's just another way the body has of turning off or ending the sexual arousal.

"Frigidity"

Sometimes a woman's fear will present itself as primary anorgasmia (she cannot have an orgasm under any circumstances), or secondary anorgasmia (she can't have orgasms during intercourse, only through manipulation), or disperenia (painful intercourse), or vaginismus (involuntary contraction of the vagina). These are also maintained by anxiety.

A woman's body may terminate sexual feelings by either turning off all the way with vaginismus, which makes insertion impossible, or just part way by being able to be penetrated but not being able to reach orgasm. The cause of anorgasmia in the female and retarded ejaculation in the male are the same—fear, which prevents complete orgasm. It's as if you had to urinate, but couldn't because someone was watching. The defensive reflex takes over and blocks the normal activity.

There are women who, just like a man, will have as much sex as possible after a split, but again, it's never as good as with the old lover. Even if she does reach orgasm, there's something missing. This is more common in women than men because men expect to be satisfied with an orgasm. A woman has been taught that sex should be more. That it must include romance and "being in love."

Then the orgasm somehow seems better, but actually *everything* seems better when you're in love.

If you are having reasonably satisfactory sex now with someone besides your ex, you are doing fine. It may not be as good. You may even feel detached, as if you want the person to go away immediately afterwards, or as if you don't care if you ever see them again. It just doesn't seem to have the impact making love used to have.

That's because you don't have the emotional attachment and involvement you had with your ex, the memories you shared and the feelings you had. You haven't learned each other's reactions, turn-ons or -offs.

Worrying about your performance, or not being in tune with your new partner yet, or even whether the other person approves of you or likes your body can adversely affect your sexual functioning, especially on a first encounter.

You may find yourself flashing on your ex while making love with someone else. Women especially have problems starting new relationships because they are taught to think of sex in the context of a loving partner, where men are taught to accept recreational sex. Perhaps the thing you miss with your ex is another level of sex that will take time and practice to develop with someone else.

In actual sexual dysfunctions, where the person just can't have intercourse, anxiety terminates the sexual act or prevents it from reaching its conclusion. The anxiety is the fear that the dysfunction will occur. If a tightrope walker is very afraid he's going to fall, he falls. In circuses, tightrope walkers with nets have fewer falls than those without nets. What you need now is a net, some form of security blanket, in your sexual encounters.

Abbreviated Sex Therapy

The basis for all sexual therapy is that if you can get people reintroduced to an anxiety-free sexual scene, sexual arousal will take over and they won't feel anxious the next time. A woman's anxiety may be that she will once again fail to reach orgasm, proving that only her old lover could do it for her. A man may be anxious about being impotent and looking bad to his new lover.

These anxieties can be eliminated by setting up a sexual scene without the possibility of the fear-inducing event. A man can't be afraid that he will be impotent if his genitals are not involved. He knows that if no one sees his penis, nobody will know whether it's erect or not. A woman can't be afraid she will be anorgasmic if she's not being genitally or vaginally stimulated to what ought to be orgasm.

The best cure for a sexual dysfunction is a platonic date—no kissing or hugging or even touching. Initially, put sex out of your mind and enjoy the other person. If you decide not to have sex, then there's no reason to be afraid you won't have an erection or orgasm. Make a contract with yourself not to go beyond a handshake on the first date.

Suppose step one in a relationship were calling someone on the telephone and step ten were sexual intercourse. A man who is afraid he will fail at step ten will be afraid to take step one because he knows step one will lead to step ten. His therapy might be to do step one without the possibility of step ten occurring. He is told to call a woman and simply talk on the telephone, not to make a date.

For an impotent man, each step will have anxiety, from calling on the phone, to the first date, to kissing, to petting, to undressing, to intercourse—but not if he eliminates the possibility of having to perform sexually or even having his penis visible. Until he is able to do step one without anxiety, he must not go on to step two. It's amazing how many impotent men will have an erection all during a first date when they are forbidden to touch.

At each step of the way he will contract in his own head to go just a bit further, providing that the last date was carefree. The next step might be, for example, no further than touching the breast over clothing, then no further than reaching under and touching skin, then no further than touching the pubic area on the outside, then no further than reaching under the panties, then no further than uncovering the breasts. It could be as simple as, "No matter what, I won't take my pants off."

The outcome of this shortcut sex therapy is that the sexually dysfunctional man and woman find themselves in a sexual situation with no possibility of embarrassment. Without anxiety to inhibit it, their sexual appetite blossoms, takes over and moves them into the area of sexual desire. With this behavioral sex therapy program, more than 80 percent of patients report that they become potent and premature ejaculators report a 95 percent success rate. These statistics are verified by their spouses and mates.

In order to progress in this step-by-step sex therapy, each decision to go further must be contingent on the last step being pleasurable. If you had anxiety during petting on the outside of the clothing or found that it wasn't pleasurable to you, then you wouldn't continue on to petting under clothing—until you had petted outside clothing and really experienced it without anxiety.

Women who feel they can't have an orgasm report feeling aroused after a platonic date. Some say they really didn't care whether they had an orgasm or not because they enjoyed the worry-free encounter so much.

Orgasms and ejaculations are not end products. It's okay to give and get pleasure without reaching either one. Sex is meant to be enjoyable play, not a serious search for the great orgasm.

Enjoy the process of exploring another person's body without looking for a place to ejaculate.

In a product-oriented society the end product on an assembly line is the shiny new car; in sex, it's the orgasm. Women who don't have orgasms feel unfeminine and inadequate, in a sense, sexually unproductive. We have been taught that there is "foreplay" and then sex or "coming." The implication is that the activity that precedes orgasm isn't as important as the orgasm itself, the end product. The truth is that all sexual play is equally important and equally valid—even without an orgasm.

It's the process (making love) rather than the end product (orgasm) that's important in sex play. When, or even if, you have an erection or an orgasm doesn't make you more or less lovable or valuable as a person. Once you realize that in lovemaking the play's the thing and orgasms are just part of the process, you will be eliminating the performance anxiety that prevents you from enjoying sex. The real peak could be meeting a new person and "clicking" together with your eyes. The anticipation and excitement are valid parts of sex. It doesn't have to be an erection, an ejaculation, an orgasm, being "multi-orgasmic," or "coming together." Don't become a victim of sexual fascism that dictates how sex ought to be.

It should be understood that the above treatment is for recent acute cases of sexual dysfunction that happen as a result of breaking up a relationship. If you have suffered a lifetime of impotence, you will probably need professional help with this sort of program. But if your problems started when your relationship ended, the gradual reintroduction of sex without worry will work. It is the quintessence of all the best behavioral sex therapy programs, including the famous Masters and Johnson approach.

If the treatment doesn't seem to be working for you, you may need a monitor, a professional to report to. Someone who will ask you, "Did you experience anxiety last time? Are you sure? Did you violate the contract in your head about not penetrating? I know you had an erection like a flagpole, but were you able to restrain yourself?"

The monitor you select could be a behavior specialist working in your local university's psychology, social work or psychiatry department clinics. Make sure he or she is a licensed health professional, someone trained to listen. If a behavior therapy approach like the one outlined above is used, most cases won't take more than twenty visits to cure the problem.

Dreaming of having sex with your ex or masturbating to thoughts of them isn't unusual. That's natural. It's as if you've been playing bridge with the same partner for years. Or tennis. You know each other's little secret signals, the moves before the other person makes them.

You can't expect the same "instant rapport" from a new partner, especially in sex. It's okay to go to bed with someone just because they're a nice person. You don't have to be in love right now, but that doesn't mean that you should eliminate the fun of sex from your life.

Right now you might even want to find a sex partner who is better or more experienced than you are. You were in love with your ex and that made the difference. When you love someone, they could be a really lousy tennis player, but somehow it's the best and most fun-filled game with them.

Tell your new lover exactly what you like. "I really love having my scrotum stroked, toes sucked, being ravished." Anything your ex did that really turned you on. Say it passively as a statement, "I am turned on by," not "John or Betty always used to . . ." Tell them your favorite position, fantasy, pressure, stroke or movement. You are responsible for your own pleasure.

Men often suffer less sexual frustration because our culture is more accepting of men using masturbation to relieve tensions. And they do. Women, on the other hand, often feel that they shouldn't touch themselves or that self-stimulation isn't right.

A woman who is suffering from sexual deprivation should buy a vibrator and learn to use it to stimulate herself to orgasm. Women's self-help centers teach about the female body. Masturbation does not take away from a woman's ability to enjoy sex with a partner. Having an orgasm with a vibrator doesn't mean it won't happen with a person. Actually, the more you masturbate, the quicker you will reach orgasms.

Nor do orgasms "wear out." It has been found that people who have active sex lives are sexually active later in life. In other words, to paraphrase Henry Miller, the more you use it, the longer it lasts and the better it works.

Don't be ashamed to go into your local department store and ask for a massage unit.

Women are especially apt to feel like taking a sexual sabbatical. Some men do the same. It's as if they were making sure no one except their ex could possibly satisfy them.

By cutting yourself off sexually right now, you will find that you won't want sex. The less sexual activity you have, the less you will want.

One reason gerontologists like Dr. Alex Comfort believe elderly people don't have a high sexual activity rate is because one of the two partners has been out of commission due to illness. When the illness is over, both have lost their sex appetite through disuse.

An impotent man or a woman who has problems with orgasm may think that they should save it up. That they have been doing it too much and that's why they have lost it. That's absolutely wrong. Erections are not a function of the amount of semen in the seminal vesicle—they are a function of how well you have exercised a complex neuromuscular system by early sex and/or masturbation.

If someone complained to you about not being able to run a four-minute mile, and you found out they never jog or run, you would know immediately that they were foolish to expect to run a four-minute mile without having worked out. They are not "in condition." The same is true for sexual desire and functioning. People who don't have active sex lives can't expect to enjoy sex as much as those who do.

6
THE TAN VAN

If what you love is far away, no matter; images
are there before your eyes and the dear name
Rings in your ears. Better to run away,
Escape from such illusions, frighten off
Such things as nourish love.

—LUCRETIUS
De Rerum Natura

The tan van fix is one of the most difficult to avoid, since the automobile is such an integral part of our world and since people tend to identify others by the cars they drive.

In almost every single case of a broken relationship, the person who is left has reported an insane desire to look into or chase every car that resembles that of their ex. Not only is the looking itself bad—it reinforces the habit of looking—there is also a question of *neurotic stimulus generalization* (NSG) involved.

THE SIXTH WEEK

Session Eleven: Discrimination Day

Neurotic Stimulus Generalization (NSG)

A man suffering NSG might turn and look at every tall brunette he sees, no matter where he is, as long as she resembles his former lover—even if it's unlikely she would be there at that time. A woman might actually tap a stranger on the shoulder because the back of his neck looks like her lost mate. It's a neurotic generalization to figure every tall brunette is "the one," or every man with a curly blond natural haircut is "him."

It's ridiculous to think that your ex is driving every car that resembles theirs, to drive recklessly close behind it to check the license plate number or even to open the door of a strange one parked near your house to check its registration.

If you are a victim of NSG, you will know it. Every blond girl with a suntan, or even without one, makes you think of your ex. Every car that was like theirs, every ballet dancer if she was a dancer, every tennis court if he liked to play tennis. The neurotic generalization you have made is the one that stimulates you to think of your ex when you see any ballerina or any tennis court. It's bad enough if you think about your ex when you see a movie you went to together, but not at all movies. Then it's a neurotic stimulus generalization.

You have learned to expect to see your ex. You can unlearn it by proving to yourself once and for all that every look-alike isn't your former lover, or that he isn't playing on every baseball field, or she isn't dancing in every ballet.

It isn't your ex-lover you are seeing everywhere but rather your primitive inclination to generalize to others from your specific ex. You still want to see your ex. You're used to seeing them and used to wanting to see them. It's a habit. That's why you imagine you see them, fantasize a chance meeting and even a future date.

It's not his dog, or her car, or his tan van, or her long hair you are seeing everywhere. It can't be. Not everywhere. You know that's a physical impossibility. In addition to the triggers that cause NSG, the NSG is a way of filling a wish to see your ex. You *want* to think your ex is in that car or that you see their dog because that means they must be nearby. Secretly, you hope for a chance meeting.

If you were to actively seek out your ex, to call or go to their house, you wouldn't get the reaction you want. You might get a hang-up or a cool or suspicious reception. A chance meeting is much safer. You feel safe from rejection and you *think* you won't be endangering your Love Cure.

In your fantasy, you meet your ex accidentally, have a drink, talk and fall into each other's arms. Intellectually, you may know that's not probable, but emotionally you haven't let go of the fantasy.

You imagine the chance meeting is a last opportunity to reclaim your love. Only for you it won't be by chance. You're going to make it happen, if you only can spot that tan van driving on the freeway. Then you could pull up and wave, or follow it.

Soon it becomes a compulsion. You may see hundreds of cars on the freeway, but a green Volkswagen like she always drove still catches your eye. A golden retriever always makes you look for him because that was the kind of dog he had.

Signal-to-Noise Ratio

It's like being at a party and hearing a hum of voices or on a subway listening to the clatter of the tracks. You don't hear particular voices or words unless someone, even in normal conversational tones, happens to say your name or to bring up something in which you're very much interested. Suddenly, you will hear that voice. The sound of your name or talk about a subject that vitally interests you leaps out of the background noise. In the same way, you are still supersensitive to things that remind you of your ex. You're selectively alert to things you've always associated with them. You see them and you're drawn to them in the hope of that "accidental" meeting where you think you'll have a chance of getting the old love goodies.

Discrimination Day will teach you that it isn't your former mate you see everywhere and will make the tan van just another car on the freeway fading into the background blur of traffic.

By learning to discriminate between *the* tan van and all the other tan vans in the world, you can save the embarrassment of chasing strange cars and people. It's like flashing on your ex everytime you hear their name in a crowd. Of course you know everyone called "Dave" isn't your former mate. Every "Anne" isn't *the* one.

Another reason you must break the tan van fix is because it reestablishes your own pattern of habitually hoping to get your old lover back. It's bad for you. Every time you see your particular trigger, maybe long blond hair, you flash on your nostalgic wish for the good times you once had with your ex. Your hope is revived.

On Discrimination Day you will set aside an entire day to spend on your compulsion, no matter what it is. It could be a particular car, a special figure or build or a breed of dog. Whatever it is, spend the entire day checking out every one you can find. After several fruitless hours of looking for your ex, you will realize that the chances of finding them by accident are practically zero.

Probably, on your Discrimination Day, you'll find yourself getting all dressed up—just in case. It's hard to get rid of that "maybe we'll meet" feeling. "After all, we are meant for each other, and I may be the one to find my love on Discrimination Day." As you prepare to go out looking, you must realize how superstitiously silly it is.

Maybe you always think you see your ex in shopping centers or fashion malls or big department stores. Spending a day there looking—going from mall to mall or from store to store will be exhausting. And you have less than one-half of one percent chance of finding them.

You will soon discover how useless an activity looking for your ex is. Every time you think you see your ex, you get excited. You're stimulated by the thought of an accidental meeting, and then you're disappointed.

Simply having your expectations consistently disappointed on Discrimination Day causes extinction of the urge to seek. Chasing strange cars can be dangerous, self-defeating and demeaning to your self-esteem. You find yourself checking all the green Volkswagens in the parking lot at the bank or market. You make dangerous U-turns. You feel stupid and still hooked every time.

You don't have to forget your old lover forever, but you do have to get unhooked from silly stimuli like cars and dogs. It's part of letting go of the painful yearnings. By spending an entire day chasing green Volkswagens, or golden retrievers, or tan vans, or whatever it is that always catches your eye and makes you think of your ex, you will learn to discriminate between *all* cars and your ex's, all dogs and your ex's.

That doesn't mean that you won't always think of your ex in connection with whatever it is you're hooked on. Green Volkswagens may mean Anne forever, or tan vans may mean John forever. But you won't be hooked on them, seeking them out. You no longer will be a slave to the urge to chase.

You may see a car that reminds you of your ex, but you will also realize how very slim the chances are that they're really in it.

You will soon feel that even if he/she were there, so what. It won't make any difference in your relationship. They're probably on their way to do something and wouldn't stop on the freeway to talk to you anyway. "It's really a waste of time" will be your natural conclusion. You will realize that it's almost impossible to run into your ex by accident.

The persistent and unrealistic expectation that you will run into your ex and have a reunion sometimes reaches neurotic proportions. You may even know that your ex doesn't drive a tan van anymore, and still you seek them out. You may know that your ex doesn't live in the neighborhood or is at work, and still you chase look-alikes. That's the neurotic part. One patient burst into laughter when she caught herself checking out the license plate on a silver Mercedes 120 miles from home.

Suppose you always feed your cat from a green dish. When the cat sees you put out the green dish, he automatically gets ready to eat. He begins to salivate, even run around the room excitedly. Soon, the sight of *any* green dish, even in an inappropriate place, will bring your cat out looking for food.

Your cat is hooked on green dishes. He will automatically salivate at the sight of *any* green dish. The salivation is in anticipation of gratification, food.

You are hooked on the tan van fix in the same automatic way. You anticipate gratification when you see one, even if it's the wrong one. If your cat were surrounded by twenty green dishes, nineteen full of sawdust, he would quickly learn to discriminate the special green dish that was his food dish, using finer cues such as smell or feel or sight. The cat soon learns that his green dish is slightly different from the rest, and it won't go nosing around all the sawdust-filled dishes. He'll discriminate by learning that all the other dishes are useless to him.

In the same way, you will see that every car that looks like your former mate's or even every person that looks like them—isn't. That you won't get gratification from every one as you once did from your mate. Your tendency to seek your lover's car everywhere will diminish when your concentrated Discrimination Day becomes a fruitless and futile search.

Plan your Discrimination Day when you know your ex is at home or at work or away in another town. You will prove to yourself that the chances are zero that your lover is in every car like theirs by looking into every one you see. You will learn that every tall blond you see isn't your ex by spending a day chasing every one you see.

If the chase response to the generalized stimulus (the tan van or blond) is not reinforced, you won't keep having that shot of adrenaline every time you see one. Each time you check out another blond or tan van, you get defeated. The old stimulus isn't working because the old lover isn't there to provide gratification. By proving that the stimulus doesn't pay off, you extinguish your own response and the yearning for the chance meeting with your old lover.

Session Twelve: The Photo Finish

If the obsessions persist, schedule another Discrimination Day. Only this time, take along a camera for the Photo Finish.

You will know if your obsession is really out of hand when you begin suspecting your ex-lover is in places where you know they can't be. You may know she's in California and still persist in following green Volkswagens in Maine.

This is the time to shoot pictures of everything you are obsessed with—whether it's tan vans, brown dogs or Afro hairstyles. As soon as the photos are processed, they become a visual aid in your self-therapy. Spend an hour examining the photos. Check each carefully. You'll see it's not your ex's car, not your former lover's dog. Looking at these pictures or even carrying them around with you provides reassurance that your chances of running into "the one" are practically zero.

It's hard to chase green VWs when you know you have a hip pocket full of color slides of green VWs that weren't the right one. Use your pictures to the fullest. Look at them until you get bored. Examine them over and over again. Whenever you have the urge to chase, remember your photos.

Running around taking pictures of cars, dogs, hairdos; gathering memorabilia into boxes and closets; turning off the love songs on the radio; reading notes with your feet in a cold bathtub—hasn't your ex put you to a lot of trouble to just get him or her out of your mind and the misery out of your heart? It's enough to make a person furiously angry, even vengeful.

7
SWEET REVENGE

You'll never find another love like mine.
You'll keep searching and searching your whole
life through.
You're gonna miss my lovin'.

—R. GAMBLE AND L. HUFF
"You'll Never Find Another Love Like Mine"

As a result of sessions one through twelve, and the behavioral changes that are taking place, the end of the second month of separation will find depressed thoughts turning to anger. Instead of "poor me," the abandoned lover's thoughts change to "How could they do that to me?" or "She'll be sorry." Or "He'll never find another woman to love him as deeply as I did."

Depression has been described, psychologically, as anger turned inward. Since your depression is going away, it's only natural that your anger will become externalized, toward the person who hurt you, your ex. And that's where it belongs.

THE SEVENTH WEEK

Session Thirteen: Jealousy

Suddenly, you are shocked to realize that you really don't want your ex to be happy, you want them to suffer. Incredible revenge fantasies of getting the loved one back and then dumping them, hurting them or making them suffer are normal at this time.

If someone hit you, you would want to hit them back. Wanting to hurt your ex is perfectly natural now. In certain countries, crimes of passion are still excused. Why wouldn't you want to kill when you think of your ex-wife in her new lover's bed? Or your old boyfriend at one of your favorite spots with his new lady?

Frustration-Aggression

Researchers at Yale University have found that whenever animals are frustrated, they become hostile and aggressive.

You have just gone through a period when you wanted something, perhaps love, from someone who wouldn't give it to you. So you became angry. In the beginning, you turned the anger against yourself because you were afraid that if you got angry with the other person you would alienate them. Now you don't care. They're already gone. You might as well make them suffer. The anger goes where it belongs.

If you are angry with your ex at this point, you're already half cured. One source of your anger may very well be jealousy.

You may not want your old lover back really, but the minute you discover there's "another woman" or someone else in the picture, it's like waving a red flag. Something pops. You imagine your ex doing all the loving things they did with you, only with someone else. You imagine the new person getting what you were supposed to have. You're furious because you feel your ex has taken something away from you and given it to someone else. Or that you've been promised something and someone else is getting it.

Although it is culturally maintained, jealousy is not a man-made emotion. Jealousy is present among both animals and humans and has actual biological as well as anthropological roots.

Just as animals stake out territories, so do people. You probably felt that it was *your* husband, *your* girlfriend, a part of your belongings, your property and your territory. Someone, a stranger, using your bed, your bathroom or your car upsets you just as it did the three bears in the Goldilocks story. If someone were to get into your car and drive it away, you'd be upset and feel as if your property were being tampered with. When it happens with someone you love, it's even worse.

It's natural (although primitive) to guard other people as if they are possessions. You imagine that someone has taken your love and your lover away—a form of grand larceny.

The goodies that were supposed to be yours are being given by your ex-lover to someone else. It would seem to follow that there are fewer goodies for you.

People aren't "taken away," they *go away*. People are not inanimate, territorial objects that one possesses, ever. Also, love is not a finite quantity, like money. It is an ability that improves with experience.

The price for your jealousy is staying hooked. Jealousy makes you angry and hostile and causes you to think about your ex all the time. The fact that it's natural doesn't make it good. It's natural to want to take what you want, but society can't survive if everyone steals. It's natural to urinate when you have the urge, but society says, "Not just anywhere." Civilization helps people convert undesirable, natural impulses into constructive measures. Instead of stealing, you earn money and buy what you want. You are toilet trained at a very young age. but nobody teaches you to control your jealousy.

You see the other woman or man in your kitchen, in your bed. You can almost visualize them making love. You feel that your territory has been taken over by an alien force, one that wants to cut you out of what you are supposed to get.

Rational Emotive Therapy

"He took my girlfriend away" is a jealousy-producing thought. It makes you angry. The real truth is that your girlfriend went away. Psychologist Dr. Albert Ellis found that by removing the irrational sentences from your mind and replacing them with reason, knowledge and information, a major source of your unhappiness is removed.

Perhaps it's true that your lover went off with someone else, but they weren't taken away. A human being isn't a possession. They go or stay of their own free will. Your car can be taken away, but not your husband or wife.

Our culture subtly tells you that jealousy is a proper or acceptable emotion. A girl may be secretly flattered if her boyfriend is jealous. "I am a jealous God," says the Bible. How many times have you heard, "I wish he were jealous," or "If she loved me, she'd be jealous."

Both the church and state support one man and one woman being together and staying together. Traditionally, sex led to babies, and it was economically important to know who the father was so that he could be held financially responsible. It was obvious throughout pregnancy who the mother was, but only by licensing and sustaining relationships could society be sure who the father was.

By encouraging jealousy and teaching people that they must maintain the relationship no matter what, society is relieved of the pressure to support illegitimate children. Traditionally, for security reasons, men wrote the rules that the man possessed the woman; but for economic reasons, the woman is also encouraged in her possessiveness. She had to maintain her relationship to see that her child was fed. Today, because of birth control, that need not be the case, but like the vestigial, obsolete appendix, jealousy hangs on. Psychologically, even our use of the personal possessive pronoun regarding people has proprietary roots.

But what happens when you find out that your former mate has already replaced you with a new love? You are outraged. You throw tantrums. You become hysterical over your loss. You are, once again, responding to being put on extinction (chapter four, Hysteria).

Like the experimental laboratory pigeons who got hysterical because they were given the impression they weren't ever going to be fed again and began pecking other birds, or defecating all over the cage, you may also become irrational with anger, hate and jealousy. Finding out that "someone else" is in your territory, getting your goodies, you realize that if they're getting all the love, you won't get any for sure.

If your hysteria and rage take you banging on your ex's door in the middle of the night or drive you to phone their house over and over again, you may get sympathy or even a patronizingly nice word or two. Then you will be trapped into acting hysterical to get love, which is worse than acting hysterical because you feel angry.

Your emotional outburst can become a futile manipulative device, so try replacing it with rational statements. Instead of thinking, "She took my husband away," you will rationally know, "My husband went away." Instead of torturing yourself with "What if I hadn't done . . ." or "Maybe if I offered . . ." you have to realize, "She left for someone who offered more or different things than I wanted to offer."

If you think rationally about what your ex is getting from the new person, the odds are you would be unwilling to provide it. There is no reason to put yourself down because your relationship broke up for "another" person. If you had wanted to provide whatever that person does, you probably would have done so and the relationship would still be intact. In essence, your life-style was your decision.

It's less of an insult if your lover leaves for someone else than if they just go away because you weren't "good enough." At least you already know why your ex left and won't have to worry about figuring out what you did wrong.

Your girlfriend wants to get married and have kids. She leaves you for another man who offers a white, picket-fenced home, suburban marriage, 2.3 children and the "security" you don't offer. You are upset, but you realize that in truth you aren't willing to make those offers. You don't want to settle down—not now, anyway.

Your real problems with your ex have nothing to do with their finding someone else, whether "she's" prettier than you, or whether "he's" a better lover. It really doesn't matter. The fact is that no two people offer the same thing to anyone.

You feel loss of power because someone else has your lover and you don't. You feel your self-esteem slipping as you imagine the handsome or beautiful new person in your ex's life. You think the new person must be better than you in every way or your ex wouldn't have left you. And, of course, you feel irrational anger toward the person who has made you suffer, unbearable hate and a jealous desire to get even.

Knowing that you didn't offer what the new person does is a consolation, but it's not enough. In many cases the deserted lover never gets a chance to make those offers.

You may not know what the new person offers that you don't. Nobody told you and maybe you would have offered it, too, if you'd been asked. You're hurt because no one asked.

Deceit

"He has been seeing her all along," or "She was sneaking out," or "He met her and then started picking fights with me," or "She met him and began making demands on me." Fighting or making unusual demands are often signs that one of two people wants to destroy a relationship. They may actually be afraid of too much closeness, but the deceit involved is truly unforgivable.

Maybe your ex has been deceiving you, pretending that you were undesirable when the truth is that there has been another man/woman all along. That goes to the top of your Crime Sheet (chapter four). To deliberately make you think there's something wrong with *you* is worst of all. It undermines your self-esteem and makes you feel guilty for the demise of the relationship—when in fact, there was someone else. It is a "crime against your person."

Directed Anger

Although it's true that you may be getting less love from your ex than you did before, that isn't enough reason to be jealous all the time. If you are afflicted with the illness of jealousy, remember that's based on the view that love is quantitative and has a limited supply. Just because someone is giving love to another person doesn't mean that there isn't enough for you, too. Love isn't money in the bank. It's an ability. Every loving experience is only practice for the next one. The more practice a person gets at love, the more loving they become. Your ex's crime was *not* loving someone else, it was deceiving you.

It's not easy to let go of the anger you feel, and right now, anger is good. It focuses your attention outside of yourself. Up until now you've been thinking, "I'm no good," or, "What's wrong with me?" or, "I deserve to suffer."

By staying with your anger and hate toward that other person, you are moving into a healthier direction because you're no longer angry with yourself. Your anger is directed where it belongs.

Hatred isn't a way of life, but right now it can be a clinical technique that will save you from feeling sorry for yourself. It's a temporary corrective measure. You can use your justified anger to make you well in the same way a doctor puts a cast on a broken arm. You have a right to be angry and turn it toward the one who hurt you. In our culture, anger is usually held in and other "acceptable" ways to express anger, such as depression, are learned.

In subtle ways, every woman is taught the expectation that she will one day get married and have children. She has learned from her mother that she will be a bride. If a man encourages that expectation and then dumps her, she has a right to be angry.

Similarly, every man learns from his father that he, too, will become a father one day. That he will have a partner who will take care of him and be devoted to him. When he discovers that the woman he expected to become his partner in life isn't interested, he has a right to be angry.

If your former partner led you to have expectations about the relationship, you are probably furious because you're not going to get what you thought you were going to get. And you have no reason to feel otherwise. Your ex deserves your anger and must take responsibility for having stimulated it. You have been manipulated and treated like an object. The excuse can be "I didn't want to hurt you," or "I was protecting you," or "I didn't want you to be upset." They are all cowardly attempts to cover up a dehumanizing manipulation.

When you understand the territorial and biological sources of jealousy, you can understand why you are hurt. Now, when your hurt is changing to hate, you can feel free to enjoy it.

Session Fourteen: Healthy Anger

The question now is what do you do. Should you really report your ex to the IRS? Should you turn them in for that marijuana stash you know about? Should you sabotage their new relationship? In essence, should you take action?

You know you shouldn't, but how do you control these nasty thoughts?

There's nothing wrong with thinking these things. It can even help you. The thoughts are good—they revive your feeling of power over that person. Now you have the power to do something that could repay some of the pain. You are losing your victim status.

Use your anger constructively. You have been offended; you have been mistreated. Of course you are entitled to your revenge, but don't take any destructive action.

Aside from humanitarian considerations, there's a selfish reason why you shouldn't do anything right now: You may regret it later, at which point your guilt could damage your self-esteem badly. If you think you *must* act, wait until the hurt is all over, your emotional equilibrium has been restored and you're *sure* you won't be sorry.

Telling your ex how angry you are may be enough for you. Expressing your anger legitimizes it by giving it reality, especially if you express it to the one who caused it. After all, you don't have to be afraid they'll leave you—they're already gone. Go ahead, tell your ex off.

Until now, your Letting Go instructions were not to call your ex. Now, to express your anger, it's okay. However, venting anger is the only purpose for the call. Don't cry or expect to get anything from your ex. Only vent.

If you have a burning, raging desire to phone your ex and tell them exactly what you think of them, go ahead. But don't get into arguments. Just release your anger and hang up. Scream and yell; you may discover that you've been wanting to do that for years and didn't because you were afraid to. You don't really need a person in your life who isn't giving you anything in return but pain. Now is the time to let loose. Don't listen for replies or excuses.

Make your accusations. It's about time you were heard. It's about time you let your ex know that they're not so perfect in your eyes anymore. If calling isn't something you want to do now, write a letter. Your anger will inhibit any sad feelings you have left. It will also inhibit your anxiety. Many patients report that telling their ex off was like a vitamin B shot.

The more you can express your anger, the less anxious and depressed you will feel. Placing your anger exactly where it belongs will make you less likely to pick on innocent family members and friends, or even yourself. It keeps the anger in focus.

What if you tell your ex off and you still have the urge to do damage, to involve them in situations where they will be made to suffer in some other way? You know he lies about his income. You know she's not really married to that guy she lives with. You are tempted to tell the authorities, his or her mother, boss or whatever. You don't feel like they've really paid for the pain they've caused you.

The Blowhard Technique

To dilute that anger and the need to repay an eye for an eye, confide in friends (*your* friends, only) about the terrible things you could do. Ask questions. Could you really get them evicted if you wanted? Arrested? Investigated? Audited? Researching your revenge is almost as fulfilling as doing it. It helps to dissipate that angry energy and gives you a feeling of power.

Telling about the menacing things you *could* do is almost as good as doing them. Verbalize your anger. Tell yourself what you could do, tell your friends, even tell your ex if you want them to worry. Watch them try to talk you out of it or suddenly get nice, and suddenly you'll feel strong again.

Be careful though, of what you tell to whom. Don't go all over town saying you're going to kill your ex. What if they fall out of a window? You might be an immediate suspect. If you do have seemingly uncontrollable killer urges, vent them with fantasy or tell them only to your psychologist in confidence.

Fantasy

Another tool to control your anger without doing actual damage is fantasy. Play out your revenge in your imagination. Imagine yourself doing in your ex. Watch him become nervous when the auditor calls. See her squirm when her mother finds out she's living with someone.

Studies on imagination have shown that your nervous system's reactions to fantasies are very close to those in the three-dimensional world. By fantasizing the punishment of your former mate, you will get almost the same gratification as you would if you actually punished them. When you hear a story, your imagination can make you cry or laugh. You will feel as if you actually did something to your ex by means of your imaginative fantasies.

Pick a quiet time of the day. You might even want to write

down a list of the things you could do, recording each event as you see it happening in your fantasy. Visualize your ex being hassled, really unhappy. Nobody looks good when they have problems. See them crying, making frantic phone calls, trying to get out of the trouble you have caused.

Ipcress File

Imagination is a good vicarious way of doing things, but if you still feel as if you want to do actual harm to your former mate, make an Ipcress File first.

The Ipcress File allows you to express anger without hurting anyone. All the vengeful, Machiavellian tactics are there "just in case" you decide to use them. You feel better because you're secure in your power to hurt the person who abandoned you and hurt you so much.

The Ipcress File is a special file box where you keep the incriminating evidence against your ex. It's a place to keep your plan of action in writing so that you won't forget even one of your devious devices to make your ex suffer.

Loss of power is one of the most destructive feelings that follows loss of love. By making an Ipcress File, you'll have something to boost yourself up with when you feel down. Just reading over that letter to her mother or the IRS, not mailing it, but knowing you could, will make you feel powerful.

Into the Ipcress File go those damaging papers, tapes of telephone calls, letters, bills, the Polaroid pictures, evidence you have or can get. All the facts of every indiscretion and to whom you could show them. Knowing that you are powerful over the person who has become your enemy, you don't need to actually do anything. Knowing you can is often enough.

Remember, never use the things in the file; just keeping them will be enough. Knowing you *could* do a person in badly if you wanted to restores your feelings of power better than actually doing it. Actually doing something will only make you feel guilty.

Your loss of power comes from the feeling that things were done to you, that you were a victim and that you had no control over what happened and have no control now. One way to restore your feeling of loss of power is by restoring your self-esteem, and the other is by having power itself.

Everyone has done something wrong. And when you've been close to a person you know what they've done that they're ashamed of or that's illegal. These are the things that go in your file. If you don't have actual evidence of wrongdoing, just simply write down what you know that could get your ex in some sort of trouble—with anyone: the landlord, the babysitter's mother, the boss, the sanitation department. The things you write become evidence and you put them in your Ipcress File.

By transferring your status from victim to persecutor, and by making your ex your potential victim, you will feel powerful. The odds are there are things you could do to be very destructive to the other person. You are no longer the victim; you are a benevolent prosecutor who chooses to be merciful.

You have the power of an Errol Flynn in one of the old swashbuckling movies like *The Adventures of Robin Hood*—where he puts his sword to the neck of the evil enemy and then, winning the duel, magnanimously spares his life. There is power in being forgiving, in not doing in your enemy.

Never make threats in front of witnesses. If you want to tell your ex all the things you could do, do it privately. Otherwise there could be legal repercussions. For example, threatening bodily harm can be interpreted as assault.

Actually using the items in your Ipcress File, doing something against your ex, can backfire. You could get caught. Also, by the time you finish the Letting Go program, you'll be sorry that you did it. Right now, you may not believe that, but at least wait until you finish this book.

Live your damaging fantasies in your imagination. Use your Ipcress File to stir your imagination. Find out how to tape conversations with your ex and keep the tapes in the Ipcress File. It can't be used as evidence, but it is fun to have.

There are photographs you could send to his new girlfriend if you wanted to. There are the love letters you could send to her new boyfriend.

Guilt

If you've already done something vengeful, it's too late for you to make an Ipcress File. You've already used your damaging evidence and now you're sorry. Guilt is a heavy burden, and this isn't a good time for you to have extra problems. You may want to get professional help to deal with your guilt feelings.

You need someone to confess to, someone who will be able to explain to you the conditions that made you do whatever you did. If your ex finds out about what you've done, don't blurt out confessions. Don't cop out. Seek professional advice first. Refuse to confront your ex about it until you've met with a mental health professional. You don't want to get involved in an escalated situation of counter threats and even action.

The Sweetest Revenge

The last and sweetest revenge is living well. Being happy and starting a new and better relationship—and letting the ex know about it. If you have something nice going with someone else, it's okay to rub it in a little.

By now you want nothing from your ex. You harbor no hopes. If you're at that place, now's the time to send that card from the Club Med in Tahiti or wherever you are with a new person. Not as a manipulation, like the old days when you were trying to get them back—just good, sweet, constructive revenge.

If you've moved, bought a new car, gotten a better job, or even fallen in love, there's a lot of satisfaction in letting your former mate know how well off you are without them. Now you may tell mutual friends or even your ex. It does feel good, especially if they're not as well off as yourself. You'll feel you've passed them by.

You may not feel like falling in love right now, but it's time to start thinking about it. In the next chapters we will discuss social ways to get rid of pain associated with romantic places, finding and approaching new people, and how to turn your love life into a more gratifying experience than it's ever been before.

8
"OUR SONG" AND "THE SACRED BICYCLE PATH"

Wherever I am girl, I'm always walking with you,
I'm always walking with you, but I look and
you're not there
Whoever I'm with, I'm always, always, talking to you,
I'm always talking to you, and I'm sad that
you can't hear
Sad that you can't hear.

—Cat Stevens
"*How Can I Tell You?*"

Now is the turning point in your love cure. You have been on the run avoiding triggers, dulling and converting your dangerous, sad and anxious feelings. This is the time to deal with the old lover's memorabilia, the things you've hidden away. After your Implosion Day, those pictures, love letters, old clothes, hotel keys, and mementos will become harmless, once and for all.

THE EIGHTH WEEK

Session Fifteen: Implosion Day

Your wedding anniversary, the date of your first meeting, your former mate's birthday, your own birthday, Christmas, Thanksgiving, Valentine's Day, the Fourth of July, New Year's Eve or the day you had some plan which won't come to fruition now that you've broken up are all good Implosion Days. If you think about it, one of them is coming up soon. The reason you should set aside a "special" day for your Implosion Day is that the memorabilia will evoke nostalgic feelings and those very days certainly will, as well.

Flooding

Implosion Day is the day you will finally grieve and cry over all the love souvenirs. You will literally cry yourself out. Implosion is very much like the "flooding" technique discovered by Dr. Thomas Stampfl for the treatment of phobias. By forcing the person to go through the frightening experience (throwing a water phobic into the deep end of a pool), he discovers that the thing he was afraid would kill him really doesn't.

Research at the Maudsley Hospital in England, by Eyesenck, Marks and others revealed that if a person is phobic about a specific inanimate object that is easily confined to one place, like an airplane, or an easily re-created situation like "the dark," then desensitization (the gradual introduction of whatever the person is afraid of) works best.

If a patient is being treated for something that is always around, like *all* germs or disinfectants, flooding is preferred. An agoraphobiac (someone who is afraid of the entire world outside the safety of their doorstep) or a person who is afraid of contamination by germs, insecticides, smog or gasoline fumes and other generalized fears is best treated by the more drastic technique of flooding, because there's no way to confine the frightening object.

Desensitization, a more gentle method, can be used if you can confine the frightening object. A person who is afraid of snakes will be told initially not to go near snakes during the course of the brief desensitization therapy, except as instructed. That's so they won't scare themselves more and become *re*sensitized. Only while relaxed and under the therapist's supervision will the snake phobic be told to even imagine he is near a place where snakes are kept, like a zoo. The therapist and patient have control over and determine the patient's readiness for the reintroduction of the frightening object later, on a systematic, gradual and orderly basis.

Basically, you should be avoiding and getting rid of pain—that's what this book is all about. But in this instance, where you are surrounded by love triggers, Implosion (or flooding) is the treatment of choice. The pain you'll feel is similar to pulling off a Band-Aid quickly. It hurts for a few hours and then it's over with.

During Implosion, the internal biochemical secretions and muscular tension that cause bad feelings exhaust themselves. Your body cannot constantly stay at one emotional level and with one constant emotion. Soon you don't have any energy left for that emotion. Just as you can't keep your fist clenched for very long, your body tensions must relax if kept constant for several hours.

Shiva

Implosion is the technologically perfect way to grieve, the true grieving that is designed to stop lingering pain. Ancient Hebrews followed the tradition of mourning seven days when someone died, and today that tradition (sitting Shiva) still survives among many Jews. By sitting on uncomfortable boxes for seven days while absenting themselves from work as well as play, the bereft person exorcises their grief, in the same way you do with Implosion.

Until now, you have been told to avoid certain things that caused you to have anxiety and be depressed. You put the photos of your ex into your Implosion Box. The records, the favorite scarf he bought you, the neckchain she gave you, are all things to which you have become sensitized. Now you can take them out and stare them down.

But the truth is that you are also surrounded by triggers which you can't control, ones that you won't be able to confine.

Time

The anniversary date comes. There's nothing you can do about it. The birthday comes, and you see things that still bother you. The sun sets on Saturday night and rises on Sunday morning. There's no avoiding those nostalgic triggers.

Friends who don't know about your split ask you where your ex is or how they are. Well-intentioned mutual acquaintances tell you things "for your own good" or "to make you feel better."

So that you won't feel awful about losing your mate, people tell you how bad your ex looked when they saw them, or about the awful-looking new girlfriend "he's" got, or the bossy new boyfriend "she" has.

Implosion is the only way to vaccinate yourself against the triggers that you can't control. Pushing someone into the deep end of a pool is certainly drastic, but many good swimmers report that's the way they overcame their fear of water. Implosion will make you very sad, but if you follow the directions exactly, it won't scare or resensitize you. Instead, it will set you free from the ever present reminder.

Even the time of day can help. If you think about your ex at sunrise or sunset, schedule your Implosion then. Or even *the* day. For instance, an anniversary. Or maybe on a Saturday night when you don't have a date and feel particularly sorry for yourself. Or on a Sunday morning during the time you always used to read the paper or go to brunch together.

Exorcism

Earlier, you learned how to stop crying. Now is the time to actually make it happen, to "implode" yourself with a "flood" of triggers, and to cry your heart out once and for all. During Implosion Day, you will bring your sadness under *your* control. Because you make it happen when you want it to, you learn you can control and thereby exorcise your own sad feelings and your tears. Today unexpected triggers in the world don't make you cry; you do it intentionally.

Opening the Griefcase

Implosion Day is when you pull out the sad records you bought that you really wanted to send your ex—they can be anything from Barry Manilow or Frank Sinatra to Linda Ronstadt or Peggy Lee. It doesn't matter. If you don't have any "special" records, use the popular music on the radio. Read the old love letters your ex sent you when things were good. Go over your emotional Bankbook. Pull our your Last Love Letter. The clothing your former mate never picked up. His golf clubs, her bathroom supplies, cosmetics, shaving cream, especially their favorite cologne. The most endearing photographs, the gifts you exchanged. Get all your most poignant memorabilia ready.

The technique that you use for your Implosion Day is called

flooding because you are literally going to flood yourself with as many of the emotional triggers as possible. If you have home movies, now is the time to watch them. If there is anything around your house that you have covered up or hidden, now is the time to bring it out. If it's a thing you can't move, like a bed, then have your Implosion Day right there, on his or her side.

Smells, like his favorite food cooking, or her favorite cologne, or even their old clothing that you never washed . . . anything that triggers your sad, longing memories should be included in Implosion Day. Put on the articles of clothing your ex always loved you in, or what you wore on a particularly happy occasion, or even something that they gave you as a gift.

Keep looking at the photos, the trinkets, and even the clothing. Cry until you are absolutely unable to work up any tears over any of it. The reason some people still cry years after a breakup is that they have interrupted their crying with their activities of daily living. They haven't gone through it and beyond their tears.

All interruptions should be shut off before you start your Implosion Day—the telephone, the doorbell, your friends. Since you must go *past* your crying, interruptions only prolong it and keep you from getting over your sad feelings once and for all. Keep crying until the particular stimuli (even something as silly as his shaving cream or her razor) become boring to you.

Disconnect your telephones if possible or at least take them off the hook or connect an answering machine. Put a "Do Not Disturb" sign on your front door if anyone is liable to knock. Schedule no appointments for that day at all, and don't answer the door or phone, no matter what.

Think of your Implosion Day as going in for treatment at a hospital or clinic, and pretend you're a patient in bed. Close the shutters and blinds and curtains. Cut yourself off from anything that could interrupt your grieving and keep your Implosion Day from working.

Because your body can only respond with a certain amount of grief, biochemically it will exhaust itself. You won't be able to respond to the sad stimuli after a while. Soon, instead of looking at a wedding ring and feeling sad (the only association you've had with it for some time), you'll associate such stimuli with a new feeling—the feeling of boredom.

Spend enough time looking at each particular stimulus trigger, and you will get bored. Then, keep on looking at the thing to reinforce the new feeling you associate with the particular object—boredom.

Arrange to have a few nostalgic foods, whatever your ex always liked to snack on, screaming Yellow Zonkers or organic grapes. Other than that don't eat much because food can become an emotional pacifier, as can booze or drugs. Keep to an austere diet and something nonalcoholic to drink. Gather your food before you start, so that you won't have to interrupt yourself to get something to eat.

In addition to "his" or "her" favorite foods, coffee, tea, a little cottage cheese or other protein food is allowed, but that's it. If you use food as a comforting device, you not only sabotage your Implosion Day, but you may develop the bad habit of eating when you're unhappy. No fun foods, desserts, candies, wine or recreational drugs, no sedatives or uppers or other deterrents to your feelings. Even the nostalgic foods that remind you of your former lover shouldn't be eaten all day—only until you get bored with them.

Fear of Fear

If you still have a lot of fear concerning the triggers that you have been avoiding, you may find that you have the same fears about your Implosion Day, too. "Will I be able to stand all that grief and sadness, now that I have been avoiding it for so long?" you wonder.

If you feel like you're going to throw up just thinking about facing your Implosion Day or are afraid you will kill yourself with grief, get help.

Since this is the first time you have faced all your grief fully, you do not have to be alone if you feel frightened. Ask a good friend to stay with you for your Implosion Day, someone who will spend three or four hours at your house that day, but who won't be in the same room with you. It's important that you feel you are totally alone. The aloneless is part of your grieving; that's why you are grieving.

Your friend shouldn't talk to you or spend time "taking care" of you in any way. You must be alone with your grief.

If you decide to have a friend stay with you during the day, explain that they are not to come into the room with you, comfort you, discuss things with you or run to your aid unless you deliberately call them. Tell your friend that you are doing a special kind of therapy to get over your ex and that no matter how much you cry and scream, or what they hear, they should stay out. The point is to feel pain, not to have it dulled with sympathy.

For the day to be completely successful, you should plan to make it last at least six hours. If you find after unpacking that you no longer have any emotional connection to the things in your Implosion Box, you are already better off than you thought you were.

Fond Memories

Remember all the good qualities that other person had, the things you miss, the reasons you fell in love with them in the first place. For Implosion Day, forget the Crime Sheet and only think about the things that were so wonderful about the person, the little endearing words you used, the things you shared, the love you gave each other. Whatever will make you feel sorry that you're alone now.

It could be the way he always held and stroked you, or the

way she appreciated everything you did for her, how he looked when he was shaving or her taking a bubble bath. His boyish playfulness, her girlish shyness.

Favorite expressions or little pet names, or the way his hair felt, or her skin, or even the brand of cigarettes they smoked. All these things can be added to your Implosion Day, plus any "special" reminders.

One girl's former husband was a high fashion photographer. Everywhere she went, she saw his work and on her Implosion Day she was surrounded by photographs of beautiful women. A man who went with a newspaper reporter surrounded himself with her byline stories for his Implosion Day.

Mourning

Don't do anything on your Implosion Day that will make you feel happy. You don't want to break the mourning spell. Call your ex if you want, but only if you feel the call will be depressing. Ask if they're happy with their new lover or if they'd come back to you. You know the answer. It's going to make you feel more sad and rejected.

You've written your Last Love Letter; now you are going to cry over your lost love as if they had died. Let yourself sink into an abyss of self-pity. Wallow in it before your Implosion Day is over. By experiencing the triggers you thought could harm you, you will learn they really can't. You will discover that you can live through looking at your wedding or vacation pictures and you won't die from sorrow.

After spending an entire day looking at the sacred or nostalgic things that remind you of your lost love and crying yourself out until you are bored, you will find that you no longer have any feelings one way or another about them. The engagement ring that not only represented your fiance, but also marriage, a home and children is now simply a ring given to you by a former lover. The "special" photograph is only a picture of someone you once loved.

Overkill

Even when you get tired of a special thing, say a gift your ex gave you or a love letter they wrote you, don't put it away. Try different things with it. Fantasize about the day you got the gift; recall the way things were when they wrote you that letter. The day you took that picture. The trip you took together when you bought the statue of the Hawaiian money god.

You will know when you reach your point of exhaustion and boredom because the stimuli will no longer affect you, no matter what you think about. When you have gone through all the triggers that you have in your Implosion Box and all the things that you haven't been able to put in the box, and they are all boring, you will have successfully completed your Implosion Day.

Boosters

You may find that two weeks after your Implosion Day, a particular lovesong still "gets to you." If it does, schedule a "booster" Implosion Day for another time, your anniversary, a birthday or vacation time when you were supposed to go somewhere together. Spend another day wallowing in your grief. Think about the happy times you had together and how they're ended. Dwell on the photographs you took when you were happy together. Think about the future you'll never have now that you've split. Re-create your first Implosion Day as much as possible except for the time period. Your booster day can be as little as two or three hours.

Just as you did for your original Implosion Day, plan ahead for your booster Implosion Day. Arrange for small spartan snacks ahead of time and a friend, if you think you'll need one again.

Victory Celebration

It's a good idea to schedule something for after your Implosion Day, as a reward to yourself and to celebrate your new freedom. You may want to have dinner and see a show with the friend who stayed with you, or go out on a date or even throw a party.

Get a massage, join a health club or start a new class that night. Do something that will give you positive, good feelings, something that says you deserve to be treated well. Have a gourmet dinner. Go to the fanciest hair salon in town. Buy yourself a present. Be good to yourself by arranging for someone to be good to you. Schedule a social activity, something where you come in contact with other people.

By the time your Implosion Day is over you will be able to go out and enjoy yourself. Suddenly you'll be bored thinking and talking about your ex. You'll want to have new experiences and forget the old ones. Make a date with a friend who has been listening to your separation anxieties and celebrate your newfound freedom with them. Your friend will probably admit they too were becoming bored with your problems and will be glad to celebrate an end to your sadness.

By confronting and conquering your emotional triggers, you become strong. You should feel proud and successful. With Implosion, you have overcome the inanimate objects in your life which have been making you sad. But what about places—the restaurants where you always ate together, the bars you went to, the foreign film cinema where you saw *A Man and A Woman,* the areas of town your ex hangs out in, the bicycle paths, the tennis courts where you played, even a special freeway sign that points to the route you always took or a special vacation spot? All the things you can't put into your Implosion Box and all the haunts you still avoid because they remind you of your ex can be exorcised just like the memorabilia.

Session Sixteen: Systematic Desecration

Avoidance

Suppose you are invited to a party in your ex's neighborhood. You are afraid you might run into him or her with their new lover. You imagine friends you knew as a couple showing up at the party and embarrassing you by asking how you are or whom you're with when you're obviously alone.

On the other hand, you know it would be good for you to go. You might meet someone new or simply get out of the house for an evening. If you don't go, you are reinforcing your withdrawal and allowing your ex to still affect your life in a detrimental way. By the next party, going to that neighborhood will have become even more frightening to you. You will have reinforced your fear.

This doesn't mean that you should grab each chance to go into your ex's neighborhood, but don't avoid it if you have a truly *legitimate* reason—if you are doing something good for yourself.

When someone has a serious phobia, say they are afraid to fly in airplanes, every time that person manages to avoid flying by going by train, car or even cancelling a trip, they think, "Well, I got away with it that time." And that feels good. Not only is the person prevented from experiencing the airplane flight and finding out that they can survive it, but it also reinforces the idea that they can get away without doing it.

Since it feels good to avoid potential pain, your instinct will be to avoid your ex's neighborhood. Like the airplane phobic who soon avoids not only airplanes, but airports, you may soon be avoiding not only specific streets, but whole areas of the city. Your ex's friends' neighborhoods, the places where they work, even the bars and restaurants they might frequent or the park they play ball in—not only will you want to avoid these places, but it will become attractive to you to be away from them.

Never go somewhere your ex might be because you have the urge to meet them. That only reinforces the indulgence. It must be when you feel like avoiding or have anxiety about it that you should go.

Certain places will be harder for you than others. Specifically, it might be the restaurant he proposed in, or the place in which she first said "I love you." In the next session you will learn ways to violate these "sacred" places, to desecrate the holy spots so that old associations with them won't bother you anymore.

Take care of yourself when you feel you may be in a threatening situation. Go with a friend or even check out the cars before you go into a party. If your ex or one of their close friends is there, decide what you'll say. It probably won't happen, but if it does, you'll be prepared and you'll feel safer.

More specific preparation for a "reconnecting" meeting with your ex will be given to you in the last chapter of this book.

Because you can't put a neighborhood in a box, nor a favorite restaurant, you must go there.

By diluting or replacing the unpleasant, sad or nostalgic memories you have associated with certain places you went to when things were good, or even when they were terrible, you can make those places yours again. Some people avoid these places for a lifetime, restricting their geographic freedom, a prelude to agoraphobia.

Naturally, you've been avoiding the sacred bicycle path you

always rode on when you were happy together. Of course you feel that you never want to go into *that* restaurant again where you had your last fight. It's all too painful.

Competing Responses

Rather than continuing to avoid the painful places at this stage of your Love Cure, begin setting up Competing Responses to the emotional triggers that certain places have for you.

To create a Competing Response you must go to the sad places, or even better ones of the same type (Squaw Valley instead of Mount Baldy) with someone new and dynamic. Set up a more impressive experience there that will outweigh the old one.

To "detrigger" the places that make you sad, the honeymoon hotel, the beautiful vacation spot, you have to go there again, but not alone. By "defiling" the sacred places with another person, you make those places less unique, less powerful, less intimidating. You recapture a large part of the world that would have been lost to you.

If you don't have an impactful, important or exciting person in your life right now, don't worry. By going to these places many times with lots of different people, you can dilute the memory.

Until now, you always thought of your ex when you thought about woods and cabins and streams and raccoons because that's the single strong association you have with him/her—your camping trip at Big Sur. You went there with your former lover when you were in love. That's heady stuff. In your deluded "in love" state, everything looked wonderfully beautiful to you. Since Big Sur was where you had your happy association with your love affair or mate, and you know you can't be there with that person, it becomes a sad place for you now. Systematic

Desecration can keep you from becoming phobic about going there again.

In order to reverse the natural phobic reaction to going someplace you think will make you unhappy, you have to reverse the association and make the place a "happy" place for you again. Treat yourself as if you were a child who is afraid to go to school.

Suppose you were nine years old and your mother told you that school was going to be fun and took you there. You look forward to school and associate it with your mother who is with you. Then, when your mother leaves, the kids discover your inability to throw a ball or that you're too fat or too short or wear glasses. They tease you unmercifully. Suddenly school is associated with the bad feelings of being teased and you develop a fear of going back, a classic school phobia.

To help you enjoy school again, your behaviorally enlightened teacher might allow you to bring a pet turtle to school or to throw a party in your classroom. Or your mother may resume going with you to school. She might give you ice cream on the way to school or a new bicycle to ride to school—anything that would make the school a happy place for you.

The ice cream, the pet turtle, the new bike all create Competing Responses to the bad feelings. By substituting a more powerful response (the joy of showing off a new bicycle or eating an ice cream cone for breakfast) for the unhappy response, your mother sets up favorable Competing Responses in you.

Approach each anxiety-producing place or thing in the same way. Figure out how you can go there and make that place even more fun than it was before. Whom can you take there? A friend? A neighbor? A relative? A lover? A new and exciting person? Or even a child? It must be someone who will hold your attention, who will compete for your memories.

What can you do there that you didn't do before? Go skin diving in Catalina if you spent your honeymoon there dancing in the casino. Ford the rapids if you just watched them when you visited the Colorado River. Do something exciting and maybe even just a little dangerous in the old place with the new person and you will be setting up a Competing Response.

If you went camping with your ex, don't go to the campsite with a new person whom you aren't interested in. Instead, go into a wilderness area, or take survival training, or climb a mountain. Don't just reenact whatever it was you did before. That may not be effective enough and if so, will just make you flash on your ex and feel sad.

If a particular place is associated primarily with your ex, if you just went there with them or went there time and time again together, and you find that you are avoiding that place because it makes you sad, then you should set up a Competing Response. Invite someone to help you.

Inform the new person what's going on and why you need them. Invite them on a trip with you, or to a restaurant, or whatever—your treat, of course. Include the new person in your planning. "For this trip to Brooklyn, will you be my Competing Response?" Most will accept.

Facing and conquering your fears about certain places that you associate with your unhappy love affair is important because phobias about places tend to generalize. There are tens of thousands of people being treated in the United States for agoraphobia (fear of any place away from home). Most started out with a fear of just one single place that generalized to include all places until everything beyond their front doorstep seems frightening.

If you spent your honeymoon in Bermuda and your husband left you, you won't want to go back there. It's too sad. Soon you will skip the travel section in the newspaper because there might be an ad for Bermuda or even "that" hotel. Soon, Bermuda becomes Barbados, and maybe all islands. If you took your fiancee to Hawaii before she broke your engagement, then you could find Hawaii becoming Tahiti, and all tropical places like Mexico, the Bahamas, even Florida.

By setting up Competing Responses for the places that make you sad, you won't completely erase the memory of your love and the wonderful time you had there. You will remember the nice things you did and you will remember your ex, but you won't have the painful memories, you won't have the fear, and you will be able to go back again without anxiety. Just as your flag will always remind you of your country, especially if you are away from it, certain places will always remind you of your ex. But they won't make you feel sad. You are not erasing all memories, just the painful, sad ones that cause you unhappiness.

Frequently, one trip will do it. You'll find that you can enjoy a place, and it won't kill you. If one trip doesn't make it, then do it again and again until you feel good about that place again. Until it's *your* place. Three trips to a sad place with a new person or a series of new people or the same person over and over again will certainly dilute and compete with the painful memories you have associated with it.

Competing Response can be used for the time of day as well as for places. If you and your ex were always together when the sun came up on a Sunday morning, if you always went to Sunday brunch together, if you spent every Tuesday afternoon together or every TGIF at a special bar together, set up Competing Responses at those times. Do something better or the same thing with someone else.

Make a list of the places you have been avoiding and think of ways to set up Competing Responses there. Make a list of people you haven't seen or have neglected who might be willing to go with you to those places. Ask around. There's probably someone you know who's anxious to go. Take someone who has no transportation to the beach. Take a relative whom you've been neglecting.

By now, you have Letting Go techniques for dealing with all of your emotional triggers. You've used Implosion for those objects that you can put into a box, the photos, records, etc. Discrimination Day and the Photo Finish for the things that move around, Competing Responses and dilution for nostalgic places, Implosion and Competing Responses for special days and times. And you still have a bunch of your ex's belongings around your house.

The Remains

Disposing of an old lover's remains is always a problem. Even after you've had your Implosion Day and are over the fear of the object, there's still the question of "What do I do with it?" The stereo he bought you that you still use. The robe she picked out for your birthday that you really love. The painting you bought together.

If some of your lover's leftovers are things you like and they don't make you feel bad when you see them, it's okay to use and enjoy these memorabilia.

Then there are things that just bug you. His old pajamas, the ones you always wore the tops of and that he told you you looked stupid in. The extravagantly expensive bikini she left at your house that you fought over when she spent so much. Or even things that remind you sadly or angrily of happy times and love you shared. Those are the memorabilia you should give away. Surely you know someone who would really like whatever it is. Endear yourself to someone else by giving away you ex's old things.

You'll feel like you've betrayed your ex, but the defiance of giving away their things helps break the attachment.

Some seemingly valueless trinkets represent your cherished memories, your personal history, a record of your life. Keep the photos for your album, they are part of your personal history. You may want to show them to your grandchildren one day. Mementos of happy times are the only ones you should keep. Bad memories automatically fade with time, but who wants to be reminded of them?

When you look at a picture of a relative who died, you don't relive the pain you felt. It's nice to have the photo. In the same way, you may want to keep photos of you and your ex or gifts you were given during happier times.

Certain things of value, like wedding rings, or sentimental things like valentine cards, may still evoke some pain. If they do, put them away somewhere for a "booster" Implosion Day. Perhaps by then you'll be immune to those things anyway.

Valuable jewelry can be taken apart and redesigned. A wedding ring or engagement ring can be turned into a dinner ring. Or a charm. Or it can be traded in for something else with no bad memories attached.

Old love letters are full of promises that weren't kept and may make you sad. Throw them out. Don't let them get you angry anymore. Almost everyone (maybe even you) made the same "forever" promises once. Figure they were written "under the influence" of a love addiction.

Don't be tempted to make a reconnection with your ex by using articles of clothing or belongings they left behind as a bribe. Don't see your ex to return anything. Wait until chapter twelve for that.

Right now, you may want to throw the remains at your ex, dump all their things on your betrayer's lawn. Instead, put them away and wait until you have been prepared if you want to return your ex's belongings.

Don't steal anything. You'll probably feel guilty later, even if you feel justified now. That gold watch he left, her ring—you'll feel better if you give it back. You may feel that you deserve whatever they left, and maybe you do.

If you are at all unsure of what your feelings are going to be or what your future relationship with your ex will be, this isn't the time to make a decision about valuable belongings that aren't yours. Put them away until you have made a successful reconnection with your ex, then decide.

In many cases, a deserted lover is left so thoroughly and absolutely that they have no idea what happened to their former mate. If you don't know how to get in touch with a person, if they have simply disappeared from your life, then keep or dispose of anything you want, any way you want. But don't use a forgotten trinket as an excuse to launch an exhaustive search for your ex. If they wanted whatever it is, they would get it. The obvious truth is that it was more important for them to get out of the relationship than to recover their belongings. In this case, sell, trade, give things away or adopt them as your own.

If you feel guilty about anything—money you owe your ex, something of theirs you have—it's bad for you. Pay back owed money if you can. Don't have leftover obligations. You can give back anything you've appropriated, but wait until the time is right (chapter twelve).

By using the principles of dilution and Competing Responses as well as flooding, Implosion and Discrimination, you will find that many of your painful memories are leaving.

But the strange thing is that people get used to pain. They get used to feeling bad. When the pain is gone, they actually miss it.

Or perhaps people are reluctant to move ahead because all change is painful, even getting rid of pain. It's frequently easier to stay the way you are, even if you're unhappy, than to go through the trouble of changing your familiar (and so, unthreatening) sad state.

9
REGROUPING

Hey—have you ever tried
really reaching out for the other side,—
I may be climbing on rainbows,—
But, baby here goes.—

—DAVID GATES
"Make It with You"

In order to go out and make contact with the opposite sex after a disastrous love affair is over, you have to rebuild your self-esteem.

Someone has left you. You feel it was because you weren't worthy of their love. The reality is that your ex didn't leave you because you're a rotten, unlovable human being, but because you chose to continue to live the type of life-style they no longer liked.

You know you would like to find someone who will love you just the way you are, but underneath, the old rejection still hurts. You believe the only thing that will reassure you is being loved again. That's what you miss.

It's hard to get over the feeling that you were rejected. You wonder if your body wasn't good enough, your personality, your sexuality. But people do change. It may be that your husband became insecure with middle age and needed the assurance of a younger woman, and you couldn't reassure him enough. Or your wife was lonely when the children left home and needed the outside world of work and excitement, and you couldn't stand her dual allegiance. Or even that you changed and were no longer able to supply the things your mate wanted. Or didn't want to.

Our culture has talked us into a need for one person of the opposite sex who will be always available for sex and love. Real dependency needs develop from the imagined ones.

For a man, at a most primitive level, it might be someone to take care of him and his daily needs of food, clothing and housekeeping. For a woman, it might mean having a man to support her emotionally and financially. Whatever the former lover supplied in the way of "love tokens" (gifts, concern, loving touches, etc.) has to be replaced.

How does someone who feels unattractive, rejected, depleted and without assets get up the nerve to try a new relationship?

It's really not true that you don't have resources. It's just that right now, because you have been left and because you were so involved in your old relationship, you have been neglecting many of your own valuable resources. You have been "on the shelf" and probably letting your real talents and assets slide. Your recent depression helped keep you from realizing your own strengths. The supposed security of relationships often makes people comfortably self-neglecting and keeps them from becoming more than they already are. Until their relationship deteriorates, most people suffer neurotic security about themselves.

People who are involved in long-lasting, committed relationships, particularly if marriage and children are involved, do let themselves go—or simply remain the way they always were. They take a hiatus from personal growth.

Women quit school and devote themselves to home and family. Men take "secure" jobs and pass up chancy ones that could advance their careers. The feeling is "Let the competition fight it out among themselves, I'm satisfied just as I am."

Newly separated people are often out of touch with contemporary mores. Men don't run around opening car doors for the modern woman, and today's liberated man doesn't expect you to cancel a date with a girlfriend for him. He disrespects catty, competitive comments about other women. She disrespects bossy, macho displays even in the bedroom.

You may feel unattractive to the opposite sex and as if you have no assets that anybody would be attracted by. Face it! The truth is that you've neglected your assets. Now is the time to take them out, dust them off and sharpen them up.

THE NINTH WEEK

Session Seventeen: Social Security

Self-Instruction

The rejected lover is frightened of coping alone and afraid that a successful relationship will never happen.

Many fears and phobic reactions are caused by the sentences running through a person's mind. A devastating love affair or a divorce, especially when there's "another woman or man" involved often leaves the rejected person many phobic-causing sentences.

When you're left, you think, "I'm not sharp enough." Or, "I'm not as good as my replacement." Or, "I'm not a good enough lover." Or, "I'll never be able to make a relationship work." The results of those sentences can be "I better not go to the beach because I'm too fat." Or "I better not date because I can't have a relationship that works anyway." Or "I better not go to a dance or party because I'll be a wallflower." Or "All any man wants from me is sex." Or "Women are only after my money so I won't date." In other words, the sentences cause phobias to develop about the beach, parties and relationships.

Self-instruction consists of changing the sentences that cause phobic reactions. Instead of "I'm not good-looking or young enough anymore," it would be "I'm an attractive, mature person." Instead of "I don't feel sexy anymore," "I'm an experienced and sensitive lover." The idea is to put on the look of someone who is self-confident and appears to have it all together; then people will assume that you do. "Dance the attitude dance," and people will assume you're a good dancer. Act the attitude, and you'll begin to feel the part.

Beginning actors often have trouble assuming a character in a play until they put on their costumes. An awkward girl puts on a long flowing Elizabethan gown and suddenly she feels like a princess. She acts like a princess, and the audience believes she is.

If you find that you aren't able to assume the character of a self-confident person, a nonwallflower, a popular, outgoing person, it may be because you have negative, phobic-inducing sentences going through your mind. By changing the sentences, you will automatically start to change your attitude. You will appear self-confident, and people will assume that you are. When you see the response that other people have, when you see that the audience believes you are indeed a princess or a king, then you too will be convinced and learn to act the part even better.

Minimally brain-damaged or hyperactive children who display disturbed behavior will calm down under the influence of a psychoactive drug. Amazingly even after the psychoactive drug is withdrawn, the child still performs better in school, remains calm and adapts better.

During the drug treatment the child discovered that when he quieted down and began doing homework, the teacher and other children responded to him in a more positive way. He learned that good behavior was rewarding because of the nice way people responded to him. And he learned that while calm, he could pay attention to school work and even do well in it.

In the authors' research with animals, it was found that a large male Doberman named "Killer," adopted from the pound where he was to be destroyed for biting a small child, became docile and lovable in a very short time after his name was changed from "Killer" to "Baby." The reason is that people responded to his new name by treating him with affection and love instead of fear and hate. When "Baby," né "Killer," found that he got sweet, loving pets and nurturing strokes from people, his personality changed totally. He became sweet, affectionate and responsive because he was enjoying the new way people treated him.

In the new field of "social ecology" we learn that no human being is totally independent as a unit, but rather interdependent with the universe. Therefore, what a person does affects others, causing them to respond in a way that has an effect on that person's behavior.

A man who is known as a tough businessman will always be treated with a certain fear and respect in his business dealings. Other men will assume that he is going to win out over them in some way and will treat him with suspicion and mistrust, even when he has no ulterior or harmful intentions. A woman with a reputation for being super sexy may find that other women regard her with mistrust even when she has no design on their husbands or boyfriends, which could drive her to fulfill the prejudicial expectations of her peers.

When you go out in the world to find replacement love sources, and you act like you don't think you are worthy or deserving, people will respond to you like you're not. That response "proves" to you that you are "too ugly, too fat, too unsociable" and makes you act as if you were uglier, fatter, and less sociable because erroneous beliefs about yourself have been reinforced by your peers and so confirmed in your mind. You may be overlooking the fact that *you* caused their response by presenting a bad attitude initially.

The robberies and burglaries that have always been most perplexing to police officers are the ones where someone walks in and loads an entire household into a moving van and drives away. Simply because the burglar has dressed in a moving man's uniform, acted like a professional mover and shown up with the accoutrements of a moving van, proper packing crates, padding and an assistant mover, neighbors have assumed he was a mover. He is able to walk away with anything he wants because he looks the part, and people treat him like a mover, not a thief.

You, too, must learn to look the part of the person you'd like to be. The way you look on the outside reflects the thoughts you have on the inside. That's why self-instruction, or prepared, rehearsed, prelearned thoughts are important. Talking to yourself (which used to be considered a sign of craziness) is now a therapeutic device.

If you have a party to go to, rehearse positive sentences in your mind over and over again, replacing the negative thoughts you have about yourself.

Self-Instruction for Going Out

Don't say	*Do say*
I won't have any fun.	I'll enjoy myself.
Nobody will talk to me.	I'm going to start a conversation.
I won't know anybody there.	I can meet someone (or several people).
I won't look as good as the others.	I look terrific.

Right now, as an exercise, make up your own "don't say"–"do say" list. Try to think of at least ten pairs of sentences about a social situation that causes you anxiety, makes your palms sweat or your stomach quiver.

If you were an airplane phobic, there would be two things that would be frightening you. One would be the airplane, and the other would be the sentence that is going through your head that says, "What happens if the airplane crashes?" Both the airplane and the sentence would be actually stimulating the emotional electrochemical fear-reaction in your body. Seeing the airplane would start the adrenaline pumping, trigger your defensive reflex and make you scared. The mere sentence "What if the airplane crashes?" would also stimulate the same adrenal-nervous system reaction and make you just as scared.

Anticipatory Anxiety

Because there are two causes for phobic reactions (the frightening thing itself and the sentence in your mind about it), there are two ways to attack phobias. One way is to slow down the adrenaline by getting used to the actual threatening object, either under safe, relaxed conditions (desensitization) or by exhausting the fear (implosion). The other way to fight phobias is to change the fear-inducing sentences. An airplane phobic will avoid flying by thinking the magic sentence "What if the airplane crashes," even when there's no airplane nearby. In the same way you can scare yourself into avoiding social situations by thinking scary sentences when there isn't even a social situation happening. You might say, "Nobody will like me," and certainly scare yourself by thinking about a party before you even get there. You don't even have to be going to a party to scare yourself. You can do it anytime.

The good news is that you can also unscare yourself anytime by changing the sentences in your head. Instead of allowing yourself to say, "Nobody will like me," get in the habit of saying, "I have a lot of very likable qualities." List your likable qualities, the things you do better than other people, the way you are with people—honest, sincere, sensitive and caring. If you think them often enough, the "I'm lovable" thoughts will replace the "I'm unlovable" ones. You'll begin to think of yourself as a lovable person, and so will others. They will treat you in more loving ways and their reinforcement will actually cause you to become even more lovable.

If you had an airplane phobia and the sentence that frightened you was "Most crashes happen on takeoff and landing," you would substitute another sentence, "Almost 100 percent of all takeoffs and landings are safe and without any problems at all." Or, "There are six billion passenger miles before there's one mishap." Or, as Ralph Nader points out, "You're safer flying in a plane than driving to the airport."

Love Phobias

Your fright at starting a new relationship is completely understandable. You have become phobic about breakups. You have learned a phobia—relationships. It's like a person who becomes an airplane phobic after experiencing turbulence during a routine flight. Before that, airplanes were okay, but suddenly the person who has experienced the turbulence imagines that they may die in the airplane.

"My life is over," thinks the potential airplane phobic, as scenes of funerals, crashes and past life flash through his head. Even though the plane doesn't crash, the person develops a fear of airplanes because in his imagination, he died. Even though the plane didn't crash that time, the phobic reaction is, "Phew, I got away with it that time, but next time I won't. I may not be so lucky." Even if their next flight is smooth, the phobic imagines death with every off sound of the motor and every "fasten your seat belts" sign. That's how many airplane phobias begin—with one bad experience.

The same thing is true for your fear of new relationships. You were in love and had a wonderful relationship. You weren't afraid until you experienced the turbulence that upset you to the point where you thought you might die. Your turbulence is the loss of the person who gave you security and provided for your dependency needs. Suddenly you have to take care of yourself, and you don't know how. You feel as if you may die. You don't know how you will pay your bills, take care of your daily living needs and keep your emotions under control.

You experience the equivalent of the airplane phobic's turbulence. Your life security has been cut off. Just as the airplane phobic doesn't see how he can survive another flight, you don't feel as if you can cope with another scary relationship. Your life-style is in turbulence and you don't want that to happen again, so you begin to avoid relationships. You become a relationship phobic.

Thoughts like "I'm not worthy of a relationship. I can't have one without upsetting myself. I'm unable to survive another breakup" race through your mind. A secondary phobic reaction develops that says, "I'm afraid I will be alone forever because I can't have a committed relationship." You become like the airplane phobic who thinks, "I will never be able to fly in another airplane because I might die." His secondary phobic reaction is "My business will suffer if I can't fly to places. I won't ever be able to vacation far from home. I won't have any fun."

In treating an airplane phobic, a psychologist will use self-instruction to change the sentences that are frightening and desensitization to gradually get him back near the airplane until he feels safe inside and is convinced that he will indeed be able to fly with impunity. Your fear, or phobia, caused by the turbulence you experienced from the breakup of your relationship, is just as real and requires the same treatment, only you can do it yourself. If you continue to be afraid to develop another relationship, you may develop a secondary phobia about whether you can indeed cope with life alone.

Loneliness Phobias

The loneliness at first seems unbearable, and you're sure you will die from it. Of course you won't, and chances are you can do most of the things for yourself that your ex did for you. You can have security, you can drive yourself around, you can cook for yourself and you can still go out on Saturday night—even though you have developed phobias that say you can't. In combatting your fear of loneliness, you can use the same techniques of self-instruction to switch the sentences in your head. People suffering from separation anxiety report amazingly similar unrealistic fears and unrealistic sentences. Your mythical catastrophe fears of being alone forever and of never finding someone to love can be replaced by rational alternatives.

Self-Instruction for Loneliness

Mythical Catastrophes	*Rational Alternatives*
I will be alone forever.	I have had a relationship in the past, and I'll have one again.

Mythical Catastrophes	*Rational Alternatives*
No one will ever want me.	Just as I want someone, others are looking, too.
I will never have another relationship as good as this one.	Because I've learned from this relationship, a future one will be better.
I can only have physical relationships.	As I gain confidence, I'll allow myself to become vulnerable.
I will never have a committed relationship.	Nothing is "forever."
I'm so unlovable that no one will ever want me for myself.	I am intrinsically lovable for my true self.
I'm too old to start again.	I have a head start with valuable experience.
My life is over.	I can make a "new beginning."
Everybody has someone, and I don't.	I have the incentive to make a "new beginning."
Even if it looks good, they'll reject me eventually.	All relationships end one way or another.
I'm incapable of sustaining a committed relationship.	The quality of a relationship is more important than its length.
I'm better off without a relationship.	No relationship is better than a bad one.
Relationships only make me unhappy.	My happiness does not depend on a relationship.
I'll be lonely every Saturday night from now on.	I will find fun things to do on Saturday night.
I won't have anyone to spend Christmas and my birthday with.	I will arrange now for Christmas and my birthday.
There's no one I can call.	I will meet new people.

Mythical Catastrophes	*Rational Alternatives*
No one every really loved me.	I have loved and been loved.
What if something happens to me?	I can always find a way to take care of myself.
Things are more than I can handle.	I have friends who'll come through for me.
Suppose I'm sick and alone?	There's a pharmacy that delivers.

Relationship Phobias

The phobic "mythical catastrophe" sentences, first identified by Dr. Albert Ellis, often prevent a new relationship from happening. For fear itself can make you pull back from social contacts and alienate otherwise compatible people who would really like you.

Today, 40 percent of all marriages end by divorce, and that's if you're in the lucky "success-possible" age group. If you are under twenty-five, the statistics are really discouraging. And if you live in California, you can predict your chances by the flip of a coin, fifty-fifty. And of course, all relationships end eventually. No one can keep the emotional level of "being in love" for very long. Even the marriage vows are " 'til death do us part." The truth is that if a breakup doesn't end a relationship, death eventually will. The ending of a relationship isn't unusual and doesn't signify that you are incapable of having another, even a better one. But first you must change the phobic sentences you have in your head about what "might" happen in the future by using self-instruction.

It's true that separation and terminated relationships do cause pain. It's not only a psychological assault on your mind, but a physical pain as well. As cardiologist Dr. James Lynch's recent medical research at Johns Hopkins Hospital on loneliness and broken hearts proves, people suffering from terminated relationships have a higher incidence of actual heart disease and even cancer, our two deadliest diseases. Dr. Lynch confirmed that psychologically broken hearts often cause medically broken hearts.

The tremendous pain you suffered from your rejection accounts for your anger, for the feeling that you want to hurt or even physically injure your ex (see chapter seven for controlling these urges). If a man with boxing gloves punched you and broke your nose, you would be able to understand why you had a fear of even going to a boxing match and certainly why you avoid all men with boxing gloves.

Breaking someone's heart is just as much of a physical assault on them as if their nose had been broken—even worse. Your fears seem indeed justified, but if you continue to let them control your life, you will find it difficult to establish better new relationships. You will be avoiding all relationships just as if you were going to get a broken nose instead of a broken heart. The pain is real. Recent studies show that a majority of female alcoholics turned to alcohol immediately after a broken relationship.

Your phobic sentences are not frivolous. They started as observations based on bad experiences, ones that are indeed worse than turbulence in an airplane. The irrational conclusions from those observations are what started and maintained your love phobia. Divorce is still rated one of the three most serious emotional traumas that a person can experience.

There are degrees of phobias, but all phobic sentences keep you from enjoying fully the experience you might have. Some airplane phobics can go to the airport without anxiety, but can't actually get into a plane. Others can get into a plane, but panic when the engine starts.

Relationship phobics also come in varying degrees. You may be unable to even talk to someone attractive who might interest you because of your phobia. You may be able to talk, but not to make a date. Or make a date, but not keep it.

Or make a date, keep it and not be really warm and open. Or make a date and even make love with someone, but really keep the relationship shallow. All these phobic reactions defeat your recovery. The degree of resistance you have to new relationships is directly related to how long it takes you to start one.

Using the technique of self-instruction, substitute optimistic sentences for the ones that frighten you. New sentences will change your mind, improve your attitude, your behavior, your future and even how long you will live.

The odds are very high that you will indeed find another person who will care for you. If you were really as bad and as unlovable as you may think you are, you wouldn't have had the relationship that you did have, no matter how long or short it was. An obnoxious person wouldn't have been loved, ever. You were, and you will be again.

Friends and Lovers

Naturally not everyone will fall in love with you or you with them, but there will be people who are interested in you who are just as lonely as you are and who will be grateful for your interest in them. If you are willing to give and provide love to other people, then they will want to be around you and your loneliness will dissipate.

Right now you are between lovers, but you haven't had your last human contact. Your friends seem too busy and involved with their own lives to take time to comfort you. If they thought you were really in trouble, they would help. Unfortunately, people don't see loss of love as being as much of a disaster as say loss of your home by fire or earthquake or flood.

Friends will rush to the aid of someone who is in the hospital or ill or involved in some sort of physical disaster without thinking about it for an instant. But it's unfortunate that those same friends may not see your emotional loss (unless someone dies) as such a serious thing. Or they may think you want to be alone with your hurt.

If you feel that your friends are unsympathetic about your loss, it could be because they don't realize the seriousness of it. Separation (by divorce or breakup of committed relationships) is a relatively new phenomenon in our society. The physical and emotional toll on the newly separated is just being recognized.

If one particular friend doesn't seem too receptive to you, call another one. It may be a bad day for them or you may have called on that person too many times in a row for favors. If you were ill, you wouldn't ask the same person to do your grocery shopping, clean your house and get your prescriptions. In the same way, you can't expect the same friend to comfort you *all* the time.

It isn't true that no one cares for you. You could probably list several people who love you in a caring way, but not in a primary relationship way. Don't automatically eliminate all formerly not-so-close friends from primary relationship possibilities. Call them and see if they've changed their attitudes or developed new ones that are more compatible with yours now. Old friends can become more attractive, more stimulating and even closer to you than they ever were before. It is possible to make a new relationship with an old friend. It could be that your former mate was the one who turned them off—not you.

If you have negative-loneliness sentences that run through your head, you might consider replacing them with sentences like:

"I have made it alone in the past."

"Being free of the responsibility for him/her is a relief."

"I can be as clean or sloppy as I want."

"It's nice not to be subject to criticism."

If you think that the process of dating is "getting into the singles rat race," and that's frightening to you, it may be because you see dating as a means to an end (relationship), rather than a fun process by itself. Don't think of dating as a project to "get someone." Instead, think of fun places you could go, the excitement of discovering another human being and of finding out about a new friend. It's not true that casual encounters, dates and even recreational sex aren't fun; they are. You just haven't tried them for a long time and may be experiencing a phobic reaction about "going out there."

Think of yourself as an explorer setting out into a new world. Instead of setting off across an ocean, you are exploring people. Find out what's going on in the world today, how people are and how they think. You'll be amazed at how people are drawn to you. People like people who are interested in them.

If you see dating as a means of hooking someone, of getting out of the dating rat race, dating and new contacts will indeed become a chore.

Instead of seeking a "special" someone who will devote their life to you forever, find people who are willing to give you their full attention for an hour or an evening. By reducing your expectations (from a "forever" relationship), you will find them easier to fill.

The fact that one person left you doesn't mean that no one will ever be with you again. You found that person and you will find others, perhaps even *one* other, when you least expect it.

"I feel like I'm too old to find someone new" is one of the sentences that the newly separated individual feels most strongly. It's true that you are older than you were when you met your ex, but it's also true that there are more people in your age group who, just like you, are newly separated. You may feel that as you grow older, your chances of finding someone are diminishing. Not true! More people are getting divorced even after twenty years of marriage. Your chances are just as good now.

Years ago, it was the first year of a marriage that was most hazardous. The seven-year itch caused divorces. Now twelve-year and twenty-year divorces are becoming more common.

Because people are getting divorced later in life, they are returning to the dating circuit at a later age. You will find more of your peer group living alone and suffering from the same loneliness and hungers you have.

When you do meet new people, remember that today, age differences are routinely ignored. Don't pass up spending time with someone you enjoy because they are ten or twenty years younger or older than you are.

A younger man is attracted to an older woman because she is more relaxed and experienced in pleasing a man, in being comfortable at home. She is less demanding financially and emotionally. The younger man's sex drive is likely to be more compatible with that of the mature woman.

Young girls are attracted to an older man. He can afford to entertain them in a way a young man can't. A younger woman wants to be taken out, not made comfortable in a homelike atmosphere. Her less strong sex drive is more in tune with that of the mature man who is often less demanding and more skilled. Years ago, height (she's too tall, he's too short) made a difference that few care about today. Age differences, too, are going the way of religious, nationality, ethnic, class and even racial differences.

In general, compatibility is more important than how old a person is. That really doesn't matter at all if two people are happy together. In chapters ten and eleven, you will find out exactly how to go out and meet new people. But first, if you have sentences in your head that are frightening you and keeping you away from new people, use self-instruction to overcome them.

Self-Instruction for Relationship Phobias

Mythical Catastrophes	*Rational Alternatives*
I'm afraid I won't find anyone to love.	I will find someone to love who will love me. *Or:* In my future there is someone who will love me and

Mythical Catastrophes	*Rational Alternatives*
	whom I will love more than anyone I've ever loved before.
I would be afraid to fall in love with someone again.	Loving again would give me so much pleasure, it's worth taking the chance.
I can't face another breakup.	My last experience has prepared me for anything that might happen in the next one. *Or:* I will survive breaking up if it does not happen because I'm surviving this one successfully.

One of the reasons many people avoid falling in love again after a divorce or a terminated relationship is because they're afraid of the breakup. How many times have you heard a divorced man or woman say, "I'll never marry again because I couldn't stand to go through another divorce."

Your fears are normal. Even people who have never been married or really involved in a committed, close, loving relationship are secretly afraid that they'll be left. They feel that they couldn't deal with the pain.

Now you have been left. You know that you will indeed survive if it happens again. There really is no reason why you shouldn't allow yourself to relate on as warm and intimate a basis as you like—since the worst that could happen is that you would break up. Then again, you could stay together. To find happiness in a relationship, you have to take that chance.

Self-instruction can facilitate increasingly more difficult and threatening situations. Suppose you are invited to a party where you might run into some of the people who work with your former mate or were your mutual friends. For many newly separated people, that's a frightening situation.

You think: "Suppose I run into someone who doesn't know we broke up and asks me where's my partner?"

Self-instruct yourself to be prepared for whatever situation might arise. Prepare and rehearse answers to "embarrassing" questions.

Your self-instruction sentences might be:

"Most people know we've separated."

"It's unlikely that they'd ask."

"If anyone asks, I will simply say: 'We're not seeing each other anymore. We've separated.' "

Practice saying, "We're not seeing each other anymore, we've separated." Say it in front of a mirror. Repeat it several times. Practice different emphases on different words in the sentence. Put an "Oh, well" in front of it. Tack something on the end like "That's just the way it is," or "That's the way things go," or "I'm happier now." Practice immediately talking about something new or unusual. It might be "Maybe you know someone I might enjoy meeting." Or "How are your kids?" Or "I'm going to Japan." It's a good idea not to let those "what happened" kinds of conversations drag on.

If someone asks you what happened, tell them, "It's rather complicated," or, "Who knows?" or, "I'd rather not discuss it," and don't. Go on to ask a question about them or ask them to introduce you to someone.

If you're afraid no one will talk to you, your sentence might be "I'll be ignored. I'll feel unimportant." Self-instruction could include, "I'll ask someone the time." And practice asking the time. "What time do you have?" Or, "I'll ask someone where the john is." And practice asking "Where's the bathroom?"

There are other specific techniques for making contacts with people.

The Sherlock Holmes Technique

Pretend you are Sherlock Holmes. Investigate the people who are around you. If there is someone you think you would like to talk to and you just don't know how to make an opening, see if you can find something unusual about the person. For instance, they might be wearing a Norwegian designed sweater with reindeers on it. You could say to them, "You must come from New York." Or any cold climate.

Even if they say no, you have made an opening. The person will probably respond by telling you where they do come from or asking what made you think they were from that particular place. Your answer could be that you've never seen a sweater like that sold anywhere in Southern California or Florida or wherever.

Always try to make your Sherlock Holmes investigation question complimentary. If you walk up to a long-haired type and say, "You must be an artist, writer or musician," they will probably be flattered. But if you say, "You must be a dropout," it just isn't as good.

If you ask whether someone is a lawyer, doctor or other status profession, they will be flattered, even if they aren't those things. Your clues could be jewelry, dress, a briefcase, or just the way a person talks. If you do happen to hit their profession right, they will be amazed at your Sherlock Holmes ability and will ask you how you knew.

You have already started a conversation.

It's easy to follow your Sherlock Holmes investigative question with "Who else but an artist would appreciate a painting the way you do" Or "Who but a fashion designer could put together such a great outfit?" Or "I thought you must have made that shawl, ring, dress, etc., because it's so original."

If the person says they didn't make whatever it is or aren't the profession you guessed, don't panic. It's easy to make your next question "Well, if you didn't make it, where did you get it? I'd love to have something like it." Or "If you aren't an attorney, what do you do?"

Undercover Agent

By saying nothing about yourself and attempting to discover everything about the other person, you can be a secret agent. Dr. David Badell suggests that you actually pretend you are in the CIA and it's your job to find out as much as you can about that particular person.

Ask as many questions as you can without divulging anything about yourself until you are asked. Find out what the person does, where they live, their hobbies, where they've traveled, who their friends are. Eventually, they will ask you about yourself, but in the meantime they will think you are absolutely enchanting for having the good taste to be so interested in them.

Never ask a question that can be answered with one word. Always ask something that will require a more complete answer, a discussion or an explanation. If you see someone on the beach or in an airplane, and they're reading a certain book, don't say, "That's a great book, I read it," because the answer could be just a grunt. Do say, "What do you think of that book? I've been meaning to read it." If the book is science fiction, say, "How does it compare to *Star Wars*?" If it's a murder mystery, ask, "Who do you think did it?" Asking someone "What do you think" gets an answer.

In a museum, you might ask someone to explain a particular piece of artwork to you or what they think the artist is saying. It's okay to criticize the artist's work, but in opening conversational moves, it's especially important not to put down the person you're trying to make contact with, even indirectly.

It's okay to criticize other people in the room, but never say, "They don't make these barstools big enough for fatties like us" or, "I suppose if you're over forty nobody talks to you in a place like this."

You can say, "This is really a dull night here. You're the only interesting looking person." Or, "They sure seem to have started watering down the drinks." Or, "Do you know a place that's a little more lively, or has dancing?" Or, "This can't be a good place to eat. Do you know one?"

Never put yourself down or the person you're talking to. The best person to put down as an opening conversational gambit is someone who isn't there. If the person you're talking to looks like a liberal type, and so are you, pick on a conservative political figure. If they are your conservative match, put down a liberal. Always pick the most conservative or most liberal, someone you're sure can be criticized by almost anyone.

If you're in a quiet place, like an art gallery or museum, a noisy person is easy to put down, or a drunk at a party, or a boor, but be sure it's not a friend of the person you're talking to. If it turns out that you're putting down someone they like, you've still opened up conversation by letting them convince you you're wrong.

Ask directions. You can do that in the supermarket or the Paris metro. If you can't find a spice or a boulevard, it amounts to the same thing—a conversational opening with a stranger. It doesn't hurt to lie a little, either. Ask how to pick out a melon, even if you already know. You could learn something new. Ask which plums are sweet and which are sour. Notice something in someone's basket and ask them if they like that particular brand. You don't have to seem unknowing if that bothers you.

Go shopping when family people are having dinner, or after the kids come home from school, or even at night. Those are the best times to find single people out doing their marketing. If someone is standing in front of the coffee, ask which is the best.

Contemporary moves and ways of meeting people have

probably changed while you were involved with your old relationship. Today's cunning linguists have already replaced words like "bitchin'," "cool," or "wow" with "bad," "trash" and "super." Women and men both make approaches more easily to each other, and there's no stigma attached to making the first move. It's just an easy way to say, "I'm interested if you are."

Coming Out Party

If you don't feel up to making the bar scene or even the supermarket approach, practice by giving a party. As a redebutante, invite everyone you know, even slightly, and tell them to bring their friends. Coming out parties for divorces and separations are becoming more popular than coming out parties for debutantes. Try to invite as many single people as possible because their friends are likely to be single, too. Put a guest book by the front door so that you don't have to worry about remembering names. It's also a good way to gather telephone numbers for your next party or even to contact a particularly attractive person later.

Creating Social Obligations

The good thing about throwing a party for everyone you know and all their friends is that you put them in a position of having to reciprocate and invite you the next time they have a party. It might not be until next year, but you will be expanding your social horizons. Think of the party as an investment—in your future social life.

You may not want to call it a coming out party because at this point you may want to forget all that. If so, any excuse for a party is a good one. Your cat's birthday, a friend's birthday, your birthday, a housewarming, moving party, barbecue or even Beethoven's birthday. Surely there's some sort of holiday coming, Columbus Day, Purim, or the Chinese New Year.

Being up front about why you're having the party has one definite advantage. It encourages people to bring eligible members of the opposite sex and also to come without dates.

Don't forget to play Sherlock Holmes again at your party. It's easy to look for wedding rings or committed couples and stay away from them. Many married men and women are just as involved in outside affairs as single, committed couples. So if you're picking someone up, say in the supermarket, be sure to check the cart out first. Remember that a basket full of milk, bread, and family groceries usually means a mate and a family somewhere. Look for the people who buy just one or two of something, not six (except beer and Diet Pepsi).

Don't sit around waiting for someone to take you out. Go by yourself.

Unfortunately, most restaurants sit a single person alone at a table. Search out the ones in your city where sharing a table is the usual thing, and frequent those. Or you could tell the maitre d' or hostess, "Feel free to have another person join me at my table." Restaurants aren't really thrilled to have one person taking up a table, so the chances are pretty good that you won't be eating alone.

Since men eat out alone more often than women, you are most likely to be joined by a man. That's great if you're a woman and beats eating alone if you're a guy. Even another man or woman could open a whole new black book for you.

If you like sports, or just lying in the sun, an easy way to meet a stranger is to ask them to watch your belongings or to hold your place in a ski line. You could be going for a swim or to the bathroom, it really doesn't matter. The important thing is to open communication.

Pick the times and places you might meet the kinds of people you're interested in. The best way is to do whatever makes you happy. If you're interested in backgammon or bridge, take lessons or participate in a tournament. After a party, when you're still dressed up, or a night out when you still have energy and no one to share it with, you could forage at the all-night market. Only single people shop after midnight.

You can usually assume that someone alone is out looking, just like you are. They may even be interested in you, or desperately seeking someone, anyone, to talk to, but too shy to make the approach. If you see someone sitting alone, either in a restaurant, at an airport or a party, there's nothing wrong with saying, "Is this seat taken?" Or, "Is someone sitting with you?" Or, "Do you mind if I join you?" Or, "Isn't it awful to sit alone and wait?"

The worst that could happen is that the person will say they're expecting someone. The best is that they will be grateful to you for alleviating their own loneliness.

Personal confessions of weakness are always likable. You could precede your overture with "I'm really afraid of take-offs and landings. May I sit here?" Or "I hate to eat alone. Could I join you?" If it seems too frightening at first to do that with a member of the opposite sex, practice on a member of the same sex.

A tiny bit of self-disclosure, like "I'm on a diet," or "I can't eat cholesterol," or "I've never been here before. Do you know what's good?" makes you seem warm, human and without ulterior motives—safe. Believe it or not, as afraid as you are, you could scare another person who's even more frightened. Self-disclosure makes you vulnerable, open, and, therefore, safer.

Meeting Stars (Not Losers)

Don't become intimidated because the other person seems "too good" for you, too young, too handsome or even too rich. Go right to the star, if you're attracted to them. Don't necessarily strike up a conversation with an obvious loser because they're in such bad trouble that they won't dare reject you. Stars get lonely, too, and are often neglected because everyone thinks they're too busy. Besides, you'll feel much worse if you get rejected by a loser than by a star.

Picking on the most neurotic-appearing person, the obvious social misfit, is asking for trouble. A person who doesn't have too much going for them anyway will demand more from you. They'll want someone to make up for their own inadequacies. An attractive, more secure human being won't expect you to be perfect. They'll know they're not and they'll be adjusted to their own imperfections. The loser knows he's so bad that only the most perfect human being will do—he wants someone to copy, someone so beautiful that nobody will notice his ugliness. Losers are looking for reflected glory, a decoration to prove that if they can get someone special, then they can't be that bad after all. Or they want an attractive partner who will prove to others they can get someone in spite of their obvious flaws.

Losers, because of their previous bad experiences, will give you a hard time, testing you and making you prove you want more than a one-night stand. Since others may have used them for an easy lay or a free dinner, they may be more likely to hold out on sex or be selfish. They'll make you prove yourself a lot before they give anything of themselves.

Approaching a star can be intimidating, so think of some reason why you must talk to them. If your particular star is a contractor, ask about work on your house. If they're in real estate, say you're thinking about buying and which area would they recommend. If they work for an attorney or are one, ask if they know a good person to handle a suit for you. But remember, don't ask a doctor for medical advice.

Your approach must have something in it for the star, not for you. Ask a doctor if he treats a special disease (anything from hearts to bad backs) because your mother, aunt, grandfather, etc., has one. That way it's in his interest, not yours. Don't ask for a diagnosis of your troubles from a shrink or your car's engine from an auto mechanic. They'll feel used and it sets up negative vibes toward you before you even get to know the person.

If you already know someone's occupation, ask questions *about* what the person does, particularly questions that are in their interest. If you're talking to a doctor or lawyer, ask where they get referrals or how to refer someone. Ask a mechanic where their garage is.

People want to be judged on the basis of how they relate, rather than what they do. If someone is proud of their job or occupation, they'll probably volunteer the information.

Instead of worrying about someone's job status or how much money they make, try to find out their values. What do they think is important in life? What do they want to accomplish? Watch how the person relates to you. Is he or she conning you, seducing you, looking at other people around the room while they're talking to you? Are they open, manipulative, friendly? Instead of worrying about whether someone likes you, find out if they're the kind of person *you* like.

Self-instruct yourself to say, "I wonder if I'll like him or her," instead of "I wonder if they'll like me."

You may be one of the people who has been out of circulation for so long that you really don't know anywhere to go or anyone single who you could invite to a party. The way to meet single people of the opposite sex is to find out where they typically go. Look in the "happenings" section where monthly events are listed in your local paper or magazines. Find out where there are lectures that interest you, especially those that would attract members of the opposite sex. Sign up for courses and seminars.

A man who's interested in the occult or poetry or cooking has it licked. Chances are most of the people in those kinds of classes are women. If you're a woman who has an interest in photography, engineering or golf, try those classes.

Stay away from group grope, five-dollar-a-night encounter sessions. The only people you will meet there are lonely neurotics who think they can pick up (along with the wholesale "therapy") a member of the opposite sex who can make them well. Drop-in therapy encounters prey on hungry, love-starved people who may really need a one-to-one intensive therapy. Sure, it's easy to pick up someone there, but do you really need somebody with more problems than you have?

Do political volunteer work. Pick a candidate whom you would like to support and offer to work for them. The marvelous thing about political volunteer work is that the group becomes very close and is accepting of newcomers very quickly. Political bedfellows are a reality. Community action with a cause and a common enemy will automatically make a group draw close together. Join an antinoise group, a food co-op. Stay away from family-oriented groups like busing or antibusing, antipornography or school milk programs. Instead, stick to the causes that draw single people, like Young Republicans, Students for Democratic Action and ecology groups.

Stay away from discos and singles bars. First of all, in a disco there's no way you can be heard, so there's no way to find out if you like someone. It's often so dark you can't even tell what the person looks like or the expression on their face until you get outside.

Men make out better in discos because women usually feel that they have to wait for someone to ask them to dance. But where do you go from dancing? Immediately ask the girl to leave with you and go elsewhere, for coffee or a drink, so you can talk. If she's interested in you, and you can get her outside of the disco even for a few minutes, you'll have a better chance.

If you're a woman, you're taking your life in your hands by going alone with a man in a car, unless you know for sure who he is. But there's nothing to prevent you from walking outside to cool off and asking a man to come with you. That way you'll be able to find out who he is and what he looks like, without hassles.

Even though they're not the nicest places in the world, with their meat-market reputation, everyone winds up at a singles bar at least once. It's okay to go for a drink after work on Thursday or Friday, especially if you don't have anything planned for the weekend. The unfortunate thing is that people in singles bars usually are there to score that night. They don't want to wait for the weekend.

Rejection is a way of life in a singles bar. It's a scene where a guy figures that if he asks ten girls, maybe one will say yes. A girl figures she'll smile at ten different guys and maybe one will want to start a conversation with her. Never take singles bar rejections seriously, and never go to one expecting to fall in love.

The only good thing about singles bars is that there are a lot of single people there. That doesn't mean that you don't check for wedding rings or live-in roommate arrangements, but rather that you get lots of chances. Among a hundred people in a TGIF bar, there may be one you'd like. The same is true for a ten-member art class. If you are determined to only meet artists, then you'd obviously choose the art class over the singles bar.

If you only want tennis players, go to tennis courts. If you want to camp out, join the Sierra Club. You have to decide on your requirements for compatibility. Go where you will find those people. The largest group of people with the same interests as you will yield the most possibilities.

Any activity with tournaments is a great way to meet new people. Tennis clubs match up beginners with each other and advanced players with each other. Then they usually have social affairs where everyone gets together. The same for golf, backgammon, bridge or chess. By joining one of these groups you are assured at least a minimal compatibility, at least one thing to talk about. Look in the yellow pages if you don't know how to find groups interested in what you like to do. Sign up for one and you will find yourself swamped with mailings from affiliated interest groups.

If you have no strong interest and don't want to join any groups, then you'll have to simply expose yourself to the largest groups you can find. It's a pretty competitive scene at the discos and singles bars. If you're not especially physically attractive or exceptionally outgoing, chances are you'll be ignored. These are not the places to display any talents you may have beyond the way you look. Obviously, the singles bar scene is superficial. If your assets aren't immediately obvious, they're not the place for you.

The only thing in favor of mass gatherings is that there are so many people that you have better odds of finding someone you like. If you don't get at least one rejection when you go to one of the mass single gatherings, you haven't been assertive enough. Set one rejection as your goal at first. You'll be surprised how much fun being assertive is and how hard it is for you to get rejected. Other people are as lonely and insecure as you are. A large group gives you better odds and the protection of a certain amount of anonymity. Each time out, increase the number of rejections you try to get. Making rejections your goal will automatically increase your chances for acceptances. Most people are there just like you, hoping someone will talk to them.

Even the most self-assured-looking person has fears about going into a mass singles affair. They, too, are worried about things like, "What if nobody talks to me?" But you are one step ahead; you know how to use self-instruction and also how to practice opening lines like "Do you have a light?" Or "Do you know what time it is?" Or even lines that will definitely start conversation, like "Do you know a place near here that has dancing?"

Scoring

Men who start going out after a relationship breaks up often judge the success of their evening by whether they get a girl to go home with them, whether they score. Chances are that you won't score, and if that's your expectation, you will be disappointed. Even regulars on the circuit don't "score" every time, and you haven't even practiced.

Start out by trying to make friends with a woman instead of trying to score. Make communication, not fornication, your first goal. Even though today's morals say that it's okay to "go all the way" on a first date, don't feel rejected if your date doesn't. She may be making sure she really likes you before she gets involved in a sexual relationship.

Women who've been "on the shelf" for a while are often surprised at how quickly a man expects them to bed down with him. It may be true that "all men want to get into my pants," but it's not necessarily true that's *all* they want. Men are often looking for someone to relate to beyond a sexual level, but they do want to get laid. That's a man's way of assuring himself of his adequacy.

Odds are that whether you are a man or a woman, the person you're just meeting has also broken up with someone, especially if they're the same age that you are. When they lose their mates, people need to know that they are still attractive. For a man, this means getting laid. For a woman, it often means being taken out without getting laid—just to prove she's more valuable than that.

Women can let men off the hook by simply stating, "I would like to go to bed with you in the future. You're attractive, and I really look forward to spending more time with you, and I definitely want our relationship to include sex, but not tonight." That takes away the expectation-disappointment factor, and the man feels validated in his attractiveness.

A man, when he hears that, makes himself doubly desirable by not being insistent, by not saying, "Why not?" and by not trying to seduce and convince. It's her body, and she has a right to do what she wants with it. Also, by not pushing, she'll become intrigued. You won't seem so hungry, and she won't feel that's all you want her for. You may reassure yourself that possibly she's just getting over an illness or is old-fashioned about sex during her period. You've heard "Yes," so cool it.

If you get a flat rejection, don't try to analyze why. Simply let it pass and enjoy your evening. A conclusion that your date doesn't like you because they won't bed down with you right away can ruin a perfectly fine evening and any future chances you might have.

Never play shrink. Don't tell your date, "It's because you're uptight, had a puritanical upbringing or have hang-ups." Nobody likes someone who tells them they're not okay just the way they are. Anyway, they've heard it all from the last person.

Although it would be nice in the dating world if everyone were honest and said exactly what they want and don't want, we all know it doesn't happen that way. Women do say "no" when they mean "yes." Men pretend that they want sex because they think they're supposed to, when they'd often be happy with a home-cooked meal and good company.

Learn to pick up nonverbal clues instead of asking. You can tell if someone likes you. You don't have to ask. You can also tell if someone is going to want to kiss you. If a woman pulls away when a man puts his arm around her, it's really silly to ask her, "May I have a kiss?" Besides, it's just not done. Allow the other person's response to your nonverbal approaches to clue you in to whether they want to go further. Holding a cold, limp hand is enough of a clue; don't press for a more obvious rejection.

The world isn't ready for you to ask someone to go to bed with you the same way you ask them to dinner.

Many women are still stuck with the idea that nice girls don't do certain things on a first date. In today's social situation, that just doesn't hold up. Nice girls do. So do not-so-nice girls. Most men are usually flattered if a woman goes to bed with them on the first date. Since dating standards have changed so drastically, you can only be guided by your instincts.

If a man turns a woman on, if she likes the way he talks, the way he touches her, the way he acts, she often panics. How should she act? What should she do? What will he like and what will turn him on?

"If I'm too aggressive, I'll turn men off," or "If I'm not aggressive enough nobody will pay any attention to me," or "If I don't play hard to get, he won't want me," or "If he knows how much sexual experience I've had, he'll think I'm not nice" are all typical sentences that bother women who are reentering the dating world. They want to know how much of themselves to reveal, if there's a special role they should play. Men often experience similar feelings. Nobody knows what game to play when they reenter the dating scene.

The answer is to be yourself. If you try to be someone else, eventually you'll be discovered. Besides, by being someone other than who you are, you never find people who will like you for you. Instead you'll be spending time with people who like what you're pretending to be.

Don't be ashamed to admit that you have just broken up. Tell new people you meet, but factually, without sympathy-inducing sobs or a list of your leftover symptoms. They've probably broken up themselves at least once. In one way, having just broken up makes you seem more desirable because you're new on the market. Let people know you are capable of having a relationship that lasts, and that lets them know you'll probably have another one. They may decide you're ripe and snatch you up before someone else does.

Plan to reach out and do things you didn't do before. If you go to a bar or a party, take a cigarette lighter, even if you don't smoke. Carry matches so you can offer someone a light.

Learn to share. Offer suntan lotion to someone who looks like they're getting burned at the swimming pool. Learn to borrow. Bum a cigarette, ask for a light, ask an attractive neighbor for ice cubes. Practice making contacts without expectations.

When you go out hoping to meet new people, do something you'll enjoy even if you don't meet anyone. If you go out on a date, make sure you go where you'll have a good time even if the date bombs. Take care of yourself—don't leave it up to someone else. There's really no reason why your happiness and pleasure should be dependent on the whim or mood of another person.

If you agree to see a movie you've seen ten times or one that you know you'll hate, just to go out with someone, then you're not being fair to yourself or to the other person. Your evening is totally dependent on them, not the entertainment. And they don't even know that.

Beware of compromising yourself and contriving with the sole goal of seducing someone. The big problem with that is that even if you do succeed in seducing the person you're after, it won't be you they're making love to, but rather the person you've been pretending to be.

Session Eighteen: Hidden Resources

Many people have trouble reaching out to others because they don't think they have any assets worth offering.

Assets Inventory

Making your personal assets inventory is a "must" assignment for this session. Your assets inventory will list everything you have going for you—from simply being a male or female to actual skills and abilities. Sit down with a paper and pen and start your list. Be honest. This is no time for modesty.

Number your assets. Start with number one, the simple fact that you are either a male or a female, which makes you potentially attractive to at least 50 percent of the people in the world.

Check out your physical appearance. You may not be happy with every part of your body—practically no one is. But you know you have some very nice features—maybe a straight nose or blue eyes or long hair or nice fingers or great legs or super skin. Everything good you can discover about yourself makes you attractive to more people—all the people who like that particular thing.

You're attracted to a certain type. Maybe tall men or short women. So are other people. There is someone looking for every asset you have.

Next list your nonphysical assets. Your ethnicity (say you're German or Italian) would make you attractive to certain people. Your nationality, your accent, your education, your religion, the part of the country you were born, the way you were raised.

Finally, list your special skills and abilities, the things you know you do well. It could be anything from cooking a special dish to sailing a boat. You could even list special possessions that are assets, like a bicycle or a great house, a bowling ball or a business.

Rate yourself for special intellectual abilities, for reading books, for hobbies, anything that would make you interesting to another person. Your character and your ability to love are also important assets. Your sensitivity. Even things you aren't can be assets. The fact that you're not a drug addict or an alcoholic, you don't have acne, aren't obese or too tall. If you're not deformed or don't have any crippling diseases—these are all attributes. Remember, even something you consider a terrible liability may be the very quality another person finds attractive.

If you do have things that you feel are detrimental—for instance, you happen to be a diabetic or think you're too short or too lazy or whatever—forget them. They don't belong in your assets inventory. Pretend you're auctioning yourself off, and you're pointing out all your assets to a potential buyer. Start with "He has teeth like pearls," or "She has the strength of an ox"—go from there. If you were trying to sell someone something you would play down its defects or even overlook them. Do yourself the same favor.

A divorced women's children can be assets. "Any man would be impressed with the beautiful children I've raised," not "Nobody wants a woman with kids." A man who's sterile should see that as an asset. Instead of "Nobody wants a sterile man," he should list among his assets, "A woman doesn't have to use risky birth control devices with me."

You'll find that many of the things you thought were irreparable deficits become assets when you look at them the right way. There's even an advantage to your new single state. The fact that you are free to do what you want, to see whom you want and even to be alone when you want are assets. The fact that you don't have to explain your actions or answer to anyone or even discuss what you want to do are all assets. You now have the power to make decisions for yourself. Your independence is an asset.

The Future Assets Inventory

This list is of your future probable assets or things you might do. It answers all the questions of what am I going to do now that I'm alone.

Your future assets inventory is broken into four different sections. Number each section separately.

1—Activities

Things I didn't do because my ex wasn't interested in them. This list could include skiing, disco dancing, scuba diving, poker, needlepoint, yoga or even getting a pet ("she" was afraid of dogs, "he" hated cats). List special vacation spots you always wanted to try but that were too hot or too cold or too far or too expensive when you were a couple.

List new things you'd like to experiment with, things you never did before but might like to try, like taking piano lessons, singing lessons, joining an acting group, learning to fly a plane, going to Europe, giving poetry readings or anything else you've always wanted to try but didn't because you knew you would have to do it alone. Politics or religion, hunting trips or garden parties, living at the beach (she burned) or the mountains (he sneezed)—what do you really want?

Now you can allow your son to be a flower child or an artist or a football hero and your daughter to be an athlete or a physicist or a ballerina. You can give your child sex education, dating advice and your personal philosophy of life.

List things you used to do but neglected because you were in love or too busy being half of a couple, like unfinished projects, redecorating, being active in a club. Are you a woman who gave up her career or a man who settled for a less enjoyable but secure one because of marital responsibilities? Have you neglected a skill like tennis or skiing? Think of the things you sacrificed, all the little things that used to give you joy and satisfaction.

2—Acquisitions

Things I want to get like a new stereo, a different apartment, a bicycle, a motorcycle, but didn't because we couldn't afford them or my ex didn't approve of them. Things you don't have to ask about now. Plants you couldn't keep around because your ex was allergic to them. The fun fur he wouldn't let you buy. The sailboat she said wasn't important. This is where you list all the material sacrifices you made during your old relationship. It could even be that you always lusted after blonds and your ex was a brunette, or fantasied a pink and lace bedroom when your ex loved wood and leather.

3–Acquaintances

Friends I've neglected because I was in love or because my ex didn't like them. Remember all those people you used to have fun with–until you gave them up. The single friends you neglected in your "couplehood."

4–Accomplishments

Things I can be now that I couldn't be before–a jet setter, a playboy, an athlete, a flirt. Change your image. Develop the ability to be spontaneous. What would you be if you could be anything or anyone? There's nobody to tell you how to dress now, how tight your pants should be, how sexy you should look or how dignified or what color you should wear. Is your secret ambition to become a belly dancer? Or a baseball player? Now you can. In the next chapter we will tell you how to exercise these new freedoms and actually become the person you could have been if you hadn't been confined in that old relationship.

The nice thing now is that you never know where you'll run into a good time, and you're free to enjoy it when it happens. You can even stay out all night if that's what you want to do. You don't have to spend time with anyone you don't want to.

Now that you have your list and know about all the things you've been missing, start doing those things. Get a date book. Find the tennis court, the diving shop, the crafts store. Call them and make appointments for lessons. Call those old friends. Make lunch dates. Call those people who always wanted to spend time with you, but who you really didn't have time for before. Ask your kids what they'd really like to do. Drive around in the middle of the night and see what it's like not to have to report in. Stay overnight somewhere, maybe at a friend's, or even a hotel or motel, and start exercising your new freedoms.

10
EXERCISING YOUR FREEDOM

Life is trouble, only death is not. To be alive is to undo your belt and look for trouble. . . . A man needs a little madness, or else he never dares cut the rope and be free.

—Nikos Kazantzakis
Zorba the Greek

The most important freedom that comes from shaking off the "monkey on the back" aspect of an old love affair is the freedom to go out and find a new one. Everybody knows that singles bars are boring and depressing, singles affairs and clubs are humiliating and matchmaking for money, even by computer, is embarrassing, expensive and unexciting.

The Letting Go method of exercising your freedom will bring new people to you without your having to do any of those frightening, self-depleting things. This week, you will begin reaching out to start new relationships—without anxiety.

THE TENTH WEEK

Session Nineteen: New Friends, Potential Lovers

Telephone Talk

Get out your phone book and start calling everyone you think will be glad to hear from you, no matter how long it's been. Tell them what happened, if you don't know what to talk about.

Get out your Crime Sheet and tell the stories of how awful your ex was and the terrible things they did, until even *you* get bored. Your close friends are bored by your stories and probably stifle sighs at each mention of your ex's name. Now you have a whole new audience.

Don't try to be "fair" or sound noble when you tell about your recent separation. You're not talking to his mother or her kids, but rather potential new relationship sources for you. If you insist that your ex wasn't so bad and that you really were to blame, nobody will believe you're ready for a new relationship. You'll convince everybody you talk to that no one they know, including themselves, could ever compete with the saintly spirit of your former relationship. Besides, those exciting "who hit who first" stories you have to tell are more interesting than your "how wonderful it was" martyrdom.

Remember, you're playing the odds. A lot of people are going to be busy, but if you call enough, you'll find your appointment book is filling up faster than you have time to shower and get ready. While you were part of a couple, most of your friends were probably couples, too. Don't skip calling couples you like just because you're a "single" now.

Couples often know unattached people. An extra man or woman at a party is a drag. It never hurts to let them know you're available. Couples love to have everyone safely attached and will try to see that you get that way as soon as possible. Make it clear that you're really interested in meeting someone new and better. Your "coupled" friends are certain to feel that any of their single friends are better than your ex, so let them prove it to you.

It's okay to tell people immediately when you call them that the reason you haven't talked to them for so long is because you were "committed," and that now you're not. Invite people to your house, a few at a time. If you "click" with someone special over the phone, ask them out. It's easy to say you got tickets to something or other.

People will reciprocate. Couples are more likely to invite you to their house than to come to you.

Make it clear that you're irrevocably through with your old relationship. A lot of people won't fix you up or take you out themselves if they're afraid you're going to go back to your ex and make them look silly. Once they're sure you're really through they'll tell you all kinds of terrible things about your ex.

In just a couple of weeks, you will get your chance to be nice to your ex (chapter twelve), but not now. It's as if you were gathering your own personal army of supporters—and having a common enemy will only consolidate your forces.

Embarrassing Questions

No matter how hard you try to avoid the people and the questions, you'll be caught eventually. Someone's sure to inadvertently ask you, "How're the kids?" when you haven't seen them for weeks. Or, "How's your golf game?" when "he" got the club membership in the divorce settlement.

"Do you still live in Beverly Hills? Or Scarsdale? Or wherever?" can come from any casual encounter. Keep your cool. A question from a stranger is no reason to start retelling the entire story. "No. She got the house, kids, dog or whatever. I got my freedom" is enough of an answer for anyone.

Or "No, he got the club membership, dog and yacht, and I got rid of him," is a shut-up-for-sure tactic. Beware of people who try to get you to feel bad by saying, "Oh, you must be so upset." Or, "How hurt you must have been." Shut these people up with the same kind of an answer.

Everybody gets hit at least once with "Was there another man/woman?" If you feel that the person is simply a gossip, the answer could be "It depends on which gossip you listen to." Another terrible question is "Why did you break up, divorce, etc.?" For an answer, prepare with self-instruction sentences (chapter nine) by saying, "I wasn't willing to give her babies and a house with a white picket fence." Or, "I wasn't willing to stay home and cook three meals a day." Or, "I wasn't willing to be treated as a possession." Or, "I didn't want to enter an open marriage, swinging, commune, etc."

Make a definite statement. You know what you are and aren't willing to do now and what you weren't willing to do before. There's nothing wrong with stating it to people. At worst, they'll think either you or your ex was wrong. At best, you'll be letting people know what you are not willing to put up with in a new relationship and eliminate the probability of repeating your mistakes. Even though you may think you would like to reverse your earlier stands on certain issues, the odds are your values really haven't changed and you're just hungry enough to pretend they have.

"Do you miss him/her?" or "Are you lonely now?" are loaded questions. Sure, everybody has twinges of loneliness now and then, times when they wish someone else was around. Don't let those little twinges and a stray remark about your ex get to you. The unspoken implication is that if you're lonely now, it's because you don't have your ex. That's not true. If you are lonely, it's only because you haven't gotten a replacement yet.

It's okay to admit you're lonely, but not that you're lonely for your old lover. Tell friends, "Sure, I'm lonely sometimes now that he/she is gone, but the loneliness is a small price for my freedom." Don't be shy about asking for help to overcome your lonely moments. "I get very lonely Tuesday nights. Why don't you come to the movies with me this Tuesday?" Or, "I get lonely when I eat dinner, why don't you have dinner with me on Thursday?" Or, "I'm not lonely, but I wish I had someone to go dancing with. Do you know any good dancers?" Or, "I miss having someone to play tennis with. Do you know anyone who plays?" That way you get to change the subject and make new connections at the same time. It's a nice way to let people know exactly what you want.

Dividing Up the Old Friends

Going through your phone book will show you how many friends you have that you think may really be your ex's friends and not yours. Because "he" or "she" may have introduced you to someone doesn't mean you can't keep the friendship—even old friends are introduced by someone. Don't worry about "taking over" you ex's friends.

Be good to yourself. Be selfish. If there's someone you especially like, don't feel shy about calling and setting up a social arrangement between just the two of you. If it works, fine. If not, forget it and go on to someone else.

People will try to stay on the fence to keep your friendship and your ex's. "No matter what you two do, I really want to be friends with both of you" is what they'll say. Unfortunately, that's an impossible situation. Eventually a loyalty test of some kind comes up (keeping a confidence or simply not indulging the urge to gossip) and choices have to be made. Someone's going to be hurt and disappointed, left feeling betrayed by a close friend. You're number one now, so let the fence straddlers stay friends with your ex.

Mutual friends, since they "mean well," will only carry stories back and forth and will never really be loyal friends to either of you. People caught in the middle can't help but keep secrets from you—either to protect you or to protect your ex. You need friends of your own, a loyal army without treason.

Turning Business to Pleasure

You don't have to date your secretary or co-worker or boss, but that doesn't mean you should overlook opportunities where you work. Smile at strangers in the elevator. Say "Good morning" each day and soon an interesting person on the elevator can become a friend. They'll begin to think they know you and you them. Familiarity is the first step.

Ride up and down at the same time each day. Go to the same lunch spot, if there are interesting people there. Sit at the counter alone. Don't read. If everyone at the counter is coupled, sit near an empty seat, or even have one on each side. That goes for bars, too. Sit in the light where you can be seen and, preferably, so you can see the door. Don't be afraid to smile at an interesting single you see come in.

Put an ad in the paper for some kind of help—secretarial, architectural or whatever. Interview people for jobs. Be interviewed, even if you're not looking for work. Get estimates for work you need done around the house. Call interior decorators. Any chore you need to do involving money can be double duty as a creative way to meet people.

A bachelor runs a regular ad for a live-in housekeeper on his ranch. He's run the ad for over a year and never hired anyone, but his social life is great. A divorced woman loves cars and spends days shopping the expensive showrooms and being courted by classy car salesmen.

Never play around with people you work with. If they work under you, you'll never get them to work as well again. They'll begin to come in late and expect extra goodies for the sex they're putting out. You can't yell at someone and expect to have a nice evening afterwards, either.

If you fool around with your boss, you risk your job. If your boss finds out you're involved with a co-worker, he'll be convinced your work is getting worse, even if it isn't, and you risk your job anyway.

Bosses make great lovers, but become demanding when they're in that much of a one-up position. You'll be expected to stay late on demand and with a smile. Having a boss-lover is like working for your father—they expect more and yell louder at your mistakes, thinking you should be perfect in bed and out.

Instead of looking in your very own business office, look at collateral events. Go to meetings, join associations, attend conventions, not for professional advancement but for social opportunities. If you sign up for a convention, forget about hearing the speakers. Spend most of your time wearing your badge in the social areas—by the registration desk, in the hospitality room, even in the restaurant where everybody eats.

If you meet people at a convention, don't go with them to hear a speaker. Instead, ask them to have lunch or a drink with you. Spend the afternoon at lunch or at the bar.

Pick societies and conventions that are one step down in the pecking order of your particular skill. If you're a high school teacher, go to an elementary school teacher's conference. If you're a computer programmer, go to a computer operator conclave. If you're a clinical psychologist, try the marriage counselor's gathering.

It's an unfair fact of life that women meet eligible men by attending affairs, meetings and conventions above the status of their jobs. A registered nurse would make out like gang busters at a doctor's convention, but probably wouldn't do too well at a practical nurses' meeting. Men meet more women by stepping down. In our sexist society, it's unfortunate, but true, the higher the status of the gathering, the more men you will find there. And the lower the status, the more women.

Ask people for advice. It's not like walking up to a stranger. You both have something in common. You have a badge with your name, and they have one, too. "Isn't this innovative, boring, stupid, great?" It doesn't really matter what you say. Anybody standing around the lobby instead of attending meetings is probably hoping somebody will talk to them. "Did you hear the last speaker?" Or, "Do you think tomorrow's seminar will be interesting?" Or, "Which are you planning to attend?"

Most people attend conventions alone. It's easy to ask an interesting person what sessions they're attending in the morning. "I'm going to that, too. Why don't we meet for breakfast at seven or eight or whatever?" Hopefully, you'll both wind up skipping the session. Nobody wants to eat alone. Breakfast may take all morning, and plans for the evening may arise as well.

Conventions have a party atmosphere, and people feel freer than they would under ordinary circumstances. Invite someone to your room for a drink or a room service meal, and chances are they'll accept. Being away from home in a hotel gives things a transitory quality, and people do things they wouldn't otherwise do.

The Podium Effect

If you play an instrument, take Music Appreciation One. If you're a social worker, arrange to speak at the probation officers' convention. You'll be looked up to there. If you're an administrator, attend the clerical convention. If you're a published author, go to the hopefuls' meeting. If you're accomplished in any field, there are people who want to be where you are. You'll have instant podium effect by speaking up at these groups. Your upgraded credentials will give your words extra credibility. You'll be noticed and admired. A well-known science fiction writer always lectures to writers' groups—especially college freshmen or housewives. He loves the podium effect.

Volunteer to help out. Just being at the registration desk or handing out folders gives you an important visibility. Wear a bright red dress or a suit if everyone is wearing jeans, or earthy guru outfits if the others are in cocktail, but make sure that your choice is consistent with your personality. Don't go formal if you're the surfer type. If it's hard for you to be "out of step" with the rest of the gang, you could always say, "I'm on my way to a business meeting," if everyone's in Levi's and you're wearing a suit. It's a good excuse to glamorously stand out without feeling self-conscious.

Session Twenty: Getting Unhooked

Defiance

You can defy the hold your former lover had on you by doing things you know would make them unhappy. Defiance is an active demonstration of your new freedom. By doing something your former lover wouldn't have liked, but that you have always wanted to do, you break the last links to your old mate. Your defiant act doesn't even have to be what you've always wanted to do. It could be something new that just came up—like a chance to go to a nudist camp or a new church!

Every recently separated person has trouble dividing their own likes and dislikes and even their own morality from those of their ex. People get and stay together because they have mutual values, and often, in a relationship, adopt each other's. Now you must find out what your very own likes and values are.

If your ex was overly cautious with your children and you think they'd like skiing or skydiving, take them! If your ex always wanted to spend vacations in the snow, and you wanted to go to the beach, go! If you always wanted to try deep-sea diving and your wife said that would be irresponsible for a family man, do it! If you always wanted to take belly dancing lessons and be sexy, but had a husband who was uptight, explore your inner need to gyrate.

Plan to do something adventurous, something you know your ex would have hated, refused to do and made a fuss if you did. Go off in a small plane if they were always afraid of small planes. Get a giant Doberman or police dog if your ex was afraid of dogs. Or a snake. Or a cat. You'll be amazed at the sudden light feeling of happiness and success.

Remember how good you felt when you took off your wedding ring, moved from the big house into a condo or even put your ex-lover's pictures in your Implosion Box? These are all defiances against your ex.

Take your son to ballet classes or on a survival trip. Show your cleavage if your ex always wanted it hidden. Go to Las Vegas and gamble if your ex thought it was sinful. The combination of doing something you've always wanted to do but couldn't do because your ex didn't approve is unbeatable. You'll feel better than a kid with the whole cookie jar in his hands. You'll also be getting out in the world and meeting people by doing things you want to do. You'll have fun, whether you meet anyone or not.

Defiance not only makes you feel good, it's another way to break the hook to your ex. Any assertive act inhibits anxiety. Your defiant act will inhibit your upset over your lost relationship. Finally you are attacking back. Your ego has been battered by your mate leaving you. Your act of defiance is your ego reasserting itself.

Defiance is freedom. You are no longer responding to what your ex wanted you to do or be. You are no longer acting in a way that you hope will please someone else, but rather in a way that you know will please you. Defiance breaks the connection.

Even after years of separation, people still find themselves shopping for the kinds of clothes their exes would have liked to see them wear, or even thinking about what "he" or "she" would like when they decide what to wear.

Defiance is wearing what you want. Go all the way in the opposite direction if you want. You'll discover your own style, develop your own tastes, likes and dislikes.

People used to "someone waiting at home" still feel guilty when they are out late at night or all night, even when no one is expecting them. They still have the urge to make up a story or hide the fact that they're dating, even years after their divorce. Now you can cover your walls with pictures of your lovers, display favorite photos and gifts, even leave *The Joy of Sex* on your coffee table, or *Playboy,* or *Ms. Magazine.*

Even if you don't really feel like doing anything your ex wouldn't have approved of, it's important that you do something anyway. Start with something small. Perhaps a "no-no" extravagance. Paint the house a color your ex hated. Buy something "he" or "she" thought you didn't need.

Defiance is a silent offense. You don't have to tell your ex what you did, but you'll know.

Suppose your ex-wife discovers you took your son to the racetrack or a ballet class. So what? You know she wouldn't like it and you don't care. She's already done the worst thing she could possibly have done to you, and you've survived.

Suppose your ex-husband finds out you had an intimate lunch with a man he hates, someone he forbade you to associate with. So what? It really doesn't matter.

Show your freedom by defiance. Don't worry about what your ex will think. Do it anyway, and enjoy it. The worst consequence is that you'll make your ex angry. So what!

Why not make the person who hurt you angry? It's obvious

that they don't care about you anymore from the way they've treated you. Defiance is a way for you to get even and to advance yourself at the same time. By resolving never to give up anything because your ex will be angry, you can go forward with your own life and career.

Doing the defiant action, whether you feel confident about it or not, will give you the feeling. In other words, suppose you don't feel like being defiant, like making your ex angry. Do it anyway, and you *will* feel like it. Before Stanislavski invented the "Method" school of acting, all actors were "technical" actors. They put the costumes and makeup on and made the gestures, and then the feelings came, the character appeared. Strike the attitude, and people will believe you. More important, you will, too.

Goodies

There were lots of things you got from your former mate (and thought no one else could give as well). You may still not have found anyone who can give you those things as well as your ex could, but have you really tried getting them for yourself? You know what you want better than anyone else. You can get your own goodies or arrange to have someone give them to you. You don't have to wait for an offer.

You know it's tacky to miss the material things you had when you pooled your resources, but you do. When you were a couple you always had front-row tickets at the best shows in town, invitations to all the most exciting parties, a marvelous house at the beach, a snazzy sports car, clubhouse seats at the track and memberships in all the best clubs. Awful as it seems, you do miss those things, sometimes long after you've stopped missing your ex. Maybe it's his horse you miss, or her kids, or his ranch, or her house in the country. Or having a dog, or a backyard to sunbathe in, or just someplace to go. Maybe it was the way she massaged your feet or he rubbed your back, or her cooking, or his gardening, or "her" hostessing, or "his" fix-it abilities.

Whatever the material things are that you still miss you can get for yourself. If it's ethnic restaurants, find them and take someone else. If it's backpacking, join a group of backpackers. Put your mind to it, and you can even one-better your ex's ability to provide whatever it was that they gave you. If it was a cabin in the woods that you liked to visit, find one that is on a lake in the woods. If it's a dog, get a better one. If it's the way he kept up your garden, hire a pro. If it's her cooking, have a meal catered.

Not only won't you miss your ex providing these things, but you'll find that your life is so full, you don't have time to get them all. Don't feel shy about hiring people to provide what your ex gave. Paying in money is often cheaper than paying in other ways.

Make a checklist of the goodies you miss and see if you can figure out ways to get them without having your ex involved. One woman reported that she missed a particular dog. She finally bought the dog from her ex, and now she's happy. A man reported that he missed having his girlfriend type letters for him. He realized when he hired a typist that his ex had only typed five letters in all the time they'd known each other, and those were full of mistakes. Also, he'd always taken her out to dinner (nicely) every time she typed a letter. At twenty to forty dollars an evening, those were much more expensive letters than he'd ever realized.

The truth is that you can get front-row seats for yourself if you really try. On a budget? Buy balcony seats and move to the empty front row after intermission. You can get anything you want without your ex, and getting it for yourself builds your self-esteem. Being self-reliant keeps you from getting hooked by dependency needs.

Starting this week, make a list of the good things you've done for yourself. You may be surprised to find that you have done a lot of things for other people, but nothing for yourself. If so, your assignment is to do something absolutely selfish. Buy yourself something that nobody else can use. Take yourself somewhere you've always wanted to go.

The only prerequisite for your *weekly* "What I did for myself this week" list is that you have done something that will make you feel good, and that it be directly for you. Giving gifts doesn't count, unless you give yourself one, too. Taking a friend out to dinner counts only if you go where you've always wanted to go.

Making this a weekly assignment keeps you from getting into that old role of passive participant in life—the one who simply waits, taking goodies as other people hand them out. Now the responsibility is yours. You're the one who makes it happen. You give out your own goodies.

Once you give up the idea that only your ex could give you certain things or do certain things for you, you'll find that there are people who would be eager to do those same things for you. You now have something to offer in return—yourself. Having other people do things for you can also be included in your weekly list. Accepting an invitation to a party is doing something good for yourself. Having a cleaning person for the day is doing something for yourself.

There are lots of people who would like to have your friendship, your affection and maybe even a number-one relationship with you. They'll be glad to do things with you and for you.

Other people will want something back for the things they do, and that's okay, too. Suppose your ex always drove you everywhere. Now you're invited to a party, you have night blindness, and there's no one to drive you. See if you can bring an extra guest. Then you'll find that it's easy to find a driver—because you're offering a party in return.

Take yourself to the gym, buy a new dress, stick to your diet or even just ride your bicycle on a Sunday afternoon.

Work at making yourself more physically attractive to yourself and to others. Make it a goal to be able to stand in front of a full-length mirror naked and like what you see. Find a part of your body that you feel is really terrific—a good knee, a nice curve, a hard calf. If you turn on to yourself, others will turn on to you, too.

Do whatever it takes to be the person you want to be. If it involves losing weight, go to a doctor and lose a significant amount. Drop several sizes and at least twenty pounds. Most newly separated people discover that they suddenly feel fat. If that happens to you, lose the excess as soon as possible. While you're in the process of losing weight, give your old clothes to a friend or a tax-deductible charity. Take your favorites to a real tailor, suck in your tummy and have them meticulously done over. If you're flush, buy new ones that match your new image.

You are now free to become the fantastic beautiful person you've always wanted to be. When you do, the good feedback you get will inspire you to stay that way. . . .

If you have sex problems that require treatment beyond the therapy in chapter five, see a licensed, reputable therapist now.

Don't think of yourself as without a relationship right now, but rather between relationships. This may be your only real chance to go to the gym and work out or to stick to a no-dinner-date-diet that will really take weight off fast. How lucky you are to have the opportunity to present a whole new self when you find your new relationship. Don't waste time. The next person you meet could be "the one." Remember, you'd never be able to get yourself in shape if you were still eating those big "together" dinners every night, and you wouldn't go to the gym every day if you had someone waiting at home.

In chapter eleven you'll find out how to fall in love again when you do meet someone. After all, you'll want to be ready.

If you've always thought a new nose was the thing you really needed, take a few weeks now and get one. Maybe it's a face lift, or an emotional lift.

This is when you should devote yourself to your own improvement. Treat yourself to whatever it takes to make you the most attractive person you can be. If you have trouble meeting people, sign up for an assertion training course. If you have phobias, find a behavioral psychologist who specializes in desensitizing you to whatever frightens you.

Pampering yourself is okay now because you're not doing it for your ex, and you're not doing it to get over pain or as a substitute for love. Pampering yourself is okay now because it's part of learning to love yourself.

Upgrade your image. Get a jazzy sports car or a new paint job on your old one. Buy new clothes. Get a new hairdo. If you think you don't have time for yourself now that you have to do all those little chores the ex did, like taking clothes to the cleaners, or picking up the kids, or cleaning the house, hire someone. Don't be cheap and deny your own self-fulfillment.

Remember a few months ago you would have been willing to pay much more if someone would take away the pain you were feeling. Certainly you deserve to spend as much on your happiness.

It may seem outrageously frivolous, but you deserve it. Go to a hair stylist or beauty salon instead of a barber or doing it yourself. Have a manicure. Vacation at a health resort. Think of it as an investment in yourself. Statistically, good-looking people earn more money, are happier and more successful.

As you get better looking, the temptation to show off to your ex, just so they can see what they missed out on, is overwhelming. Don't do it. In chapter twelve you will get your chance, without risking any of the good work you've done so far.

11
ERROL FLYNN

I haven't got time for the pain
I haven't got room for the pain
I haven't the need for the pain
Not since I've known you

—Carly Simon and Jacob Brackman
"Haven't Got Time for the Pain"

Only an Errol Flynn type can throw himself into a new relationship when the last one ended so disastrously. A bad experience in a previous relationship can keep you from finding a new one because you are afraid you won't be able to survive another breakup. The truth is that you have survived this one and the next won't be so hard, but even in the best of circumstances, falling in love again is scary.

THE ELEVENTH WEEK

Session Twenty-One: Love Holdouts

Newly separated people usually fall into two categories when it comes to forming new relationships: doomsayers and colluders. Doomsayers are still frightened because of their previous bad experiences. They are love phobics constantly looking for signs that the new relationship is going to end badly.

Doomsayers

He may throw his clothes off and expect you to pick them up. The female love phobic automatically assumes her newfound friend is a male chauvinist in disguise, that he will soon be telling her what friends she should have and how to spend her money. If he also leaves the toilet seat up and doesn't put his dishes in the sink, she will silently write him off.

She might take your mail in for you and hold back the swanky mail order catalogue from Neiman Marcus, handing you the bills. The male love phobic decides his new lady friend is really a "gold digger" who will soon be telling him what to buy her and wanting property in both names. If she also admires expensive jewelry in store windows and she's always wanted to belong to a country club, he'll cross out her number from his book.

Colluders

The second danger for the newly separated is what Dr. George Bach calls "collusion." He can take the morning paper, leave the tops off the jelly jars, criticize your housekeeping, want you to cook for him and bring him coffee in bed in the morning. She can look at each piece of mail and make comments, expect you to pay for everything and buy her presents, too, and send away for travel folders to exotic places.

The colluder is so hungry, so lonely and hates sleeping alone so much that it doesn't matter what a new person does, as long as they're there. There are inherent dangers in collusion.

When you overlook lots of little things that someone does, just to maintain a relationship, eventually that person is going to do one little thing that's "over your line" and you'll blow up. Your new friend is chronically late, which you hate but choose to overlook. Or uses your belongings without asking. Or begins to restrict your personal freedom, asking where you're going and when you'll be back and who you'll be with. Or breaks dates at the last minute. Or criticizes your cherished ideals.

If you choose to ignore certain flaws in your new mate, you become guilty of collusion. You don't say anything about what's upsetting you because you're afraid of endangering your relationship—and you just couldn't take it if you lost another potential lover right now. By not saying anything, you give your silent permission to the other person to continue in the behavior that is annoying to you.

If your new lover wants to have an "open relationship" and you agree (by not saying "no"), when deep down you are consumed by anger and jealousy, you have colluded. One night, you phone your new lover and are politely informed "Tonight's Alice's (or Joe's) night, and we're right in the middle of things, can I call you later?" Again, you bite your tongue, swallow your bile and say, "Sure."

The next time you have a date, you run into Alice or Joe leaving just as you are knocking on the door with flowers and happy anticipations. You fling the flowers at your puzzled friend, shout invectives that can be heard for miles and storm away. To you, it may seem like "the straw that broke the camel's back," but the truth is that you asked for it.

By giving silent permission, you haven't drawn your own boundary lines. You have cheated yourself and your friend of a potentially loving relationship. By colluding, pretending everything was okay when you knew all along it wasn't, you have allowed that other person to take intolerable liberties with your inner beliefs. You feel violated, but by concealing the "real" you to preserve an unrealistic relationship, you have really violated the confidence of your new friend.

Remember, you're the one who acted as if you really liked everything that was going on, as if it was "cool" and you were someone other than who you really are. You have influenced the new person in your life to behave in a manner that is unacceptable to you by your collusion. You have also set up unfulfilled expectations in that person.

Your new lover can't imagine why you are so upset. To them, it was just one more liberty. To you, it was *the* one you couldn't handle. How were they to know? The only one who could have even hinted at your true values and ideals was you, and you chose to collude.

Your new lover expected you to be just as "cool" about seeing another woman or man on their way out as you were about the "open relationship" in the beginning.

Collusion can take place on many levels. Sure you thought it was cute the way her undies and clothing were scattered all over her house. And at first, you pretended it was "cool" and that as a liberated man you understood her aversion to housework. You lived up to her expectations and led her to believe you liked her just the way she was.

She spends a few weekends (with her dog) at your place, and suddenly it looks like hers. You go along, acting like you love her and her dog, too, until one night your nostrils are assaulted by the same unmistakable odor that permeates her house. And there she sits on the porch. She's still wearing that naughty little nighty that turned you on so much last night. "Oh," she smiles as you point out the mushy pile on your living room rug, "I'm waiting for it to dry. Then it'll pick right up."

It's easy to see why she doesn't understand your outrage. How was she to know that dog shit was "over your line"? Surrounded by buzzing green bottle flies and "that" odor, you tell her to leave, it's all over. You wonder how she could have done that to you.

Women, who are traditionally passive and who (according to our sexist society) must wait for the man to initiate contact, are the most guilty of all colluders. Since it's usually at his option that she sees him, women tend to overlook more than men will. "After all," she imagines, "if I tell him what I'm really like, he may not call again." A woman who is worried about having a social life or cares a lot about being taken out often feels forced to collude, to "put up with" things she hates. In a coupled society, there's safety and a date every Saturday night, if she can only keep her mouth shut and pretend he's really perfect.

His constant talking about other women in his life might be frightening and make her feel inadequate, but she doesn't say anything. He may drink too much, become boisterous and boring at the end of every date and unable to participate sexually, but she submerges her sex urge and never says anything. After all, he does have all those other women just waiting, and he lets her know it.

At first, she likes his easygoing, anything-for-a-laugh attitude. She overlooks it when he begins to demand his clean socks, expects her to be available all the time and just pops by on the spur of the moment. Secretly, she's flattered.

He's not exactly what she had in mind, but it's better than being alone. She's understanding when he wants to watch the football game and even pretends to be interested herself. She hates rock music, but never mentions it when he turns the stereo up loud at her apartment. She tries to keep her cool, being the perfect "total woman." He answers her telephone during the game one Sunday afternoon and whoops, "Barbara's bordello, she's tied up right now." Only this time, it's her mother calling about a family emergency, and it's not funny. She blows up, and he doesn't know why. Once again, collusion doesn't pay.

Right now you may be starving for love and affection. You may decide that you can overlook "little things," maybe even basic, obvious differences in beliefs and values. Being alone is too tough right now, so you "put up" with the things you wouldn't tolerate under other circumstances. You try to change, to mold yourself into the other person's way of life, to fit in with them.

A few months of lonely barhopping and a man begins to capitulate. Sure he felt stifled, restricted, a prisoner in his old relationship. Sure he wanted a woman who would give him space, who he could be his own person with. Then he meets an old-fashioned girl with old-fashioned values. She bakes bread, and it smells good. The house is warm with her presence, and he imagines he will change. The domestic tranquility that dulled his intellect in his old relationship might be okay after all. Maybe he really should settle down, become a one-woman man and raise a family. The women he really wanted don't exist after all, so this one will have to do.

Three or four weekends go by without a date and a woman begins to capitulate. It's no fun to go anywhere and watch those obviously "in love" couples cuddling together when she doesn't have anybody. Sure, she wanted a man who would make a commitment to her this time, who would give her security, love, a house, babies, and even that big wedding with all her friends and family there. She meets a tennis pro who's living in his van and trying to break into the circuit by giving lessons. He's handsome, has a good body and thinks she's just the greatest. The other side of her bed has been empty for a long time, and she feels great in public now when he puts his arm around her and pulls her to him despite his minimal earning capacity and obvious unsuitability for a long-term relationship. After all, the perfect mate may never turn up, and as long as she doesn't make any demands, she'll still have an arm around her shoulders at the movies. Maybe she'll become a liberated woman instead of a mommy, she thinks.

The choice is yours, but you must recognize the price if you do decide to collude out of hunger or loneliness. You can indulge your inclinations to have a relationship—any relationship. You can try to change; you can give up your dreams of what you really want in another person. But it's important to recognize the consequences of your choice.

At some point in the future, when you're not as needy, when you're not missing the "coupled" feeling, the compromises you've been making combined with the minor issues you've been overlooking are going to become too much, just like they did in your last relationship either for you or your partner. You will have set up expectations in your partner that you will behave and react in certain ways and they in turn may behave and act in a manner you have pretended to like.

Recognizing that their "colluding" capabilities are enormous and seeing how destructive it has been in the past, many newly separated people vow *never* to collude again. There have been so many disillusionments in the past that they become inflexible.

The slightest infraction, and a new lover is crossed off their potential relationship list. Reformed colluders do not have to behave like reformed alcoholics, never taking a drink (or a chance in a relationship) again. There are other options besides cutting off all chance of having a relationship develop when you discover that your new lover does things that are intolerable to you.

In the past, every time you've lied to someone, pretended to be someone you're not, put up with something you hate, overlooked something you really didn't like, bit your tongue or walked on eggshells so you wouldn't rock the relationship boat, it's been a disaster. Being untrue to your inner self has left you frustrated and unhappy and destroyed the relationship in the end anyway. This time, you vow, you won't "put up with" things just to maintain a relationship. The first time you see something you don't like, that's it.

You assume that dating a pet owner will lead to dog mess on the living room carpet. Dating a beer drinker means an impotent drunk in your bed forever. "Never again," you think, sending what might be your next "soulmate" out of your life forever.

Collusion doesn't work. Sending everyone who shows the possibility of future disappointment out of your life doesn't either. You'll never find a "perfect" person. You could become so sensitive to every little fault even remotely connected with a past disappointment that you will never fall in love again.

Before you start falling in love again, you will be prepared to handle any possible shocks or disappointments by using the behavior technique of Stress Inoculation developed by Dr. Donald Meichenbaum at Waterloo University in Canada. Just as a child is inoculated against measles, you will be inoculated and made immune to the frightening stresses (either real or imagined) of your potential new relationship.

Right now, you may even know someone who just might be interesting to you, who might be someone you could fall in love with, if you weren't holding back so much. "I'm waiting to see if I really like him/her," or "I'm waiting to see if they really like me," or "I don't want another situation like the last one" are all love holdout thoughts.

Overcoming Love Phobias

Stress Inoculation can help you overcome the anxieties that may be making you a love holdout. If you knew you were going to a country where there was a chance of a diphtheria breakout, you would inoculate or vaccinate your body against the disease before you went. You can also inoculate yourself against "love stress" the same way.

You may have already used a form of Stress Inoculation in your everyday life. A wedding rehearsal is Stress Inoculation for the anxieties and last-minute tensions of a wedding. In the military, a form of Stress Inoculation is used to prepare for capture by the enemy. Soldiers are actually rehearsed in the correct answers if they are captured, interrogated and even tortured. A play dress rehearsal is a form of Stress Inoculation, in that not only are the lines practiced, but the stage fright is dissipated.

Even though your potential new relationship hasn't caused you any problems yet, you are imagining them happening. Imagining an event has the same effect on you as the actual event happening. Remember the airplane phobic who became frightened at the *thought* of flying in an airplane?

Stress Inoculation

Using desensitization, a psychologist might ask an airplane phobic to imagine a frightening experience that he has already had, like taking off in an airplane, in steps that take him closer and closer to actually getting in an airplane and taking off. Desensitization works best when a person remembers experiences that were frightening.

Desensitization is the gradual reintroduction of a frightening situation under controlled, relaxed circumstances (in a psychologist's office). Stress Inoculation is used to prepare people for future frightening events that they have not experienced, such as a new lover leaving. Stress Inoculation uses the same basic techniques as desensitization, but works for those fears you have about what "might" happen if you fall in love again with a new person.

Often when a person has had bad experiences in an old love relationship, they develop fear about getting into a new one. Even though the new relationship is with a different person who would never do the same things the old lover did and who relates and interacts differently than the old lover, the projected fears still exist.

When you become involved with a new person, you relate in a new way, and the new relationship has new problems. You are probably already mentally preparing for the worst by imagining all kinds of terrible catastrophes that could happen in your new relationship.

Separation Anxiety

What do you imagine could go wrong with your new relationship? Your old lover may have been a dumb but gorgeous blond who was lured away by a ski instructor with a chalet in the mountains. Or a singer who went to travel the country with a rock band and was more interested in groupies than you. Chances are pretty slim that you would have those same problems with a new person.

Your new lady friend could be a bright brunette instead of that gorgeous but frivolous blond. Instead of risking loss by a ski instructor, you are afraid she'll find you too intellectually lacking. The exciting new male in your life could be an athlete, and you may fear he'll leave you because you can't keep up jogging. The new relationship situation is full of new, intimidating situations, and you imagine them all happening, leaving you heartsick and rejected all over again. Your imagined fears keep you from starting a new relationship and falling in love again.

Scene Cards

To start your Stress Inoculation, write scenes that you imagine might happen in your new relationship. Put each possible traumatic event that you think could happen on a separate index card.

For each scene, imagine yourself and that particular new person in your life. Where are you? What are the circumstances? What is happening? What are you wearing? What did the new person do or say in your imaginary scene? What is the hurtful outcome? Make the scene vivid. Don't get involved with your emotional response to the scene at this point—concentrate instead on the stimulus.

Fear of Intimacy

As Dr. Irene Kassorla discovered, many people don't even allow themselves to get to know a new person well enough to develop fears about a new relationship. They are the people who are afraid of new relationships in general. If you still haven't been able to meet someone who interests you and who offers the possibility of a new relationship, you may be developing a love phobia.

"I won't get involved," says the love phobic, "because I know that if I do start a new relationship, it, too, will break up just like the last one. I will be hurt again." Some people start a new relationship, but keep it shallow. Their fear is even more common. It is the fear of intimacy.

If you feel that way, put the circumstances of the imagined breakup on your scene cards. How will the new relationship break up? What do you imagine will happen? Why will a new lover leave you? Your avoidance of a relationship is also a phobia. Ask yourself, what is the scene that makes me afraid of new relationships?

The answer may be that the new person will leave. Or "We'll have a fight" or "The relationship simply deteriorates." Imagine the fight on your scene card. What are some of the things the fight might be about? Imagine a series of little "relationship deteriorating" scenes.

You may fear your own reactions to another person, that you would be the one to make the relationship deteriorate because of your own intolerances that make little things annoying to you. What are your intolerances? What are the little things you can't stand? Imagine a new person doing each of those things on separate scene cards.

On each scene card, imagine your behavioral response to the annoying occurrence. Suppose you can't stand a person who sleeps late every morning, and your new relationship turns out to be with a "night person"? Sure, you feel that you won't like that person anymore eventually, but imagine your immediate reaction. What would you do when it got to be midnight and you were the only one ready to go to bed?

Suppose you've never been impotent before, but your last breakup left you occasionally impotent. Now you anticipate being impotent with your next lover. Of course you're afraid. And this is a new fear. Set up scene cards for that, too.

How will the impotence happen? Write a script for it.

Or suppose you're afraid the new relationship will end, so you avoid real intimacy—like a classic phobic. You need to write down the scenes of how you imagine the breakup will happen.

It might be that while you are walking on the beach one morning as you always do, he seems distant, in serious thought, and simply walks away. Or is it that you'll have a fight? What will the fight be about?

Or you'll become annoyed by the responsibility of his or her constant presence. What do you anticipate you might actually do? Would you create a fight over something mundane like leaving the toilet seat up or pulling apart the morning paper? Is that how it would start?

A SAMPLE SCENE CARD HIERARCHY

Jamie asks for his morning coffee. He's in bed. I perk fresh coffee and bring it to him. He doesn't say thanks. In fact, he says nothing, reaching for my morning paper and handing me the women's section. I throw a fit, tell him he's around too much "and I'm not your fucking maid. You're intruding in my life, taking and not contributing." Jamie silently gets up, gets dressed and storms out, slamming the door.

Next card:

I am pacing the house most of the day, waiting for his call.

It's evening. The phone rings. I jump to answer it and it's my friend Mary. I am short with her because I want to get her off the phone in case he's trying to call. She's obviously put off by my lack of willingness to hear her. It's midnight and he hasn't called. I can't even call Mary because I know she's mad at me.

Next card:

I track down Jamie to apologize and try to get him to make up. He patronizingly says, "It's okay. I'll see you around. Talk to you soon." I know it's over.

Another hierarchy could be "She suddenly suggests moving in." Or, "She begins to ask what time I'll be back and where I'll be. She nags about my taking her for granted. I blow up at her. She cries and sobs, 'I've had enough abuse,' packs her things and quietly leaves."

Or, "I find evidence of an affair. She's been breaking dates regularly, and his razor is in her bathroom. I see them together in a restaurant." Get specific. How are they acting toward each other? What does he look like, how does he dress, what kind of car does he drive?

It may be hard for you to imagine this with a new lover, but whatever your area of vulnerability, make up the vivid scene cards anyway, placing any new person you've met in the role of antagonist. Be a scriptwriter. Make up dialogue. Write down their lines and yours. Describe the scene, the setting, where it's taking place.

One scene per card. Then sort the cards into a hierarchy set, the least frightening card on top and the most frightening at the bottom of the pile. For instance, the first card might be "He always leaves the jelly jars uncovered and his dishes on the table, in spite of my repeated requests," and the last, "He splits in the middle of the night without an explanation."

Or "One Monday morning over breakfast, she announces she was invited to go skiing over the weekend," to the last card, "She announces she's marrying a movie star she met on the slopes."

It's normal to be afraid when you see someone new doing something that annoys you. "This is just the beginning," you assume. "It's sure to get worse. Maybe I should cut off my feelings right now." Those are the thoughts and fears that keep people from falling in love. Using Stress Inoculation, you can prepare yourself ahead of time for what you imagine might happen after you fall in love with the new person and "things start to get worse."

Being prepared and having already dealt with the worst thing in your scene cards makes handling your inflated fears easier. Dangers exist for you in forming a new relationship, but the greatest are not the ones you think. The danger isn't that your new lover will leave, but that you'll avoid getting close for fear of losing in the end.

Using the technique of Stress Inoculation, you can not only get prepared for the worst—that the new person in your life will leave you—but you can also become genuinely comfortable with what you consider adverse qualities of new lovers and overcome your fear of new relationships.

By using the Stress Inoculation card system, you can actually learn to relax among her dirty dishes or his smelly socks. If soldiers can stand up to enemy torture without divulging classified information, you can make yourself immune to the indignities and discomforts that frighten you about your new relationship.

Your scene cards should start with the first small infraction. "He watches the waitress in a restaurant. She's wearing a short skirt and a low-cut blouse." When you get comfortable with that one, "He asks the waitress's name and what hours she works." All the way to "He brings the waitress home and makes love to her in front of me."

"She left the lid off the toothpaste tube" could be the first infringement that starts your cards. "She has her stuff all over the bathroom," when you feel all right about the toothpaste. "She spilled a drink and ruined the top of my table, the only thing I have that was handed down to me from my dead mother" might be next, and finally, "There are bugs all over the kitchen floor from the food she left out too long."

It could take twenty or more scene cards to get to that final scene of indignity you imagine might take place, but if you are comfortable with each scene before you go on to the next one, Stress Inoculation will make you immune to the most outrageous, even life-threatening and sanity-endangering things your new lover could do.

Soon you will no longer find yourself "walking on eggshells" or "biting your tongue" or even overlooking disturbing actions by your new lover. You will have become so immune that these things no longer faze you. Your sensitivity to the stress is wiped out, and you are free to discover the human being underneath the superficial. You can relate on a more intimate level because you have removed the blocks that have caused you to cut off loving.

Lots of men leave toilet seats up, and lots of women leave hair on their brushes. There are more important things to discover in a new person, but first you have to become immune to the little sensitivities you've developed, the annoyances that send your love barriers up and make you cut off relationships before they fully develop.

You're the one who's bothered by the hairy hairbrush or the uplifted toilet seat. It's really your hang-up that's keeping distance between you and a person you may want to relate to, and you're the one who has to overcome it. Instead of worrying about changing the other person to fit your mold, get rid of your hang-ups so you can discover the really important compatibilities that make a relationship work.

Just as all blonds are not dumb and not all brunettes are intelligent, not all men who look at waitresses act on their impulses. Unfortunately, the first time your new blond girlfriend does something not so bright, you may decide that, like your former blond girlfriend, she too will become intolerably dull and boring. And the first time your new boyfriend turns on the football game, you may want to write him off as another male chauvinist jock who will soon be ordering you out to the kitchen for another beer. It's your fear that things will get worse, the things you imagine *might* happen, not the thing the person has actually done, that is upsetting you.

There must be something that really attracts you about the new person in spite of your fear. You feel they might become an important relationship in your life, and you know you already like the person or you wouldn't be worried about what could go wrong. What really attracts you to that person and makes you want to put up with the problems? It could be sex, beauty, brawn, brains, sensitivity or some inner feeling that you "belong" together; but whatever it is, isn't it worth it to get past your hang-up to find out if this is indeed a person you would want in your life for a long time? Don't let your insecurities cheat you out of a chance for a good relationship.

Learning to Relax

Put your Stress Inoculation scene cards in order, starting with the least difficult for you to handle. Then relax! If you can't, learn how. Use yoga, self-hypnosis, meditation or any other technique. Make sure there is no tension anywhere in your body. Test each part. Purposefully tense and then relax everything from your fingers to your toes.

If you haven't experienced a relaxed state before, sit down in a comfortable easy chair and actually try to get in touch with the various parts of your body. Sense exactly where your tension is. Your neck? Your back? Your stomach?

All adults feel tension compared to the relaxed state of a child. Even when an adult sleeps, he has tension in various parts of his body. Are your shoulders relaxed, your upper arms, your chin, your jaw, your eyes?

Wherever you feel tension, tense that part of your body even more. If your fingers are tense, tense your hand, clench it into a fist until it hurts. Hold the tension as long you can. Then let go. Relax. Like a rubber band that is stretched as far as it can go and then released, your tense spot will relax completely.

Pay attention to the new relaxed sensation in your body. Remember how it feels to relax. Check other spots and make sure your entire body is as relaxed as the one you just tensed and relaxed. If you have other tension hot spots, repeat the process until they are all gone. Really experience the difference between how your body feels relaxed and how it felt tensed. If you can't remember, start again.

When your body reaches a state of total relaxation, your mind will also be at rest. Mental tension causes physical tension. By getting rid of the physical tension, you send relaxation signals to your brain and relax that, too.

When you are totally relaxed, take out the scene cards depicting events in your new relationship that you're afraid might happen. Start with the least anxiety-producing scenes. Read the card and actually imagine the new person acting out the scene with you in it.

Your deep fear may be that the other person will leave you and you'll be hurt. You may imagine yourself sitting alone and crying, but that's not the scene. The scene is the very first event that leads to what you imagine will be the eventual breakup of the relationship. It could be the new person in your life telling you that they won't be able to see you next weekend or calling to break a date.

The sad and lonely feelings that you imagine yourself experiencing don't belong on a scene card. Sad and lonely feelings are the emotional response to what has happened to you. Your scene cards are the actual events that start your response (sad feelings). The scenes (what happens to you) are the stimuli and have nothing to do with your reaction, which may or may not be realistically in proportion to the stimuli. You could get hysterical because your new lover "wasn't in the mood" one night, but that would be your emotional reaction to the stimulus. Your new lover actually in your bed, telling you they weren't in the mood, would be the stimulus. That's what belongs on the scene card.

The feelings you have are important. Those feelings are the gauge by which you put your cards in hierarchical order. Your emotional reaction decides which scene is least frightening and which is most frightening. Your individual response will vary from other people's even with the same stimuli. One person could turn over and go to sleep, happily accepting "I'm not in the mood." For another, "I'm not in the mood" could feel like a prelude to "I don't love you anymore." Stack your cards according to your own personal feelings. What is the thing that would upset you the least? Put that card on top. The most? That card goes on the bottom.

Your scene is the actual stimulus, the thing that happens to you in the world that makes you feel upset. It's the stimulus that starts your being frightened about your new relationship, the scene that triggers you to imagine something far worse.

The scene must relate to a particular person. Obviously, you won't have the same exact scene with your new lover that you had with your old one. They are different people. They speak differently and say things in different ways, have different actions and reactions. Put your new lover's voice and words in the scene.

SAMPLE "DATING" CARD HIERARCHY

Your first card might be: (Name) calls and cancels a date. The excuse is a good one. *Or it might be:* (Name) doesn't call when he/she said he/she would.

Card Two could be: (Name) breaks a date with a really feeble excuse.

Card Three could be: (Name) doesn't show up for a date and when you call, he/she says he/she forgot.

Card Four: Another broken date. This time the excuse is that he/she had something important come up and will discuss it with you next week.

Card Five: You call and he/she says, "I've been thinking about us. Let me call you when I get a chance."

Card Six: He/she says, "Let me get a chance to miss you."

Card Seven: You finally call and he/she says, "I'm really serious about this new person I met."

Card Eight: "I'm getting married."

SAMPLE "IN LOVE" HIERARCHY

Card One: You have pledged love and commitment. You haven't been out with anyone else for months. You go to a party and he/she responds to a stranger's attentions.

Card Two: He/she gets a call while you are there. It's obvious they don't want to talk in front of you.

Card Three: You are living together. Someone calls and hangs up when you answer.

Card Four: He/she slips and calls you by someone else's name.

Card Five: He/she shows up with an expensive piece of jewelry you didn't give them and know they can't afford.

Card Six: He/she tells you they have to go away next weekend.

Card Seven: He/she becomes morose, refuses to tell you what's wrong and says they want some time alone.

Card Eight: He/she moves in with someone else and refuses to talk to you or see you.

Stress Inoculation can free you from either of two limiting possibilities in your new relationship.

1. That you will collude out of hunger, a relationship-limiting device because whatever is irritating you will be bound to crop up later.

2. That you will be so love phobic your new relationship will be limited because you panic at the first sign of discord.

If you have decided that you do want a coupled "in love" relationship, Stress Inoculation will keep your old bad experiences from interfering with your desires.

Even if you choose not to fall in love, you may want to use Stress Inoculation against the "fears" of being single: not having a date, being lonely, feeling left out, always looking.

Stress Inoculation can free you to make a choice about a new love relationship and keep it from disintegrating because of your leftover bad feelings and the relationship phobias you may have developed.

How To Do Stress Inoculation

1. Put one frightening or anxiety-causing scene on each of your cards.

2. Put your cards in order starting with the least anxiety-producing scene as card one on the top of the pile and progressing to the most stressful scene,. numbering them consecutively. Your highest-numbered card will be the highest anxiety-producing scene and belongs on the bottom of the pile.

3. Lie down in a comfortable position and relax, using the techniques described earlier or any other relaxation techniques you know.

4. Look at card one. Imagine the scene described on that card. Feel your own anxiety level; see if you are still relaxed. If you feel tense, put the card away, do the relaxation exercise and then look at the card again.

5. When you are able to imagine the scene on card one (the least stressful situation) without feeling tense or anxious, move on to card two. Repeat the process with each of the cards.

6. When you have imagined the most terrifying scene card you have (it may be number twelve or twenty-six) and feel bored and not the least bit upset, you are ready to fall in love with a new person. You know the possible dangers, but your fears of them won't destroy your future relationship.

In your imagination you have lived through the worst. Perhaps you have envisioned the person you were falling in love with announcing they were going to marry someone else, or going on an extended trip around the world, or taking a job in another city, or dating your best friend, or just stopping all communication with you.

Having lived out "the worst" in your imagination and having survived (even become bored by the possibilities), you now realize that you won't die from anything your new romance can provide. Actually, the fearful things you imagine might happen are usually worse than anything that could really happen.

After your Stress Inoculation, your fears will be controlled, but that doesn't mean problems and conflicts won't come up. Using the behavioral methods of contracting, negotiating and facilitating, you can handle even the most difficult problems without destroying your relationship.

Contracting

In chapter two, contracting was suggested as a method of reconciling with your former mate. It works just as well for solving problems with new people you meet.

With a new person, the problems will be different, and so will the ways you react to them. Your new relationship probably isn't old enough to have problems like "I want her to quit her job" or "I want to have children, and he doesn't."

Conflicts in a new relationship are usually things like "I can't stand it when he's late all the time." Or "She insists on smoking marijuana before we make love." Or "He always wears jeans when we go out." Or "She expects me to pay for everything."

"Courtship" is the first phase of a new relationship, and then comes "intimacy." During the courtship phase, or the honeymoon, everything is perfect, and everyone is on their best behavior. But even during the utopian courtship when both partners are "in love," telling all their friends about the wonderful new person they met and even making plans for "forever," or at least the next year, little doubts and annoyances surface. During the courtship phase, people tend to ignore the otherwise unacceptable behaviors of their new lovers. Being "in love" shadows everything and makes even the most irritating behavior not so bad. This is the time when everyone colludes—pretending it doesn't matter if the house is always a mess or that an hour late is okay.

Contracting is a way of settling problems during the very

delicate and delicious courtship period of your new romance. You're on your best behavior and feel shy about bringing up anything "bad."

Don't be intimidated into thinking that if you bring up the first thing that's wrong, the spell of perfection will be broken. It's going to be broken eventually anyway. To avoid the temptation to collude, negotiate the points that are bothering you already.

Sit down with the new person in your life and tell them "I like you" [or "love you," if that's true], and I definitely want our relationship to continue, but there are a couple little things that are bothering me. I want to talk to you about them before they pile up and affect how we feel about each other."

Reassure your new lover, who may be just as insecure as you are. "It's not that these are really important things, but I'm afraid if I overlook the little things that bother me, you may overlook some things that bother you, and soon we'll both be overlooking really big issues 'for the sake of the relationship.' "

State the thing that's bothering you in a positive manner. Not "Don't open my paper before I see it, and put your coffee cup in the sink," but "I have a thing about the morning paper [a self-disclosure about your own idiosyncrasy], and I would like to see the paper first. Also, I have trouble keeping the house clean [self-disclosure], so do you think you could help by putting your dishes directly into the dishwasher?"

By disclosing a failing of your own before you make your statement, you are saying, "I'm not perfect, either." Nobody likes to think they're the only bad guy.

Follow your complaint by inviting your new lover to mention anything you do that bothers them. You might say, "I'm sure there are a couple things I do that bother you, things you've overlooked. I noticed you cleaning up after me in the bathroom, and I will try to be neater there. Is there anything else I can do to make our relationship better?"

The answers to your complaints can range from "Of course, you're right. I'll change that" to "Well, but . . . "

Suppose you suspect your partner is lying to you about where they are or what they're doing. You request that they tell you the truth.

Their answer might be "Yes, but if I don't lie to you about where I am or what I'm doing, you'll be offended by the truth. We'll get into an argument." Your answer is "I promise to sit down and talk to you about my feelings instead of yelling and arguing, if you tell me the truth about where you are going and what you're doing."

You are contracting by your use of the word "if." Every contract has an "if," a contingency clause. "I will cook dinner three nights a week, *if* you take me out the other four nights." Or, "I'll pay for the movies, *if* you make dinner."

The exact same methods of contracting that you used when you tried to negotiate a reconciliation with your old lover (chapter two) can prevent problems in your new relationship. Contracting at the first sign of a problem will keep the problems from adding up and getting out of hand and avoid the seeming "out of left field" breakup you had in the past. If you contract for small points in the beginning, you avoid the big ones as well as the "no communications" bind where you have to bring in a third party to do the negotiating, usually a no-win situation.

Facilitating

If you can stand off as if you were a third person, not one of the principals but merely an arbitrator, then you become a facilitator.

Suppose someone says something offensive to you. You could either ignore it, yell something equally offensive back or facilitate. For example, a new person in your life who you think may become important to you or who is already important to you tells you about a date they had. Of course—you're jealous. You're furious, especially at the very fact that you're being told all the details. In retribution you tell about a beautiful, romantic evening you spent that far surpassed theirs.

You experience a brief "victory-winning" sensation; by your retort, you only win a battle, but you lose the relationship. You may make your point, but you have also created hard feelings.

To be a facilitator, pretend you are a third person listening to the conversation, someone who wants to help preserve the relationship.

Instead of screaming back that you, too, had a great date—other than them—the facilitating move would be "It seems to me that you want me to know you are attractive to other people." This kind of facilitating keeps you from losing points, from engaging in destructive battles and from backtracking in your relationship. Even if your partner doesn't say so, they'll think to themselves, "I wonder why I said that?" instead of trying to think of something even more hurtful to hurl back.

A facilitator stands back and simply mirrors the feelings of the other person. Suppose the new person in your life is constantly late for everything. It's beginning to get on your nerves, and they always have an excuse that you don't believe. Your schedule is upset, your plans are ruined and you feel "taken for granted." Instead of expressing your feelings, assume the role of a facilitator and simply mirror what's happening.

Instead of demanding, "Why are you always late?" a facilitator might say, "It seems as if you may have some ambivalence about coming here." A facilitator stands back and actually wonders what are the conditions that made the other person come late, instead of hurling accusatory questions or expressing their own feelings. Instead of, "You've ruined my evening," a facilitator might say, "I wonder what prevents you from being on time?" Or, "I wonder what it is that is unpleasant to you?" Or, "I wonder what about being late turns you on?"

In facilitating, the idea is to change the other person's behavior without getting into an argument and without making them feel defensive or put down. Facilitating gets the other person to think about their behavior and to decide to change it on their own, by pointing out what's happening. The idea isn't to express how you feel, but rather to help your partner discover how *they* feel.

Once you've pinpointed what's bothering you, you can facilitate more easily. It could be that he always tells you what you should or shouldn't do in your home. Instead of screaming, "Don't tell me what to do or how to live my life," you would facilitate the situation if you would say, "It looks to me as if there are a lot of things I do that you don't think are right." In essence you are reflecting the other person's point of view.

Sex is often a problem for new couples because their different past experiences lead them to have different expectations. A man may demand fellatio, and his partner retorts, "You're a pervert. Aren't I good enough?" A challenge and an accusation. Instead, the facilitator would say, "I hear you say that you're not satisfied with our sex life."

A woman pulls out her vibrator in the middle of lovemaking. "I feel like I'm in bed with a locomotive," her partner shouts. "Aren't I good enough for you?" To which she might snap, "Almost." He would be better off saying, "It sounds like you think I'm inadequate because you need an added stimulus when we're making love." To which she responds, "The fact that I'm in bed with you and using my vibrator in front of you intensifies my joy with you."

Turning down a sexual advance, just not being in the mood or having other private reasons for not wanting sex that particular night are points of real contention among new couples. Inevitably, the one who wants to have sex is angry and feels put down. Instead of defending your right to say no, a no-win defense, the facilitating thing to say would be, "It sounds as if you think I don't care for you, or that I'm not turned on to you, just because I don't feel like making love tonight."

Facilitating is a perfect bedtime brawl preventative. Your partner says, "You never kiss when we make love." Or, "Why won't you get on top?" Or, "You always go to sleep right afterward." Or, "We never make love spontaneously."

Your first instinct is to defend yourself against the accusation, to prove you're right. As a facilitator, overcome the urge to indulge in a fight or to defend yourself against the accusation. Instead, reflect the other person's thought in a way that makes them think about how they really feel.

To facilitate in sexual problems, say, "It sounds like you feel unloved because I go to sleep right afterward, get on top all the time or don't make love spontaneously." A facilitator never says, "I do that because . . . " A facilitator first throws out a guess or a question about how the other person feels and only later states their own feeling.

Good opening lines for facilitators are "It seems to me that you feel . . . " or, "I wonder if you feel . . . " or "Could it be that you feel . . . "

Negotiating

Negotiating becomes a part of contracting when you bargain for points. In other words, "I won't make dinner for you every time you come over, but what if I do it every third time?"

Or to the "We never go out to eat" accusation, you might want to negotiate two home-cooked meals for one restaurant meal. Or to the "We never see movies I like" problem, you might want to negotiate alternating choices, or even who pays and who picks.

There are going to be points in every relationship that are basically unnegotiable. She won't give up her job no matter what. He insists on an open relationship. She's already planned her trip around the world. He has decided to take a job in another city.

If you find yourself in a new relationship that has lots of unnegotiable points, it may be that this is just not "the one" for you. Not every relationship has to be a primary one, nor does every relationship have to lead to marriage or living together. If you enjoy the new person's company enough to accept them with their unnegotiable points, that's fine, but if there are basic ideological differences, the chances are you won't be together as a primary unit for very long.

That's not to say that you should dump the person totally; just realize that the role they are going to fill in your life isn't that of a primary relationship, and keep looking. Figure he's not "it," or she's not the "dream girl." That doesn't mean that you can't have fun together and go out. It simply means that you should look elsewhere to fill your primary relationship needs or consider your new coupling as strictly temporary.

Too many unnegotiable points in the beginning of a relationship mean that even more will come to the surface as you get to know each other better. Don't try to force a new person into being what you want. It's better to go out and find someone else who shows more potential for meeting your expectations. Be careful not to put your primary relationship expectations on a new person with whom you have many unnegotiable points. Not only will you lose the primary relationship, but a potential friendship as well.

If you're honest with yourself, it should be obvious to you when there are too many unnegotiable points. The danger is that right now you may be really hungry to get back to the old familiar coupled state and mistakenly make a commitment to the wrong person. If your life-styles are radically different, if lots of things annoy you that the other person seems unwilling to change or that are just part of their basic personality, if you find yourself doing a lot of facilitating, contracting and negotiating and still being annoyed a lot of the time, keep looking. You don't have to give up the relationship totally. It's okay to relate to more than one person at a time in a loving manner, but be careful right now about making commitments just for the sake of being coupled.

A bad committed relationship is really much worse than no relationship at all. As long as you aren't committed, you still have a chance of finding "the one" or at least one of them. Once you have committed yourself to work exclusively on a particular relationship, you close out other chances. Unnegotiable points early in the game should be a good barometer for your future possibilities.

Even if you can't get totally "in tune" with the first new person you date, keep the relationship going and practice your facilitating, contracting and negotiating on them, so that when you do find someone more compatible, you'll be ready. Don't dwell on the negative aspects—that the new person in your life will never be "it." Think of the positives instead. That person could introduce you to your future mate. They may change or you may change. They may become a good friend who will last through many affairs. Relate without expectation of a permanent, coupled existence. You won't be lonely, and you may even want to consider a collection of good friends instead of a permanent replacement for your ex.

Guilt

As you begin to relate to a new person, you will be discovering things about yourself, perhaps even realizing past mistakes you made with your former mate. You called him a pervert for wanting to do certain things in bed that you didn't think were right. Now you find out that everybody does those things. He wasn't a pervert after all, and you feel guilty.

You accused your ex-wife of deserting you and the kids when

she went to work. Now you find out that most of the mothers you meet work, and it's okay with their husbands. You feel that you have destroyed your marriage.

You may even think about calling your ex and confessing how wrong you were. After you have made your reconnection in chapter twelve, you will once again be able to communicate with your ex and maybe even to tell them they were right about a few things, but it really doesn't matter. The truth is that it's too late for that old relationship and carrying around newly discovered guilts won't do you any good. If you think the way you acted in the past wasn't right, you will have a chance to act differently in the future. Instead of punishing yourself for past mistakes, congratulate yourself for seeing them and for giving yourself the opportunity to change.

Methadone Treatment

Just as methadone is used to help the heroin addict get unhooked, there are "methadone" treatments for love addicts. Now you are over the initial shock of your love withdrawal. The tremors are gone, and you're well enough to go back on the street and score again.

In our society, everyone's a love addict to one degree or another. Mechanization, family unit disintegration and depersonalization have made love a very important commodity and everybody wants some. Love, in little doses, comes easily enough, but the committed relationship, the big score, doesn't come that easily or that often. It's like a very scarce and very popular new drug on the market. Everybody's trying to get it and the price for a steady connection is high.

The addict without a connection will often settle for second best—a lower-class street drug, not quite what he wanted. It may be laced and adulterated, but it'll do in a pinch. The love addict often makes the same compromise.

You may still have the same needs for love and commitment, but you want to avoid getting hooked on "bad stuff." The next relationship you develop won't necessarily be "the one," but, when you're still hungry for a love fix, it's easy to assume that the methadone love is the real thing. It takes away the pain and the new person fills the void left in your life by your ex. You aren't lonely anymore, but just because you have stopped hurting doesn't mean it's love.

Methadone makes drug addicts stop hurting, too, but it's not heroin. Your "methadone" love may or may not develop into a real, committed love, but don't assume that because you're happy instead of unhappy, because you have found someone to fill your dependency needs, you have found "the one."

Lack of pain isn't love. Even momentary pleasure isn't love. Don't make declarations of undying devotion just because you aren't unhappy anymore. It's not fair to you or to the other person. They'll think you mean it, without realizing that what you really mean is that your pain has stopped.

Independence

By now you will have discovered that there are lots of things your ex did for you that you can do perfectly well for yourself or that you can hirc people to do. Then, after you've learned to swing a hammer and handle a power drill, along comes a new lover who wants to do all those handy things around the house for you, who wants to take care of you.

You've learned to cook, clean and take care of your laundry and along comes a new lover who begins taking over these tasks for you again. What do you do? You're afraid of becoming dependent all over again and then being left to fend for yourself.

If a man moves from mother to wife, never cooking for himself or taking care of his daily living needs, it's a shock when he finds that he has to do those things. If he finds another woman to do his cooking and cleaning for him before he finds out how to do them for himself, he will indeed be replacing one dependency with another.

If a woman has never earned her own living, if she's always been supported by her father or husband or boyfriend, she will feel devastated when she finds she has to buy her own dinner. If she finds another man who is willing to support her before she has learned to support herself, she is likely to substitute the new man for the old one in a provider role.

The answer is that it's okay to let people do things for you. It makes you both feel good. But it's not okay if you are developing dependency needs that you don't feel able to fill yourself.

One important dependency need both men and women have is the one for "company." A companion is what people miss most about their old relationship—someone to talk to, to confide in, to simply be there. A warm, loving body in your bed, someone who is always available. It's okay to let a new person fill that need, if you feel comfortable knowing that you aren't dependent, that you are able to exist without having an "always available constant companion." Then the other person is a bonus, not a way to increase your dependency needs and eventually destroy your self-esteem and your relationship. Nobody can fill the void for a person who can't stand their own company. The demands are too great. It's as if they were being company for you and them both. If you just want "someone there," get a dog, not a lover.

If you realize that you have the ability to fill whatever need the new person in your life is filling, let them do it. Letting someone else do for you what you could do for yourself is okay as long as you know that if they stop doing it you are perfectly capable of taking over and filling the space in your life by yourself.

Sexual Adjustments

Your ex used to ravish your body. You were in perfect harmony. Your fantasies matched. When you made love, it was like two hungry animals coming together, an almost unhuman mating full of lust and raw sexual enjoyment.

The new person in your life is gentle, has a soft touch, doesn't fantasize. You miss the lust. You find that you're masturbatory fantasies are always about your old lover, the one who ravished your body, not the gentle new one.

There are three ways to transfer your old satisfactory sex fantasy to the reality of your new lover. The first is to realize that it's not cheating or adultery to silently fantasize about your old lover while you're with your new one. As a matter of fact, if it turns you on, satisfactory sexual fantasies can have a healthy effect on your functioning in the new relationship. Letting loose in your imagination could actually improve your sex life.

Fantasizing about your old lover while you're with your new one will be okay for a while, but it still won't be as satisfying as you might hope. Once you feel comfortable with your fantasies (you don't feel guilty about thinking of having sex with your ex while you're with your new lover), you will find that your sexual satisfaction with your new lover is improved, and therefore, so is the relationship.

Pillow Talk

The second step in transferring your old fantasies to your new lover is by using pillow talk. You're probably not the only one that has sexual fantasies. Chances are your new lover has a few of his or her own which they haven't told you about either. The goal of this exercise is to get your new lover to confess his or her secret sex fantasies.

But by using a sort of desensitization game, you can very

gradually make it "safe" for your partner to tell you their innermost secret sexual dreams and desires. If you're a woman, start with "I've always wondered what sex fantasies men have." Or, if you're a man, "I've always wondered about what kinds of sexual fantasies women have."

Or you might say to your female lover, "What do you think most men fantasize about sexually?" Or to your male lover, "What do you think most women secretly desire?" That way you're not asking your new partner to confess about their own secret fantasies, but to speculate instead on what other people of the opposite sex are fantasizing about.

If you ask a woman about men, she'll probably guess that the predominant male fantasy is "Making it with more than one woman at a time." If you ask a man what he thinks women fantasize about, he might say, "Making it with a movie star." It's always easier to answer questions about other people. The idea is to open sexual communication.

The next logical question is, to a man, "What do you think other men fantasize about?" and to a woman, "What do you think other women fantasize about?" At this point, confessing your own secret turn-on is often a good way to free your shy fantasizer to disclose his or her most orgasm-inducing fantasies. Typically, your mate will practically blurt out, "But my fantasy is . . . " without even being asked.

Always start by asking a man what he thinks women fantasize about. Then ask what he thinks "other" men fantasize about. Start by asking a woman what she thinks men fantasize about, then ask what she thinks other women fantasize about. The last question to ask is what your lover thinks members of their same sex fantasize about. Then, after you've confessed your own most shocking secrets, you can expect to hear your mate's hidden fantasies disclosed.

If you take your time desensitizing your new lover to fantasy confessions, you will find that they very quickly start to tell their secrets. They'll feel closer to you because they have shared a secret with you that they've probably never told *anyone* before. Not their exes or their shrinks!

The only fantasy you should never talk about concerns body structure. In other words, if your new lady has small breasts, don't say your fantasies are of giant tits. If your new man has a small penis, don't tell him you fantasize about giant penises. People feel very helpless when your fantasies involve preferences for someone with a different color hair or a different size or different look. Keep your fantasy confessions to actual settings (a forest) or props (feathers) or sex actions (being ravished).

The next step is the sharing of the fantasy through whispers while making love. Suppose your new lover has told you that he's always wanted to be a shiek surrounded by beautiful belly dancers from his harem. That's your clue to wiggle your bottom and whisper to him during lovemaking, "If you were a shiek, I'd be your favorite belly dancer. You could order me to dance for you any time you wanted. Would you like that?" Asking questions while you're fantasizing is important. Ask your lover, "Then what do *you* do? Then what do I do? Am I the only belly dancer, or do you choose me from a lineup?"

If your new lady confesses to a rape fantasy or a multiple sex fantasy, whisper to her while you're making love, "I'm a stranger who comes to your door. I see you and I can't help myself, I have to ravish you. You scream out in fear and I put my hand over your mouth. I pull your legs apart." Then ask her, "What do I do next?" Surely she'll tell you.

Use whatever hint you have about your mate's fantasy to elicit a response during lovemaking. Talk about your own fantasy, too. Encourage your partner to reciprocate and participate, both in re-creating and talking about your fantasy as well as their own.

If you find that your partner is only interested in you

creating their fantasy in bed, but not in creating yours, you might have a very selfish partner—one of the ones who is going to expect you to do all the work throughout the relationship. That's a good thing to know about from the start. Fantasy revelation and sex talk can tell you a lot about how a person is going to react in other areas of relating.

Erotic Theater

The third level of transferring your old fantasies to your new lover is with erotic theater—or enacting the fantasy. Your new lover may need some reassurance that it's okay to act out certain fantasies. If that's the case, take him or her to an erotic film, an adult bookstore or just bring home some adult magazines or sex toys. If you're a woman, tell your new lover you've always wanted to go to an adult toy store or bookstore or porno flick, but you've been embarrassed to go alone. Could you go together? It's important to go as a couple so you can see what your lover is really into and can show them that others are, too.

Once you've discovered your lover's fantasies, get a few props. If it's belly dancers, buy a belly dancing costume or harem pants and beads. If it's "Patty Hearst," get a blindfold at the drugstore. Imagine that you are directing a play. Stage your fantasy or your lover's fantasy as a surprise. Have everything ready. Set up a seduction. Burn incense. Change the ambiance of your usual lovemaking environment. Be spontaneous. Do it on the living room rug. The kitchen counter. Run naked through the house playing dirty old man and little girl.

You may want to experiment with the so-called kinky erotic sex, like slave-master relationships where one person has to do the other's bidding. Or you may want to try out light bondage or discipline. If your taste runs to the more exotic, gourmet-type sex fare, and your partner's taste is more pedestrian, a good ice-breaker is a well-known sex manual you could read together, like *Joy of Sex.* When a best-selling book says it's okay, your partner may be more ready to experiment.

Never say, "John always did twenty minutes of foreplay first," or "Mary always washed me afterwards." Instead say, "It really turns me on when my nipples get kissed," or "Sometimes I get turned on again by having my genitals washed with a hot soapy cloth."

Don't insist on acting out your fantasy right away. It takes people a while to get used to new ideas. Buy sex books and look at the pictures together. Ask, "Does that turn you on?" Or, "What do you think the turn-on is with that particular picture?"

Start wherever you want. It may be *Playboy* or *Hustler* from the local newsstand or a hard-core magazine from the "adults only" bookstore. Try to go just a little further than your level, even if you find that some of the things actually turn you off.

In testimony during obscenity film trials across the country, psychologists have pointed out time and time again the social value of pornography, sexually explicit magazines, books and photos. Psychologists routinely recommend these explicit sexual materials to their patients who are having sexual problems in their marriages and relationships because the erotic materials provide a springboard for discussion and open previously closed sexual communication. *Deep Throat* is often recommended as a sex education guide. If you are still having trouble with your new sex relationship, it might be wise to consult a reputable sex therapy specialist in one of the licensed health professions.

Don't worry about fantasizing about your old lover when you're with your new one. Even pretend it's your old love, if that makes it better for you. The important thing is that you enjoy your lovemaking experiences. What you fantasize about is not important.

Obviously the new person in your life is going to have

different ways of making love, things that turn them on. Maybe you've never experienced a certain kind of lovemaking before—say fellatio or cunnilingus, or even spanking—and the new person in your bed suddenly shows you without any doubt that a particular act you're unfamiliar with turns them on.

You are going to have to make adjustments to your new lover. It's not just going to be a case of having them adjust to your sexual preferences; you're going to have to adjust to theirs, too.

You don't have to see a new or unfamiliar sex act as a permanent commitment to perform that act from here on. See it as an experiment. Many people have never tasted French delicacies like escargots or the delicious Mexican tripe or the Italian eel because of preconceived prejudices about the particular dish. Your first visit to a Japanese sushi bar could be ruined by the thought of eating raw fish, or you may discover a great delicacy. Either way, you'll never know if you like something or not without trying it.

There's no guarantee you'll get to like a sex act that you've never participated in before or even a type of lovemaking that is different from what you've liked in the past. Give the new way a fair test, just to see.

One of the things that will help you adjust to the sexuality of the new person is to assume a complementary role. Your old lover was a diamond-in-the-rough Bogie type and the new one is a romantic Louis Jourdan. Or your old girlfriend was a Jane Mansfield sex bomb and your new one is a Leslie Caron, all sweetness and lace.

Try on a new role yourself. If your new lover is romantic and soft, try becoming that way, too. If your new lover is sexy and robust, try becoming more like they are. See if you can get turned on in your new role, whether it's Monroe or Lolita, Valentino or the White Knight. That doesn't mean that you have to totally submerge yourself forever into a character that doesn't fit you and doesn't turn you on, but you might find that you enjoy playing a different role for variety once in a while.

Maybe you've always liked to pretend you were a whore or a pimp in bed, and you're now involved with a man who wants a lady and no "bad" words or a woman who wants a Philadelphia "preppie." There's no reason why you shouldn't expand your horizons and try out the new role. Maybe you'll be turned on by being a lady or a gentleman, or find that it's not so bad once in a while. Try making compromises in the bedroom with your new lover; then you have a better chance of getting them to compromise their basic patterns as well.

If it doesn't work out, if you discover that your new lover's gentleness just doesn't satisfy you or your new girlfriend's sexiness just doesn't turn you on like "a lady" in bed does, then you'll know for sure they're not the one for you. A trial doesn't consist of just once. It took a long time for you to get turned on to the style you like now. Give the new role at least five tries before you count it out.

At worst, you'll find out that you are really sexually incompatible. At best, you'll discover new ways to increase your erotic feelings and sexual pleasures, and maybe even the ultimate, to combine both your old sexual expressions and your new discoveries and take yourself on even more erotic sexual journeys than you've ever had before.

Once you've dropped into the role that's complementary to your new partner's, there are ways to turn the tables and have them drop into the sexual role of your old lover as well.

Besides eliciting sexual fantasies, there are behavioral strategies for mutual sexual enrichment—or pillow talk assertion.

Asserting Yourself in Bed

When there's a real roadblock, something you definitely want done in bed that the other person's not showing any desire for or leaning toward, what do you do?

It's true that most sex books today tell you to ask for what you want in bed, but don't, at least not directly. Because if the answer is "no," you have a confrontation. When you haven't made any demands, you can't be turned down.

A man finds that his new girlfriend never goes down on him. Instead of patiently repeating to her how much it turns him on, he shoves her head in the direction of his penis. This type of nonverbal assertion doesn't work unless the person is really willing to perform the asked-for sex act or you have some indication the person is turned on by that type of activity.

A woman finds that her new boyfriend never seems to want her to get on top. Instead of telling him how much it would turn her on if she could make love to him, she hops on top of him and tries to insert his puzzled penis. He wonders what she's doing, not knowing that it turns her on. Suppose your new lover says he or she would really like to please you, but is too inhibited.

Orgasmic Reorientation

One way to help your new love turn on to an untried sex act is to fantasize aloud about it just at their moment of orgasm. The fantasy or sex act becomes associated with orgasm in the person's mind.

This is a very subtle form of pillow talk assertion and can be used only if you're patient. It won't necessarily take the first time, but by whispering your fantasy each time your partner is reaching orgasm, you will create a need and a desire in your partner for that very sex act.

When psychologists treat child molesters, men who are primarily turned on by young boys or girls, they begin by having the man masturbate in his usual fashion, that is, while thinking of children. Then he is switched to pictures of adults at the moment of orgasm. He begins to associate adults with his tension release and so to seek out adults as companions.

Dr. John Marquis of the Palo Alto V.A. Hospital was the first to derive this technique from the theory of tension reduction. In other words, everyone seeks that which they imagine will reduce their tensions, whether it's chocolate ice cream or little girls. At the moment of orgasm, there is a natural reduction of tension. By relating the reduction of tension (orgasm) to a fantasized new sex act, your new lover will start seeking out that particular tension reducer and lose his or her earlier inhibitions regarding the sex act you both desire.

People have reported startling successes by whispering fantasies to their mates at the moment of orgasm. "Imagine we're nude, with three other people in the room," a woman whispers to her new lover who refuses to go to a nudist park with her.

Or a woman with rape fantasies whispers to her love as he's coming, "I feel like you're raping me." Done often enough, he will soon accept the rape fantasy. She definitely will get him to accept acting out a rape fantasy faster if he identifies it with his release of tension.

Power and Sex

The connection between domination, power and sex is very primitive and has been studied extensively. Civilized nonsexist human beings are often frightened by any assertion of power, especially between the sexes. Assertion in the bedroom is often frightening, too, because people often think that a person who asserts in bed will be dominating outside of the bedroom. That's one reason that the new "up-front, speak-out and demand what you want" method doesn't always work in bed. It scares people into wondering if the entire relationship is going to be a power struggle.

Sex is a time to be primitive, but the cloak of civilization doesn't always allow for that. Even if you or your mate wants to dominate or assert in bed, chances are you'll both be shy about it because you don't want to appear "uncivilized."

With birth control, sex became as much play as procreation. Just as little children try on roles when they play house, doctor or cops and robbers, there isn't anything wrong with adults trying on roles in sex play. You may want to be dominant or submissive or Queen for a Day in bed, and there's no reason why you shouldn't. In fact, take turns at these roles. By using the appropriate and effective methods of bedroom assertion, you will be able to act out any role you want in bed and have the cooperation and enjoyment of your partner at the same time.

Session Twenty-Two: The New Love Relationship

When you discover someone you could love again, you are still going to find little things that the new lover doesn't have that the old one had. It might be little golden hairs creeping down her thigh, or a patch of silken hair on his back, or the way her skin felt, or the hair he had all over, or the sweet smell of her body.

The truth is that you just can't have everything, and if the new person in your life doesn't have that special color hair or eyes, you might think about all the pain you had for that hair or those eyes. Would you really give up a potentially good relationship because your partner lacks certain superficial qualities—blond hair or blue eyes or muscles or a suntan? Of course not.

The new person in your life might want things from you, too, that you're not willing to provide or that you just don't have. Now is the time to make a decision. If your new lover says he only wants an "open" relationship and you don't love him enough to make that effort, this is the time to get out. If the new woman in your life says she can only have an exclusive relationship and you know you would find that hard to do, now is the time to figure out if you love her enough. If not, call it off.

Code of Ethics for the Newly Separated

If you think the relationship is worth doing what your new lover requires, then you should try it and see if you can acquire a taste for the new activity. You won't die from the experiment. You can decide it's not worth it after you have tried it. It may take two dates to find out something isn't working. It may take two weeks or two months before you have made a rational decision. If you try it and it doesn't work, you hate it and even the new relationship isn't worth it, it's time to move on.

Otherwise you are pretending and colluding, and eventually you will destroy the relationship and cause a lot of pain to both yourself and the other person.

If he likes Hungarian food and you are a vegetarian, you must decide if you like him enough to join him in beef goulash. If she likes the ballet and goes once a week, you must decide if you care for her enough to go to the ballet.

If she likes to ski and you hate the cold and know that you don't love her enough to spend a week in the snow (but you don't want to give her up either), then when ski season comes let her know that she's going to have to find another person to ski with.

If he loves tennis and you hate the game and are strictly the intellectual type (but you love him), then let him know that it's alright for him to line up other partners for tennis. This kind of open relationship is only for the person who is secure and has lots of other close friends of both sexes. You are going to be lonely when she goes skiing, and you are going to be jealous when he's with other partners on the tennis court, unless you have someone to be with, too.

You might make a deal, like it's okay for you to go to Aspen with whomever you want and I'll go to La Costa with whomever I want. Or, if you must have a woman who will perform that particular sex act, it's okay if you do it with someone else, as long as you let me know ahead of time so that I can schedule something else. Or it's okay for you to go to the concert with another guy, if I can take another girl to the ball game.

The options you have are to either change and provide what your potential new mate desires, to try allowing them to get it elsewhere or to split. If you decide to try changing and find that you are unhappy with the changes you have made, chances are you'll break up anyway, but with much anger and sadness.

You can only allow your mate to "get it elsewhere" without it affecting your relationship if you, too, have "other things going." To many people, having other things going means that the primary relationship simply isn't. If you try having other lovers and find it keeps you from having the committed relationship you want, you will probably wind up breaking up.

A third alternative, terminating the primary relationship and looking elsewhere, relegating your lover to a secondary position, is really a very safe one, provided that you both accept it. Think of the relationships you form now as "try on" relationships, not permanent ones. Try on the people and see how you fit together.

You've met someone interesting and you've been seeing a lot of each other. You've made love, but it's been just a little disappointing. You can't put your finger on it, but something's missing.

Often the new love connection just isn't as good in bed, and you just don't know why. You've communicated every way you know how about what you know "turns you on," and maybe you've even got your new lover doing exactly what the old lover did in bed. But there's something missing, an excitement, a thrill or a feeling that just isn't there.

It isn't a matter of bedroom technique and often not of looks either. Your new bed partner may be far superior in every way—looks, ability, endowments, affection and consideration—and still you yearn for the old one.

The Last Sex Sabbatical

For many people, the sexual hook to the former lover lasts longer than the love for them does. Total withdrawal from sex "because something is lacking" isn't unusual. It's been a normal symptom of loss of love recognized for years. But the lack of full sexual enjoyment is something new.

Modern, thinking people know that it doesn't serve their best interests to withdraw totally from sex after an affair disintegrates, but they are often upset because the sex isn't as good anymore.

The sex gratification that always came from the same place (the ex) is very much like the love gratification they gave. The deserted person often remains sexually hooked to their former lover long after the loving feelings have gone. Dreams, fantasies of the former lover while masturbating or even while making love with someone new still remain and shouldn't cause you upset.

Your new lover hasn't become a habit yet. You aren't conditioned to receive that much gratification from the new person in your life. After all, they haven't been around as long. You still have a lot to learn about your likes, your bodies, your sensitivities and favorite sensations. You still have a lot of practicing to do to catch up.

If you find that you have too much practicing to do, if sex with your new lover is so unsatisfactory that it doesn't begin to compare with the old one, don't give up. You could wind up like the woman who was still having a twice a week tryst with her ex-husband five years after their divorce "because nobody does it as well." It's not true that nobody's better, but that she just hasn't looked around enough.

Fears that it will only be a one-night stand combine with the attitude that it's the length of a relationship that determines how good it is to make many people totally reject new love affairs. Fearing that their sexual ability has been questioned because someone left them, some experience a sexual dysfunction of one kind or another.

It's highly likely that you are "in love" with a new person. You think the new person should be as sexually exciting as the old one and that you should have stopped fantasizing about your ex.

By now, you've discovered that you can indeed get the love gratification from sources other than your ex, and with practice, the sex gratification from your new love source can be even better. It's old-fashioned to think that you must get the highest sex gratification from the same source you get your highest love gratification. Your mother may love you more, but someone you pick up at the beach could prove more sexually satisfying.

Staying on Top in the New Relationship

Being on top is not just sexual in the new relationship. You want to be on top all the way, never to feel as bad as you did before.

Behavior therapy can teach you methods of constructive assertiveness and maintaining equality in your new relationship so that you don't get into a one-down position in your love life. You don't want to feel like you're the one who's making all the compromises and not getting as much as you're giving.

In the beginning of a new relationship, you are automatically on top. The pecking order hasn't been established yet. You don't want to be the king of the barnyard, but you don't want to be on the bottom of the list either.

Imagine a continuum of people who are shrinking violets, to people who are assertive, to people who are aggressive bullies. If you're a shrinking violet, you're asking people to walk on you. If you're a bully, nobody will be attracted to you except shrinking violets. If you've been either a shrinking violet or a bully in the past, this is the time to trade in your old role for that of an assertive human being.

The shrinking violet is a person who overlooks things. "It's not worth making an issue over," they say when their feelings are hurt. So, of course, their feelings get hurt time and time again. For the shrinking violet, nothing is worth incurring the displeasure of the other, no matter how much abuse or discomfort is involved. The shrinking violets sacrifice themselves rather than the love affair.

It's okay to overlook things in a casual affair, when you're just getting your feet wet again in the world of sex, but not when you've decided that you've found a person to fall in love with. Then you must stand on your own rights, feelings, actions and beliefs.

If you give in too much, play the shrinking violet part all of the time and generally collude in your new love relationship, you are doomed to wind up as a doormat again. Also, by hiding your true self, you are going to attract a person who is drawn by what you pretend you are, not what you really are. When the real you comes out, as indeed it must, your new mate will feel disappointed and angry because you're not what you seemed. Because you didn't speak up and pretended to be someone else, you will have wasted valuable time with a basically incompatible person. If you are colluding now while you feel needy of "someone," you will either:

1. Split in unexplainable anger.
2. Blow up with a list of things you've been colluding about.
3. Become manipulatively devious, getting even with nonver-

bal, positively irksome and indirect hostilities, like being late, wearing objectionable clothing, getting drunk, stoned or even attempting suicide.

4. Cause fights over red herrings—the dirty dishes, the phone bill or the thermostat.

The worst offense about presenting an "acceptable" but false image of yourself is that *that* is what is loved, not you.

Things look pretty good for you and the new person in your life. You've found someone you can love who cares for you, and it's more than just a one-night stand.

You don't want to turn off the new person who is making you feel happy again, you don't want to go out and start looking all over again, and you don't want to do anything that will rock the boat. So when little things annoy you, you try to convince yourself they don't matter. You overlook them.

This is unfair to you, to the other person and to the relationship and any future it might have. When you overlook things, you are training the other person to become aggressive and to repeatedly behave in a way that annoys you. By not saying anything, you are actually telling the other person that what they're doing is just fine and they can keep it up.

Generally speaking, the aggressive part of human nature is kept under control because people are afraid of the retaliatory anger of the person being aggressed upon. Being aggressive can get you in trouble. You can get arrested for aggressive civil disobedience, and in a relationship, you could lose your mate. But there is a difference between being aggressive and being assertive. You aren't being assertive if you overlook things for the sake of your relationship. By your lack of assertion, you are encouraging your partner to be aggressive (press their way of life on you, overriding your likes and dislikes).

People don't like to be bullies, but if a shrinking violet never expresses an opinion, it is human nature to take over. By allowing your mate to be aggressive, you show them that there's nothing to be afraid of, that they can get away with anything and that you will meet all of their demands and will just take whatever they dish out.

You have taken away all the unpleasant consequences usually associated with aggressive behavior and have created a bully. Everyone has an aggressive side and everyone is capable of becoming a bully, but they won't do it unless they think they can get away with it.

By the time you reach adulthood, you have developed pet ways, favorite foods, special concepts of how a spouse or mate should act, and so has the other adult you are relating to. It's a natural tendency to try to set up life so that it is in line with your own desires, so that your favorite foods are served, rituals are lived out and relationship role concepts are fulfilled.

No matter how irksome it may be to you, your new mate is going to try to set up life so that everything goes according to their particular schedule. If you allow it, you will be setting up your relationship so that all your partner's little patterns remain undisturbed and so that you will make all the adjustments.

In the very beginning of a relationship, when things are still on an even keel, people are afraid to impose their will on you because they are afraid you'll tell them to get lost. As the relationship progresses, there is a period of testing. If your new mate sleeps late every morning and you're an early riser, it's to the new lover's advantage if they can get you to rearrange your schedule instead of having to rearrange theirs.

If, during the testing period, you don't call your new lover on it when he or she attempts to uncompromisingly override your life-style with their own or to bully you into conforming, you are extinguishing their fear of reprisal. You are assuring them that there's nothing to be afraid of when it comes to bullying you. The thing that keeps people from hitting someone when they are angry is the fear of being hit back. If someone hits you and you don't hit back, you have extinguished their fear.

Emotional assaults are exactly the same. If your new lover makes an emotional assault on you and you choose to ignore it (for the sake of the relationship), you are encouraging their abusive behavior by taking away the fear that you will retaliate.

Your new lover may start by asking for coffee in bed, and you bring it. Next they want the paper, and finally, a hotel-style tray with a complete breakfast. One day, he/she says, "I want you to shine my shoes." You say, "What? Shine your own shoes." But what if you didn't say anything? What if you continued bringing the breakfast, shining their shoes, doing their laundry, grocery shopping and housecleaning? Because you have never called a stop, you are encouraging this sort of escalating bully behavior.

You have taken a perfectly balanced and terrific relationship and wound up as an underdog, creating a bully out of a perfectly rational human being, your mate. If your new mate begins to act exactly like your old one, it's because you trained them to be that way by reinforcing their aggressive behavior. When you provide your new lover with everything they want totally at your expense, you have trained them to expect what is not rightfully theirs.

It's not the "straw that breaks the camel's back" that ruins relationships. It's not because things have accumulated. There's no part of the body that accumulates anger. The real mechanism that causes a final blowup over what seems to be a lot of little things is the tyranny of the trivia. You can train your mate to encroach on little trivia in your life.

Eventually, because you have allowed that person to encroach on so many trivial parts of your life, they simply take one more small liberty. To them it seems like a small one, but this time it's something that's really important to you.

A man whose wife has been buying his Christmas gifts for years doesn't understand when she blows up "Just because I asked you to buy a valentine gift for my secretary." To him it was simply one more small request, but to her it was the one that was too much.

A woman's boyfriend has always taken her to the movies she picked out and the restaurants she wanted to go to. She is used to overriding his decisions. One day he comes home and announces they are going on a trip to Hawaii. "No," she says, "not Hawaii. Let's go to Mexico instead." When he blows up and storms out, she doesn't understand why.

In both cases, the partner took one liberty too many, but wasn't to blame. Their mate had been training them to take liberties for years. Why shouldn't they?

In order for your new relationship not to disintegrate and for you and your new mate not to come to the point of anger over little encroachments, you must learn to be assertive—not aggressive—when "little" things aren't quite right. Your little pacifiers can become tomorrow's big angers.

Even though "assertion training" has been "in" since the mid-seventies, most people don't know how to assert. That's because they don't realize that an assertion really is simply a verbal statement that is effective, that makes you firm, fair and predictable.

Many people are afraid that if they make a verbal assertion, they will look bad. That's not true. In reality, you will appear firm, fair and predictable.

A verbal assertion is different from a nonverbal one. A nonverbal assertion is a punch in the nose, sulking, acting depressed or even moving someone's clothing out of your house. The trouble with a nonverbal assertion is that its meaning can be interpreted in different ways by the person making it and the person receiving it. In a verbal assertion, there is no misinterpretation.

A verbal assertion is a statement that says something like "I will do it this time, but never again." Or "I will do what you want, if you will do this thing that I want done." Or "No. I have done this for you in the past, and I'm not going to do it again." Or "These are my limits. Any further demands will not be met."

The value of the verbal assertion is that it is unemotional, reasonable and rational. It must also be fair, and so you must weigh the facts before you make it. Since the verbal assertion makes you predictable, it allows people to know exactly how far they can go with you.

By making a verbal assertion when someone imposes on you, you save yourself the aggravation of having the imposition made on you again with an even more annoying liberty.

You save a lot of having to say no if you have made a verbal assertion about what you are and are not willing to do now. If you have made it clear that you won't allow something, your mate probably won't even bother asking you, knowing ahead of time that you aren't going to go for it. You won't be put into the embarrassing position of party pooper because you refuse to allow your mate to invite a lot of people home at the last minute.

One reason people resort to nonverbal communication is because they hope to be misunderstood. They may not even know what they mean themselves, and a nonverbal communication saves them the trouble of thinking out exactly what they do mean. The advantage of a verbal statement is that it's clear to the giver and the receiver.

The late sixties and early seventies saw a huge psychological push for "nonverbal communication" and the consequent proliferation of "touchy-feely grope groups" to establish connections and affection among a basically unassimilated group of people. Of course, in a group of strangers, it's not likely that you would know exactly what you want to say to someone you've never seen before. How much easier to look deeply into their eyes, holding their hands and hoping that they get a "nice" message.

Group grope was part of the counterculture, an antiintellectual movement to get people to touch and hug rather than talk. Unfortunately, overkill in the nonverbal skills lessened the importance of making a clear, concise, verbal assertion and left many well-intentioned people giving looks and nonverbal signals that are just not understood.

Unfortunately, this pseudo-humanistic approach has, in its antiegghead stance, left thousands unhappy and unable to communicate realistically. Touching may have deep meaning during a Lamaze method birth for your baby, but that doesn't mean that nonverbal communication with your mate will take the place of a verbal assertion that is fair, firm and predictable.

In matters of affection, there's no doubt that it's good to be able to show your feelings nonverbally *as well as* verbally, but when it comes to stating the ground rules of a relationship, renegotiating and modifying them as you go along, verbal assertive techniques work better.

If you find that you are unable to state your needs verbally, then you are being cowardly and taking a chance on losing your relationship anyway. You might as well say what you want and then you at least have a chance of getting it.

The world may need more nonverbal assertions of love, but it also needs more verbal assertions of ground rules, especially in relationships. It has been clinically demonstrated that of all the psychological techniques in use today, assertion training is the most powerful for overcoming social shyness due to interpersonal anxiety. The reason that assertion training is so powerful is that the world respects an assertive person and reinforces an assertion. Bullies back down in the face of assertion. It was the nonassertive pacification by Chamberlain at Munich that cost the world twenty-four million lives during World War II. By pacifying Hitler and accepting his territorially aggressive first move, Chamberlain silently encouraged the rest.

You have a right to be an assertive person. You have the right to judge your own behavior, thoughts and emotions and to take the responsibility for their initiation and consequences upon yourself.

You have the right to offer no reasons or excuses for justifying your behavior. You have the right to judge whether you are responsible for finding solutions to other people's problems. You have the right to change your mind. You have the right to make mistakes—and to be responsible for them.

You have the right to say, "I don't know," or, "I don't understand," or even, "I don't care." You have the right to be independent of others before coping with them. You have the right to be illogical in making decisions. In fact, to quote Dr. Manuel Smith, innovator of many of the following assertive techniques, you have the right to say "no" without feeling guilty.

Once you have assimilated and affirmed your assertive rights, the next step is to learn how to assert. There are several techniques which have proved to be effective as assertion strategies.

Broken Record Assertions

By simply stating your assertion over and over again in a calm repetition without arguing, you can win without getting upset. Your mate might want you to do something and you don't want to do it. Instead of arguing, you would simply say, "I'm not going to do it." No matter what your mate says in argument, no matter how they shout or plead, no matter how rationally they try to convince you, you calmly repeat, "I'm not going to do it." That's the broken record technique of assertion.

The broken record is especially good with a bully because since you're not arguing back, you're not reinforcing them. Eventually, the bully simply runs out of steam and arguments.

Allowing yourself to be drawn into a debate over whatever it might be simply escalates the argument, not the solution. By using the broken record technique, you save yourself the problem of thinking up arguments to support what you want and you also save yourself the upset of indulging in angry feelings. You will soon find that you can feel comfortable ignoring the manipulative, verbal side traps, argumentative baiting and irrelevant logic of the bully, while sticking to your desired point.

Fogging Assertions

Nobody likes to be criticized, and the normal reaction to criticism is to argue back. Fogging is an assertive technique for dealing with criticism by calmly acknowledging to your critics the probability that there may be some truth in his conclusions about you, but still remaining your own judge of what you do.

In using the fogging technique, you simply roll with the bully's punch. Instead of becoming a solid wall, you become a nebulous target. Giving way by recognizing your mate's perception of you, you take the wind out of their argument, while still leaving the final action up to you.

Suppose your mate is upset because you "aren't in the mood" for sex. He/she accuses you of not being sexy enough. In fogging, you wouldn't argue your sexiness or your right to have sex or not. That would still be up to you. You would simply acknowledge your partner's feeling while maintaining your stance. "I can understand how you might feel that I'm not sexy enough, but I just don't feel like it tonight." No matter what your mate says, no matter how bad the criticism seems, you simply fog without arguing.

Your mate might say, "You don't know anything about sex,"

and your answer would be "I can understand how you would feel that way." Or "You never take a sexual interest in us," and you would answer, "I can understand how you feel I'm not interested in sex." Eventually, your mate runs out of arguments, and you haven't been bullied into submission.

Negative Assertions

Use negative assertion when someone criticizes you about a fault that you know you have, but have decided not to change. In making your negative assertion, you strongly and sympathetically agree with the hostile or even constructive criticism without apologizing for your actions.

You don't have to be perfect; you have a right not to be. As a matter of fact, you know that you're not, but you accept yourself the way you are—complete with your faults—and you don't want to change. You don't have to be defensive and you don't have to deny that you've acted in a way that is unacceptable to the other person or that may be unacceptable to society. It is your right to behave the way you want while accepting the consequences of your behavior.

But what do you do when someone attacks you for it? You agree, "Yes, I have that fault." You sympathize, "I understand how it can upset people." That's a negative assertion. You assert your right to have your negative qualities. You say, "I am antimarriage," if that's the case. Or, "Yes, I do tend to be irresponsible," if you are.

You are asserting your right to be as you are. Your new lover says, "You have been bossing me around. You act as if I'm your slave. You expect me to do everything for you. You are sexist."

Your negative assertion might be, "Yes, you're right, I am sexist." Fogging, in the same instance, would be "Yes, I understand how you might think I'm sexist because I asked you to do the dishes."

In a negative assertion, you are saying, "Yes, I have a right to be a sexist or antimarriage or antigovernment, and I am." You are also saying to the other person, "You have a right to leave me for it."

A negative assertion is a way of saying "I am." Fogging is a way of dealing with an attack that admits the possibility that the other person's conclusions about you might be right, but in both cases, you stick to your original point.

When a person criticizes you for something you do wrong, they expect you to fight back. By agreeing, you dissipate the anger and refuse to fight back.

Negative Inquiry

Making a negative inquiry is another way to avoid hostility. When someone attacks you for something, instead of fighting back, you simply ask, "What makes you think I'm antisex?"

Ask a lot of questions and continue asking in the honest pursuit of the truth. But don't argue. Don't make statements. Instead, inquire about your negative traits. "What else gives you the impression that I don't like sex?" Eventually the attacker loses ammunition. They just can't think of anything else that makes you antisex. In the meantime, you may have learned something about yourself.

Negative inquiry exhausts your mate's anger because you're not arguing back. It allows you to feel more comfortable about getting criticism in close relationships and also prompts your mate to express honest negative feelings. Negative inquiry can improve your communications with your new mate without bitterness.

Self-Disclosure

When you find yourself in an argument about something in yourself (for instance, you are always late), self-disclosure is an excellent way to handle the situation. You may want to say, "Being late is a problem for me. It always has been. As a matter of fact, I'm usually at least two hours late for everything." It could be something humorous. "You think this is late? I was once so late I missed a cruise boat and was stranded for six days."

Or, suppose your partner says you're frigid or just not sexy. You could say, "I've been told that before. As a matter of fact right after my divorce I didn't have sex for two years."

By disclosing something about yourself, you encourage the other person to disclose a secret about themselves. You may be surprised to find that your new lover admits, "You know, I used to have a problem being on time myself." Or, "I once didn't have sexual relationships for a long time myself."

Self-disclosure allows you to openly admit things about yourself that you previously hid because you were afraid to tell people. It also keeps the two of you from arguing.

Humor Assertions

If it isn't bitter, humor is a most desirable and tension-reducing form of assertive communication. A sense of humor is developed and can't be taught here, but if you've got a slightly cockeyed view of the world, use it as the most subtle assertion. When she's late getting to bed and you're lying there waiting, "If you come to bed with me, we can start and finish together."

When he calls and announces that he and his buddies are coming to your house for dinner after the ball game, "Sure, honey. I have three cans of tuna and two boxes of oatmeal—which do you think your friends would prefer?"

Once you know the basic assertive techniques, you still have to practice in order to become an assertive person. You may have a lifetime of nonassertive activity to overcome, and like an actor who is assuming a new role, you must rehearse.

Behavior Rehearsal

Get a tape recorder and simply practice saying what you'd like to say to your mate using one of the assertive techniques. Say it over and over, louder and better, until you sound like you mean it without shouting or becoming emotional.

Practice with a friend, having the friend play the role of your mate. Start when your problems are little; begin asserting before the encroachments on your personal freedoms pile up.

Suppose you've been dating a new person and even have fallen just a little "in love." The only thing is that every time you go out, it's where they want to go. You only eat where they want to eat, you only see the movies they choose. You might want to practice saying, "Sometimes I would like to be consulted on the decision about where we go." Or, "I would like to pick what kind of food we eat, if you are going to pick the restaurant." Or, "I would like to choose the movie tonight."

It's very hard for you to say that. You're really not unhappy with your new lover, just a little disturbed at the way they make all the decisions. If you don't use an acceptable assertive technique to let your new lover know how you feel, you are going to either shut up and take it or you will wind up saying something irrational and manipulative like "You always decide everything and I never get a chance to have any say in what we do." That is not an assertion, it's whimpering, a crybaby manipulation.

Devious, subtle bully techniques taught by generations of pseudo-martyrs, and laced with a secret hostility, are meant to make the partner suffer. Don't be a guilt-inducing, long-suffering "mother." Don't assert yourself with devices that use veiled threats like "Oh, we can go to the Mexican restaurant. My ulcer won't be too bad if I take my medication." Or "Go, my love. Have a good time with your tennis teacher. I can stay home and try to find something to do." Or "Sure, we can visit your family again tonight. I can catch up on my sleep another time."

You now have the opportunity to be both effective and fair in your communication. Practice saying what you want to say. Make a firm, verbal assertion that is fair and makes you predictable. It's not hard to say the words "The next time I would like us to plan our weekend together." But it's not easy to suddenly change from a shrinking violet to an assertive person, while not coming off as an aggressive bully. In a culture that glorifies "intimidation," honest and clean assertiveness remains the style of the honorable and fair individual.

Rehearse with a friend who will play the role of your mate, or just yourself and a tape recorder if you feel shy. For starters, try saying something close to what you mean, like "Do you think that one time next month I could pick a movie for us to see?" Gradually build up until you can say the target statement loudly and clearly.

It's important to have eye contact when you are making your assertive statement. That's why it helps to have a friend play the part of your lover, so that you can get used to making your assertive statement while looking straight into the other person's eyes. If you don't have a friend to practice on, get a photograph of your lover, look at the photo and say your target assertive statement.

A lot of people give themselves away. They let the other person know that they don't quite mean what they say by looking at their fingers, the ceiling or their toes when they are making their assertive statement. If you don't have a picture, use a mirror and look yourself in the eye while you're practicing.

If you find that it's hard to look people in the eye, start by looking at their forehead. Talk first to their forehead, or chin or even start at the belly button and move up. Hopefully, you will eventually be able to make your assertive statement looking the person directly in the eye.

For some people, it's always impossible to look right in the eye of their adversary. If you're one of those people, look at the bridge of their nose and it'll have the same effect. You'll appear to be looking the other person square in the eye and your assertion will be effective.

The Pursuit

Until now your new relationship has been on an even keel. You have been assertive about the things that bother you, and you haven't been bullied.

You have both initiated contacts, phone calls and dates, and suddenly you start to feel as if you are making all the moves, and maybe the other person is beginning to disrespect your pursuit. That's the time to become assertive. "It would really make me feel good if you were to start making some phone calls to me. I assume you like me, but it feels like I am initiating all our contacts, so I would like you to make phone calls to me at least as often as I call you." That's making a fair, firm statement about how you feel and more important, what you'd like.

Another area of conflict at the beginning of new relationships is the amount of time people spend together. The person who wants more time feels as if they are in a one-down position. If you find that happening to you, you're not supposed to sit home alone and cry about it. Nor are you supposed to complain to all your friends. A gossip talks about people, a friend talks to them instead. Make an assertive statement. "I would like no more than a week to go by without our seeing each other." You may be tempted to simply say, "I would like us to see more of each other," but that is just not as effective.

Workable Compromises

To be effective, you must be specific. The ultimate purpose of all assertions is to arrive at a workable compromise. That means that everyone gives a little and everyone is satisfied.

Making workable compromises and effective assertions has nothing to do with loving or not loving. A lot of people assume that if they make demands, they'll be considered unloving. On the contrary, if you don't make demands, maybe the other person will believe you just don't care enough. As Erich Fromm pointed out, you can't love someone else until you love yourself. If you don't take care of yourself by making demands to insure your own happiness, then you aren't loving yourself and won't be able to love someone else. It is not a loving thing to sacrifice and to forego your own needs without recompense. It's unloving and creates distance and resentment between lovers.

Even if you never say, "Look at all the sacrifices I've made for you," you'll think it. Use your assertion technique to make a compromise. If you're not getting enough time, love or attention, you can bargain. In other words, you might say, "I want us to have at least three nights a week together." While your mate may not agree to that, you may be able to bargain for two nights a week, but special ones—like the weekend.

If it's important to you that you see your lover on Saturday night and he or she has been making other plans for Saturday nights, then you have to assert yourself. Speak up. Simply say, "It would make me happier if we see each other on the weekend, especially Saturday nights, because they are important to me." Or, "Saturday's the most important night to me, and I would like to generally keep it for the two of us."

Creating Instant History

One of the things you miss is memories. You have so many that involve your ex, and since you've just met your new lover, naturally you don't have a history together.

Every time you remember some pleasurable moment in your past, it seems as if your ex was there. The time you went to Las Vegas, the time you went to see two plays on Broadway on two consecutive nights, the time you camped under the California redwoods and got caught in the rain or the time you were in New York during the blackout. What you need to do now is to create memories that don't involve your ex. Create instant history with your new lover.

The wonderful things you did with your ex were done over a period of at least months and probably years. You went to Paris and your cousin's wedding together. As a matter of fact, you and your ex did everyhing together. No wonder all your fond memories involve them.

Instead of waiting for memories to evolve in your new relationship one at a time during the natural course of events, cram them into as short a time as possible. Set up important new things to do together, attend events that are memorable and that have an impact. Use the weekdays and weekends, too, daytimes as well as evenings. Go places and do things, don't just lie around in bed. Schedule trips. Involve your families. Plan a party. Involve the new person in your life thoroughly—in your finances, too, if possible. Involve yourself in their career.

It's amazing how quickly you can have many, many things to look back on, memories that would normally take months, maybe years. By accelerating the events, you create instant history. Making new, pleasurable memories for yourself that don't involve your ex is one great way to clear your mind and make your new relationship even richer than the old one.

Rebound

Rebound is a double-edged sword. Most people will advise you not to fall in love on a rebound. The reason for that advice is that you are hungry and tend to overlook things, to collude or become a doormat out of neurotic love starvation. But you've already learned how not to collude and how to assert yourself in a new relationship. You won't allow your hunger for a relationship to cause you to compromise beyond what is reasonable and what is in your interest.

It's true that you have an artificial or ulterior motive for getting involved in a relationship now. You need love; you're tired of being alone. However, there is always an artificial or ulterior motive for starting any relationship. It might be that she's pretty or has big tits or he's rich and successful. Or she's got a nice smile, or he has a great sense of humor. Or we like the same things. I'm horny, or she's a good cook, or he plays a great game of tennis.

Maybe it's convenience—we live so close. Or friends encourage you by saying you're meant for each other. How the relationship starts, or why, is not important. The fact that it is stimulated by the new person's physical attributes, wealth or ornamental value, or pheromones (biochemical body aromas) or success doesn't mean anything. It's what *sustains* a relationship, not what starts it, that's important.

Relationships don't fail or succeed because of how or why they start. Whether or not you meet someone on the rebound doesn't matter. Thinking it does is as silly as saying they fail because they started as a physical attraction. Relationships fail because people interract in wrong ways, and therefore can't *maintain* the partnership. Don't be afraid of relationships that start on the rebound.

12
THE RECONNECTION

There'll be good times again for me and you;—
But we just can't stay together,
Don't you feel it, too?
Still I'm glad—for what we had and how I once loved you.—

—Carole King and Toni Stern
"It's Too Late"

When someone has been an intimate part of your life for even a few months, when you feel you have a friend in the world who cares about you, it seems foolish and wasteful to just toss them out the window.

Surely there were things in your former lover that were truly endearing, qualities that were only theirs, the things that made you love them in the first place. It's possible that you still miss the good, lovable and attractive qualities your ex had and would like to have those back again—without pain or re-establishing the old "in love" relationship.

Or it might be a simple matter of logistics—you live close by, shop at the same market, work together or frequent the same social group. What do you do if it's awkward, inconvenient or impossible to avoid the ex—or if you simply don't want to?

THE TWELFTH WEEK

Session Twenty-three: The Geneva Convention

Once you have established new relationships, it's okay to make a reconnection with your ex, as long as you are sensitive to the problems and prepared for them.

If you have a new lover or new lovers in your life, it's important not to hurt them. It's also important not to hurt yourself (most of all) and even your ex. Only when you're feeling good about yourself, when your life is in control, when you no longer have a driving need or inner turmoil when you think about your ex-lover, should you reconnect.

The reason you should be sure that you feel good before you reconnect is because otherwise you may be giving in to the old fantasies and yearnings about getting "him" or "her" back. If you are confident, the meeting is sure to be less traumatic and won't pull you off-center emotionally.

The reconnection itself is not part of the Letting Go process. It's only after you've let go that you can reconnect on a whole new basis and begin developing a new relationship with your ex. If you aren't sure that you've totally let go yet, don't make your reconnection. You must be "unhooked" before you can make a logical, well-thought-out choice as to whether you really want your ex as part of your life.

A driving need to see your ex again means you shouldn't try

for a reconnection now. It may take you months or even years, or you may not ever want to make a reconnection. Or it may be impossible.

How can you tell if you're ready? Retake the test in chapter one. If you score yourself less than five on most of the symptoms, you should be able to handle the meeting with no trouble. The lower your score, the more evidence you will have that you have indeed broken the hook to your ex. Don't just skim the questions. Actually take the test again and compare your score and symptoms with your earlier scores before reconnecting.

If you take the test and find that your improvement in certain areas isn't at least fifty percent, check carefully to see what things are still bothering you. If it's thinking about a place you were once happy together and haven't gone to yet, then plan a special Competing Response (chapter eight) for that place. If it's memorabilia or pictures that are bothering you, try another Implosion Day (chapter eight). High scores mean you shouldn't try a reconnection without reviewing the chapters and sessions that concern your particular weak spot. Your anxiety and depression levels should be gone or totally manageable by now. If not, you may want to see a behavior therapist for a personalized review of your "special" problems.

Reconnecting with Your Ex

The reconnection is your show, and you're the one who has to run it. Think of it as an opportunity to find out about an old friend. Aren't there things you'd like to know? Aren't you curious to find out if your ex is happy, sad or even alive? You may not be, but if you are, the reconnection is your chance.

It's not the time to ask, "Why did you leave me?" Even if that's the question that's foremost in your mind, forget it. You'll only cause an argument if you try to find out in this first meeting.

If you hadn't seen a close friend for three months because you'd had an argument, you wouldn't ask, "How come I haven't seen you for three months?" first thing. You'd know why you hadn't seen them for that long.

There are easier topics to discuss than your breakup. Ask how business is, where they're living, if they've seen old mutual friends and how the friends are. Chances are you were involved in your ex's career to some extent. Ask about that. Ask what a caring person would want to know about someone they had been out of touch with. Don't make points or try to prove any. Don't argue or rehash old stuff. If you can't think of anything else to talk about, work up a list before the meeting. You want to be "rational" and together.

The last time your ex was exposed to you, your emotions were raw. You weren't at your best. Don't worry, though, you don't have to apologize for anything you said or the way you acted. If you feel that you have to make some excuse for anything you've done, do it simply, quickly and only once.

Many people report that they just don't want to see their exes ever again. If you feel that way, then you may be avoiding—still phobic about that one person in the world. Why should you be afraid to see them? If you're still angry, you are allowing your ex to run your emotions. Only by making a successful reconnection will you truly be free.

Don't get stuck with being angry. If you are, review chapter seven. If you feel afraid, chapter nine. You have the right not to reconnect, but there's more in it for you if you do.

Your reconnection is a good opportunity for you to re-establish a friendly relationship with your former mate. If you have children, it certainly can't hurt them to see that grownups can make up. Think of it as being civilized.

Decide exactly what you might get out of a meeting with your ex, so that you aren't disappointed. Don't set your expectations for the first meeting too high. Your ex is going to be experiencing as many qualms about it as you are. And so is someone else.

Tell your new lover (if you have one) about your forthcoming meeting in as nice a way as possible. You might say, "I'm considering having lunch with him/her. How do you feel about that?"

You don't have to ask permission; simply be sensitive to the other person's feelings. You already have permission. You gave it to yourself.

If your new lover throws a fit or repeatedly restricts you from making your reconnection, you may have a very insecure person in your life. The value you place on your new relationship should be in direct proportion with how much reassuring you want to do.

Your reconnection is strictly your business, and you may realize there's nothing between you and your ex anymore that would make you get back together again, but your new lover doesn't know that. You are having your own anxieties about the meeting, hoping it will go well, while your new lover is imagining you and your ex walking off into the sunset.

If not handled right, your reconnection may seem like a threat to your new relationship. First, you must decide and truly believe it's not, and second, you must convince the new person in your life.

If you have a new person in your life, arrange for them to be with you immediately before and immediately after the meeting. If you decide to reconnect with your ex over lunch, have your new lover (or any new friend) stay with you the night before. Have breakfast together and make plans for the afternoon, too. Treat your reconnection like a business meeting that interrupts an otherwise perfect day in your new life.

Where to Meet

Meet your ex at a restaurant or other public place where you can have some privacy but also the protection of other people. Nothing keeps voices and tempers civil more than peer disapproval. Think of a fairly sedate spot where the clientele is "nice." Good vibes from the people around you can't hurt, either.

Find a meeting place that you associate with someone else, not your former mate. Seeing your ex again at any of the "special places" you went to as a couple will only resensitize you and reassociate that place with your old lover.

Make the appointment for breakfast or lunch. Pick an off hour, so you're not rushed or bothered by a waiter who's worried about his table or a maitre d' who wants to move in a new party.

Who Should Be There

Don't take anybody, not your new lover, not your dog, not your shrink or best friend. If your ex insists on bringing someone, don't take it as a personal insult, but rather as a signal of their insecurity.

Firmly assert yourself by saying "No, I want just the two of us this time." If your ex isn't ready to meet with you alone, then simply say, "Okay, let's give it some time and I'll call you again."

Notice how good it feels when you shift the burden of who's neurotic onto your ex and off yourself. Anyone who needs an arbitrator is too scared for honest communication. Look for the secondary motivations if your ex wants to include a third party. He/she might have a new mate to show off, to neck with in front of you, just to make you feel bad. Or it could be a lawyer to make sure you're not trying to get more out of the community settlement. No matter who your ex insists on bringing, you insist on meeting alone.

Setting Up the Meeting

Make arrangements exactly a week in advance, not two months off. Get it over with. The longer you have to wait, the more expectation anxiety you will build up. Yo have already succeeded with your therapy. This is not the hardest thing you've done, so don't allow it to become more important than it is.

If you can't schedule a lunch when you'll have a couple of hours, schedule to meet after work for cocktails. Under no circumstances should your meeting last more than two hours. Make your time schedule clear when you make the appointment. "I'm going to leave at . . . "

Don't get smashed or stoned either before, after or during, and don't even fantasize about the meeting turning into a sexy interlude. Not this time.

Calling Your Ex

Before you make that call, fantasize that you are really calling a friend of the same sex that you haven't seen for a while. How would you say hello? What would your tone of voice be? Practice with a tape recorder, or even call a friend and tape your side of the conversation first. Then see if you can practice calling and saying hello to your ex until your voice sounds the same. Use the same intonations, the same words. Pretend you're talking to a member of your family, a younger sister or brother you haven't spoken to for a while.

Make your voice happy. That's one good way to make sure you're not turned down. Nobody wants to go to a meeting where they know they're going to be hassled. Nobody wants to meet with an unhappy person, especially if they feel responsible for causing the unhappiness. If you worry about phone fright or the words coming out wrong, write a practice script. Use a tape recorder until you sound the way you want to sound, like a person you'd like to meet for lunch or a drink.

If your ex thinks you're going to dump on them as soon as you get them to see you or that you're sad and you're going to cry all over them, they won't want to come.

Make notes before you call. Write down the exact words you are going to say, and practice them. Know what *you* want to say and stick to your purpose. Here are some guidelines for you, but the words should be your own.

1. Say a cheery "hello" and identify yourself.

2. You may want to say you're sorry you haven't been in touch, but you've had a lot on your mind. Or that you've been busy getting your life together, and now that you have things under control, you didn't want to lose touch.

3. That although you've been into a lot of new things lately, you don't want to lose contact with old friends, and you thought it would be nice if you were to get together.

4. "I was thinking about lunch or a drink after work. Are you free any day next week?" This is the best way to ask because you have left them with their options open. It's their choice, and if your ex chooses to tell you that they're not free the next week, then you must say,

5. "Okay, you still have my number [or give it to them]. When you get some free time, maybe the week after next, give me a call."

6. If your ex says, "I don't know" or, "I want to think it over," don't argue. Simply say, "You have my number, let me know."

7. If you haven't heard from your ex in a week or two, make the same call again. Use the same cherry hello followed by "I guess you forgot about our lunch. How about this week?"

Remember, if your ex refuses, it may not mean that they

don't want to see you. Maybe she's waiting 'til after the next session with her shrink, which is still a week off. Maybe his mother is sick. Or your ex may still be afraid of you. Even the person who ends an unhappy affair often has leftover pain or guilt they haven't dealt with.

Session Twenty-Four: Meeting Without Fear

Before your meeting with your ex, solve all the logistical problems ahead of time, like whether to shake hands or who pays (you do) or what to wear. Work out your own problems and fears about the confrontation by following the step-by-step directions in this session. You will be more comfortable and better prepared than you ever imagined. Your ex will be the one on the spot. You'll *know* what to do, no matter what happens.

By the time you get to the meeting, you will be well rehearsed. Like an actor who really knows his lines and his business (stage moves), you will be confident that nothing can trip you up.

What'll He/She Think of Me?

It's natural for you to want to show your ex how happy and together you are and that you will indeed survive very well without them. You want to show off, to flaunt how good you look and that you haven't fallen apart, to prove you have become a better person than you were when you were part of that particular coupling.

Think of your reconnection as a business meeting. Keep it clean. Don't wear your sexy clothes, or something they always liked you in, or even the type of clothing they always wanted you to wear.

Don't dress to prove a point—that you're thinner, neater, better looking, sexier or richer. Nor should you dress like a slob because you want to prove you don't care. Forget about wearing your most seductive outfit to show the ex what he/she can't have. Wear something you feel good in. Everyone has one particular outfit that they've always gotten lots of compliments for, or that they've always had successful times wearing, or that just feels comfortable. If you have a special outfit you feel reflects the new you—wear that.

Overdressing will make your ex suspect that you are still trying to get them back. But you don't want them to think, "How smart of me to get rid of that slob," either. Start with a clean, neat, well-groomed you and add things selectively. Women shouldn't look like they just came from the hairdresser. And men shouldn't wear that super-jazzy, new three-piece velvet suit at lunch. You'll only look like you're dying to be touched or on your way to a wedding.

If you play it right this time, you'll get another chance to meet with your ex and show them how sexy you've become and/or how you don't care by being extra sloppy. But not now. Wear clothes you feel confident in; be neat, clean and well groomed, but not ostentatious.

Pretend you are going to a normal event, among very good friends who like you, not an "important" viewing by your ex. Don't ask for approval by investing too much into making a good impression. If you make too much effort (more than for an ordinary occasion, say a stag party or a shower), you'll look like you're still asking for your ex's approval, even if you're not. The bad part about expecting (wanting or needing) approval is that if you don't get it, you'll feel turned down. You don't know what's going on in your ex's life right now. Suppose an uninsured teenager in a red dress rammed your ex's car last week, and you're wearing a red dress. Or a guy who looked just like you stood her up. Or a girlfriend is giving him trouble. Or her mother is sick again. Or it's just a bad day at the office. If you invest too much effort to get your ex's approval and don't get it, you'll be disappointed.

Don't wear special false eye lashes if you never wear anything but mascara. Don't go to the fancy men's beauty salon for the full treatment if you always go to Joe the Barber's on the corner. Don't invest any money in buying a special outfit for the occasion. Don't make a serious investment of time or money. If your ex had a bad day, you're liable to be hurt . . . just because your investment didn't pay off. How much better to do the primping for an occasion with someone you know will be thrilled with your efforts.

Don't starve yourself to lose weight especially for the meeting. Don't wear that special piece of jewelry your ex gave you, either, the one when you were "in love." Don't bring any old photos or sentimental letters or other trinkets you want to return. Leave the picture of your new lover at home, too.

Remember your only goal for the meeting is to make contact with an old friend. Concentrate on making your poor nervous ex feel comfortable. After all, they probably don't know how to handle the situation. You do.

For you, the meeting can be a chance to regain a lot of lost self-respect. Don't expect any miracles or that things will ever be "the way they were." The new relationship you establish with your former mate will be entirely different. You've changed and so have they. Make the day you meet the first day of a new relationship—a comfortable, hassle-free time for the both of you. Expect and demand respect, not love.

Limits

This isn't the time to ask or volunteer favors. Get your own ride if you need one. You don't want to rekindle dependency needs now that you're taking care of yourself so well.

If you have a new important other person in your life, it's

considerate to call them as soon as the meeting is over to let them know that you haven't run off with your ex. It's also good for you to obligate yourself to calling the new person at a certain time, so you have to draw the meeting to a close.

If things are going smoothly, it's okay to stay until the outer time limit. If you sense a tension about yourself or your ex, keep things short and sweet. Leaving before things go bad is the only way to feel good afterwards. Be sensitive to when to leave. Unfinished business and questions can be taken care of at a later meeting.

Preparation

Pull out a picture of your ex. See if you can mentally superimpose a friend's face in place of your ex's. Talk to the photo as if it's your friend and not your ex, and rehearse what you want to say to your ex.

By pretending it's someone else's face you're talking to and not an old lover's, you won't feel anxious when you actually see your ex. You can even put your friend's face on your ex's across the lunch table. Predetermine a face. If you have trouble superimposing your friend's face on your ex's photo, try putting them side by side or even cut out the friend's face and paste it on your ex's. Then remove the friend's face and see if you can imagine it's still there.

During your meeting, if you feel yourself getting overly emotional or losing control, flash your friend's face on your lover's. Try to talk to your ex-lover like you would your friend.

Dress Rehearsal

Do a dry run at the restaurant. Pick a table and set the entire meeting up just as if it were the real thing. Even order lunch. Wear the exact same clothes you plan to wear for the meeting.

Invite your superimposed friend to go along and sit at the same seat your ex will occupy at the meeting. That will make it even easier to flash your friend's face on your ex's if you have trouble maintaining during the meeting.

Take a picture of your ex along with you to the restaurant. Talk to it, or at least look at it, while you run over the things you want to say at your meeting in your mind. Lack of familiarity is the keystone of fear, so rehearsal is the best way to overcome it. Rehearsal erases the fear that some unknown thing will go wrong and you won't be able to cope, so don't skip yours.

Stress Inoculation

There may still be some things that are pertinent only to your relationship with your ex. Fears that only you have. Things that worry just you.

If specific and unique fears having to do with your situation with your ex are bothering you, use Stress Inoculation techniques outlined in chapter eleven. For instance, it could be a touchy situation about money or children or family members or things you did that you're afraid might have been discovered, lies you think they might have found out about, even verbal or physical abuse.

For a woman, it might be "What if he yells at me about . . ." or "What if he tries to hurt me by flaunting his new girlfriend?"

For a man, "What if she shows me pictures of her new baby?" Or, "What if she threatens to wipe me out financially?" Or, "What if she tells me she's getting married or living with someone?"

Write down your fears about what "might" happen on three-by-five cards and stack them in a hierarchy. Pretend you're taking a lie detector test and try to look at each one without getting upset or excited.

Imagine your ex-lover saying or doing the thing you're most afraid they'll do. Start with the least frightening, and when you can imagine that happening without getting upset, without losing your relaxed state, go on to the next card.

With Stress Inoculation, even if the worst possible, the most threatening thing happens, you will be prepared.

Card One might be: Your lover comes to the lunch and says, "I really think it's nice of you to call this meeting, but I want you to know that I think we shouldn't try to see each other again."

Card Two: He/she comes to the meeting furious with a list of all the things you ever did wrong.

Card Three: He/she says, "You were always terrible in bed. I was just pretending to like it. My new lover really turns me on for the first time in years."

Refer to chapter eleven for more detailed Stress Inoculation instructions.

The Arrival

Since you're the one who's done the inviting, you should arrive early. Besides, you don't want to be rushed and add that anxiety to the stressful situation. Getting there early gives you time to compose yourself and relax.

Prove to yourself how together you are by taking control of the situation right from the beginning. Make an early arrival, get a table that will give you the right amount of privacy and leave your ex's name with the maitre d' when you arrange for the check to come directly to you. Have no more than *one* glass of wine (if you don't have a drinking problem) or cocktail and a cigarette before your ex arrives. Relax, think of it as an enjoyable outing.

Food

Enjoy yourself. Don't eat anything spartan. As a matter of fact, order the "best" thing on the menu, whatever it might be, if that's what you want. Indulge yourself. If you want dessert first, have it. Remember you're the one who's okay now, so whatever you do is just fine.

The Greeting

Don't get nervous waiting for your ex to show. If he/she is late, it may be they're subconsciously frightened. Don't panic. If more than a half hour goes by, order your own lunch, have it and really indulge yourself. You deserve it.

He/she shows up. It's up to you to set the pace for the meeting. Pretend it's a stranger who is coming to your home for the first time, and you want to make them comfortable. If you're the type who would ordinarily peck on the cheek, do it. If you suddenly feel like throwing your arms around your ex and hugging, do that. If you think a warm handshake, a pat on the back or just an arm on the shoulder feels the best and easiest for you, do that.

At the very least, you must stand up and give the greeting. A happy, smiling, big hello, even if you're not sure you feel that way inside. This is the moment that sets the pace for any peace you and your ex will find. Make it a good one. It's up to you.

The next thing you must do is touch them. Start with a handshake. Break the touch barrier and you're halfway home. Try for a peck on the cheek. It's a cinch you won't get turned down in a public place. Do whatever is the warmest thing you can pull off, but don't forget to touch.

Decide ahead of time what you think you can carry off, and do it. Don't be put off if you don't get as much back as you put out. Your ex may be thrown off balance by your newfound confidence and take-control attitude. No matter how he/she reacts to your greeting, you must act as if they had reacted in the same smiling, friendly, open way you did. Treating people as if they're going to be nice often makes them just that way.

No knee in the crotch during the greeting. No rubbing chests. No blowing in the ear. No tongues in the kisses. Keep it warm, but not hot. Sex with you will scare your ex now because they're afraid it still would have all those relationship problems attached.

What If . . .

. . . your eyes suddenly fill with tears at the sight of your ex. Take Kleenex with you. Dry your eyes and carry on. You don't have to be ashamed of honest emotions and/or feelings. You're entitled to them. But you should try to maintain. After all, you don't want this meeting to dissolve, literally, in front of you.

. . . your ex suddenly becomes amorous and seductive.

Ignore it. Keep things light and easy, and pretend you don't even notice their advances. Ignore that special look and that spark in the eye. It'll only get your head in trouble if you take it seriously or react to it. Your ex's flirting is a way to test their old sex hold on you.

What to Say After You Say Hello

The easiest thing to do is make a fuss over the restaurant or offer your ex a glass of wine, the menu or even a chair. If you want, order a light appetizer. Offer your ex one, too. Order a carafe of wine and pour them a glass.

Even if it's raining, propose a toast to the day, or to your new hat, or to the raindrops. All those things like what to order take up lots of time and keep things from getting uncomfortable during the adjustment period.

"It's great to see you."

"You look wonderful."

"I like that suit."

Think of something to compliment your ex with right away. You know what they will like. Say something about how great her hair looks, if it's her pride. Say you like his new shirt, or how terrific he looks, or how much weight she's lost. If you can't think of anything else to say, practice saying, "It's good to see you again." Or, "How's work?" Or, "I saw Aunt Jane last week." Exchanging news about mutual friends by asking or offering information is a very good conversation maker. There must be something you can say that isn't controversial and that will put your ex at ease.

Since you're doing the inviting, you might want to pick a place that you have been to before, but not with your ex. One where the specialties are your favorites. Then, make recommendations. Hopefully, the menu will be big and you can always spend time reading it if things get awkward.

Digs

Don't. No matter how tempting it is, don't say, "This is where I've been coming to a lot lately with my new friend" or, "It's a shame we never came here when we were together."

Emotions

It is possible that you will be overcome with anger or sadness or whatever. Or that your ex will do something that will be just the same type of thing that they did that always upset you before. If they do, it's a top dog game. They obviously don't like your new "in control" self and are trying to destroy it. Don't play it. Get out immediately. Excuse yourself and leave. If your ex shows up with another woman or man, you may feel that you can't handle that situation, or suddenly you're overcome with unexpected emotions.

If you can't excuse yourself to make a phone call or go the rest room and quickly get yourself back together to the smiling, confident person you were, then you should leave. If you don't want to face your ex and whomever they might have brought along, you don't have to. Just excuse yourself by saying that something came up (that's true, isn't it?) and that you'll call for another meeting later. You could even send a note with the waiter or maitre d' that an emergency came up.

You don't have to stay somewhere where you are uncomfortable. There's no reason you should stay and get dumped on, either. If your ex seems determined to dump, get out. Don't wait for them to do it twice.

It's better to leave and try another time than to allow yourself to get sucked in.

If you find yourself getting overwhelmed, throw the burden for making conversation back on your ex. "How's your life? What's happening with you? How's work?" Ask questions and study the menu while you regain your composure. After all, you initiated the meeting. Try to pull it off, just so you'll feel good about yourself. Ask for news about people you know mutually. Ask about pets, tell little stories about family happenings. Find out if the roof still leaks.

Tell your ex about some of your new accomplishments, all the things you've done.

The New Person in Your Life

Don't be shy about letting your ex know that you've been dating a lot, if you have, or that you have a special new person in your life. If your former lover seems interested, tell them about your romance, but don't indulge in private sexual disclosures and discussions of who's better.

Don't rub it in if your ex doesn't have a new lover or if they seem unhappy. Portray your new affair as news, just as you would to your best friend.

It's not important to impress your ex by telling them how happy you are or how successful you are in the dating world. Be yourself and tell the truth. Remember, the best answer to a question you're unsure of is, "I don't know." That can go for anything from "Are you happy?" to "Are you going to marry?"

Sirens and Flashing Red Lights

Your reconnection is a lesson in objectivity. You are now a separate entity from your ex. You are no longer connected in any way, and you are now establishing a new connection. You don't want to base it on the old emotions that tore you apart in the first place. How can you keep yourself under control?

If you always imagined that there was a cop following you while you were driving, you'd never get a ticket. In the same way, imagine that someone you want to impress with your rational behavior is at the table. It could be your therapist, your best friend, a new lover, a potential new lover or employer.

Imagine someone whom you would like to have think you're perfectly together—a well-balanced, well-centered individual. Picture that person, someone you respect, sitting beside you and quietly listening to your conversation. What would they think of you? It could even be a parent or a child. Don't say or do anything that you wouldn't want that person to hear or see

Sex

People often still feel sexual attraction long after the original love is gone. It's a habit. It doesn't mean that you are still hooked on your ex if you see them and feel turned on or even fantasize about wanting to go to bed with them. It shows you're normal.

You were attracted sexually to that person in the first place or you wouldn't have been together. It's natural that you would still be attracted to the same physical type that turned you on before.

It's even possible for you and your ex to have a sexual relationship again in the future. But this isn't the time. Sexual advances now will only complicate your first meeting and probably scare your former mate. They'll be sure that if they go to bed with you, the rest of the terrible things that happened before will happen again. Consider you're now treating a phobic who's afraid to have sex with you. Don't resensitize your former mate.

Before you can have a sexual relationship, you have to

reincorporate the old lover into your life in a new way. The best start is to establish an easy, tension-free friendship first.

Now you may find, much to your surprise, that you are no longer turned on by your ex and have lost any sexual desire for them. Happy for you. A major source of your addiction is over.

Friendship

Relationship separations and divorces often leave one partner or the other angry and hating for years afterwards. The real problem with that is the destructive possibilities in hate. It's an emotion that eats up the person who's doing the hating and drives the hated person into despair.

If you allow your ex to hate you, you are allowing them to not only destroy themselves, but to also run terrible guilt-induction numbers on you. The guilt is that you've done something so terrible that a person who once loved you and whom you once loved now hates you and refuses to talk to you or see you. Rationally it doesn't matter whether you did hateful things or not. It's up to you to dissipate the hate for your own good and for the good of your ex.

Don'ts

Don't get into a business relationship of any kind with your ex. Don't work for them or let them work for you. No strings at this time. Don't lend money or ask to borrow any. Don't create any future commitments or obligations that would tie your lives together in any way. Be satisfied with a simple, friendly lunch. Don't make a future date for anything.

Don't say when you will call. A simple "Let's keep in touch" or "Feel free to call me, and I'll talk to you soon" will do.

New Freedoms

You can call your ex after the meeting without worrying if you're going to get a bad reception. You can have a party and even invite your ex (with a date). You can reestablish contacts with mutual friends.

Cured!

If you can handle your reconnection with your ex in a civilized way, you can handle almost any socially stressful situation. By taking on the one person who has been most threatening to your social security, you will learn that you can take on anyone. The social confidence you gain by reconnecting with a once-alienated mate is invaluable.

You will go on to new relationships feeling secure. You will know that if things do go wrong, you won't have invested lots of time without at least making a friend. You will have a new stronger self and the certain knowledge that you will live no matter what happens in your next relationship.

EPILOGUE

And these mem'ries lose their meaning
When I think of love as something new,
Though I know I'll never lose affection
for people and things that went before.
I know I'll often stop and think about them,
In my life, I'll love you more.

—JOHN LENNON AND PAUL MCCARTNEY
"In My Life"